CULTURAL LIBERALISM IN AUSTRALIA

CULTURAL LIBERALISM
IN AUSTRALIA
A Study in Intellectual and Cultural History

GREGORY MELLEUISH

Department of History and Politics
University of Wollongong

CAMBRIDGE
UNIVERSITY PRESS

CAMBRIDGE UNIVERSITY PRESS
Cambridge, New York, Melbourne, Madrid, Cape Town, Singapore, São Paulo, Delhi

Cambridge University Press
The Edinburgh Building, Cambridge CB2 8RU, UK

Published in the United States of America by Cambridge University Press, New York

www.cambridge.org
Information on this title: www.cambridge.org/9780521479691

First published 1995
Re-issued in this digitally printed version 2009

A catalogue record for this publication is available from the British Library

National Library of Australia Cataloguing in Publication data
Melleuish, Gregory, 1954– .
Cultural liberalism in Australia: a study in
intellectual and cultural history.
Bibliography.
Includes index.
1. Liberalism – Australia – History. 2. Australia –
Intellectual life. 3. Australia – Social life and customs –
1901–1945. 4. Australia – Social life and customs –
1945–1965. I. Title.
306.420994

Library of Congress Cataloguing in Publication data
Melleuish, Gregory, 1954–
Cultural liberalism in Australia: a study in intellectual and
cultural history / Gregory Melleuish.
p.   cm.
Includes bibliographical references and index.
1. Australia – Civilization. 2. Liberalism – Australia – History.
I. Title.
DU107.M4 1995
994–dc20   95–11413

ISBN 978-0-521-47444-3 hardback
ISBN 978-0-521-47969-1 paperback

Contents

Acknowledgments		vii
Abbreviations		viii
1	Introduction: Culture, Tradition and Modernity	1
2	Traditions of Modernity in Australia	26
3	Ethos and Myth: The Dynamics of Cultural Liberalism	50
4	Ethos and Myth: The Humanities Strike Back	81
5	Liberalism and Its Critics: The Realists	103
6	Liberalism and Its Critics: The Idealists	137
	Epilogue and Conclusion: Cultural Liberalism Spurned?	176
Notes		191
Bibliography		211
Index		222

*For my undergraduate history teachers
at the University of Sydney who first
made me appreciate the value of tradition.*

Acknowledgments

This book began life as a thesis, initially at the University of Melbourne and subsequently at Macquarie University. It was completed while I was teaching Australian Studies at the University of Queensland. Parts of this book have appeared in earlier forms in a variety of places, including the *Australian Journal of Politics and History, Political Theory Newsletter,* G. Melleuish (ed.), *Australia as a Social and Cultural Laboratory* (St Lucia, 1990), G. Stokes (ed.), *Australian Political Ideas* (Sydney, 1994), L. Dobrez (ed.), *Identifying Australia in Postmodern Times* (ANU, 1994) and P. Gathercole, T. Irving and G. Melleuish (eds), *Childe and Australia* (St Lucia, 1995). The section on V. Gordon Childe appeared in an earlier version in *Quadrant,* January 1989.

I should like to thank all the people who kindly provided me with ideas and suggestions while work proceeded on this study. I have particularly fond memories of long discussions with Dr Bob Dreher and Dr Geoffrey Sherington of the University of Sydney. I benefited much from the advice of my colleagues at the University of Queensland, Professor Geoffrey Bolton and Dr George Shaw of the Department of History and Dr Geoff Stokes of the Department of Government. I should especially like to thank both George Shaw and Geoff Stokes for the moral support they provided during difficult times.

I learned much from discussions with Dr John Moses on the responses of Australian academics to World War I and on George Arnold Wood. Dr Wayne Hudson of Griffith University provided assistance both academic and practical. I should also like to thank all of those who bore the burden of supervising the PhD thesis from which this book is derived, my original supervisor at the University of Melbourne, Dr Ian Britain, and my supervisor at Macquarie University, Associate Professor Jill Roe. I should also like to thank my students in ID 218, Australian Cultural

Studies at the University of Queensland from 1988 to 1992 on whom many of the ideas in this book were first tried out. In particular I am thankful for a period of study leave from the University of Queensland that enabled me to complete the manuscript of the thesis in 1991. I would also like to thank the Burgmann family for permission to consult the Burgmann papers held by the National Library of Australia.

In addition I should like to thank my wife Diana, without whose support and assistance this work would never have been completed. She typed and edited both the original thesis and this manuscript, correcting some of my more fanciful prose constructions, dealing with textual minutiae as well as suggesting some of the sub-headings in the text. Long has she struggled to get this work into proper shape. Along with our children, Alice and Helen, she has had to live with this work for many years. Finally, I am always grateful to my parents Des and Rita Melleuish, who first encouraged my interest in matters academic and made possible an appreciation of the phenomenon that was Cultural Liberalism.

Final responsibility for any errors remains as always with the author.

Abbreviations

AAAS   Australasian Association for the Advancement of Science
AJPP   *Australasian Journal of Psychology and Philosophy*

CHAPTER 1

Introduction: Culture, Tradition and Modernity

Modernity and Post-Modernity

All historians write within a particular present. As such, they are granted certain insights but denied others which those writing in future ages will see with clarity. In an investigation such as the one which this study sets itself – the elaboration and analysis of a specific tradition of thought and action – it is useful to attempt to establish both the particular present and its relationship to the topic under review. In this way the precise contribution of this study to Australian cultural and intellectual history, both at the empirical and the methodological levels, can be established. The approach of the Introduction is fundamentally Socratic; by discussing and criticising existing approaches to Australian cultural and intellectual history it can establish its own approach to this field of learning.

The most appropriate way to consider this relationship is first to state the topic of the study and then the nature of the particular present. The study deals with a particular tradition of thought in Australia as it developed during what may be described as the period of 'modern Australia'. (Modern Australia may be used as a term to cover that period of Australian history inaugurated by Federation and which came to an end in the 1960s.) This tradition, which was developed in the main, by university educated intellectuals during the period c. 1880–1960, is summed up most aptly by the term 'Cultural Liberalism'. It covered a range of concerns, from political and social matters to general cultural issues, and it possessed a powerful religious dimension. The central ambition of its adherents was to maintain the spiritual and intellectual integrity of the individual while at the same time providing the basis for a rational and humane social order.

The particular present is that of post-modernity in which many of the ideals of the tradition which we seek to explore have been scorned or

rejected. Significantly one aspect of post-modernity has been the assertion that we live in a 'post-humanist' age.[1] More generally, as we shall see,
one of the most important features of the adherents of post-modernity is
the tendency to emphasise discontinuity, plurality and uncertainty or, as
Richard Rorty sums it up, 'contingency and irony'.[2] This is complemented by attempts to dissolve or 'deconstruct' all fixed and certain
positions.[3]

Whatever may be one's attitude to some of the more dubious aspects
of post-modernity, the power of many of its arguments should be recognised and the challenge that it poses cannot be ignored. Nowhere is this
need stronger than in the study of Australian cultural and intellectual
history. Traditionally this has been a relatively underdeveloped field of
intellectual enquiry.[4] Moreover, the association of intellectual and cultural history is by no means uncontroversial. There is a battle raging in
Australia as to the meaning of culture, a debate with which this study
must engage. Before the framework necessary for our needs can be constructed we must first try to understand how ideas about the development of Australian culture have changed during the past forty years as
modern Australia has given way to post-modern Australia.

This task may be carried out most economically by first examining the
radical nationalist conception of Australian culture which was the key
expression of culture in modern Australia. Then it will be possible to
consider the somewhat anarchic situation which has arisen in the wake
of the sustained attack launched on that ideal of culture during the
1970s and 1980s.

Australian Culture: Radical Nationalism and its Aftermath

Although radical nationalism had existed in Australia since at least the
1890s, it is true to say that it was given its ripest expression in the 1950s
with such works as Russel Ward's *The Australian Legend* and Vance
Palmer's *The Legend of the Nineties*. There is a great irony in the fact that
these mature expressions of Australianism occurred at the very moment
when post-war immigration was transforming the culture they purported
to describe. Both works look back to an Australia which, whatever its
virtues and vices, was to die slowly over the next thirty years as the policies which had maintained it, from 'White Australia' to economic and
financial regulation, were dismantled.

Palmer's *The Legend of the Nineties* may be taken as a fair representative
of this genre. It is a work in which the need to demonstrate the growth
of a unique Australian culture is balanced by a despair that that culture
has degenerated since the golden days of the 1890s. In a sense, for
Palmer 'legend' plays a similar role as 'myth' did for Georges Sorel – as

that which motivates people to participate actively in the life of their community (or, as in the case of Sorel, make a revolution).[5] Palmer was nothing if not a vitalist. He had been profoundly influenced by Hilaire Belloc's *The Servile State* and came to see the National Culture as some sort of vital animating principle fighting the modern tendency towards servility.[6] For Palmer, culture did not mean the actual way in which people lived their lives but the ideal of activity which inspired them to break the chains of servility.

Palmer believed that Australian culture existed in the ideal sense as the legacy of a decade in which 'a scattered people . . . had a sudden vision of themselves as a nation with a character of their own and a historic role to play, and this vision set fruitful creative forces in motion'.[7]

In effect, the 1890s had given expression to these creative forces, even if imperfectly and naively, so that they had established the true, living Australian culture. As Palmer put it, there was an 'intensity about the spirit of the early nineties that created images and ideas having a continuous force'.[8]

How did this Australian culture come to be? For Palmer it was the culmination of an evolutionary process through which migrants coming to Australia had grown into harmony with the soil. Although his position is not stated explicitly, Palmer was of the school which believed that Australian cultural development had passed through the evolutionary stages common to all cultures.[9] He described a group of people isolated from the rest of the world, and placed in an environment which set to work moulding their characters: 'the people beyond the coastal ranges . . . had a common face, for the same influences, physical and spiritual, had been at work on them for nearly half a century'.[10] Palmer owed a debt to nineteenth century evolutionary thought, in particular to Lamark's theory of acquired characteristics and Tylor's anthropological model of the stages of social growth.[11] The anthropological influence becomes especially strong in the following chapter, 'Myth-making', in which Palmer contended that: 'It has been said that men cannot feel really at home in any environment until they have transformed the natural shapes around them by infusing them with myth.'[12]

Palmer's evolutionary model of Australian cultural development (by which he meant white European development) proceeded as follows. Firstly, the people were brought into the Australian environment which then began to mould and shape them. The race evolved in its own peculiar way: 'three or four generations of life under semi-tropical suns had coloured his [the Australian's] skin with protective pigment'.[13] Like any people they developed myths and expressed them in the traditional forms of the ballad and the song. Out of this earlier myth-making emerged a national ideal which Palmer described as 'the dream of a self-contained country, secure from the outer world, developing its own resources, and gradually building up a society that would be a pattern for free men everywhere'.[14]

This ideal found its expression in Utopianism and the flourishing of literary activity but came into conflict with reality. This led to compromise and the eventual fading of the dream, leaving behind the Legend as an inspiration for future generations. In Palmer's scheme there was also a belief in the idea of the 'saving remnant', of a fragment of the pure white race living in isolation from the world preserving democracy for the world. A similar belief was expressed in P.R. Stephensen's *The Foundations of Culture in Australia*. This vision of Australia as the last bastion of European civilisation in a world of strife and decay reflects the crisis through which both Palmer and Stephensen lived. Australian culture could be made to seem a beacon of light in an age of gathering darkness.[15]

The major problem with Palmer's model is that it will not bear the weight of the facts it seeks to explain. There is a quaint charm in his attempt to construct an Australian national ideal using scaffolding derived from out-dated nineteenth century anthropological and historical ideas. (The model is also exceedingly Eurocentric.) At most, it is what Palmer called it – a legend, a myth: not entirely false, but then also, not substantially true. This is not to accuse Palmer of ignoble motives – far from it. Palmer's desire was to create a more alive and vital culture in a disappointing and disheartening era.

One can reject much of Palmer's argument and yet concede the basic point: that something which can be termed Australian national culture did come into being during the latter part of the nineteenth century. Palmer's real problem was that he claimed too much. He placed the development of Australian culture on a single track using a dubious model. But the incorrectness of the details of Palmer's analysis does not necessarily contradict the appropriateness of the two key elements of Palmer's position: national culture and evolution. Rather, it is a matter of examining more closely what is to be understood by these two terms.

Palmer's conception of national culture also illustrates some of the fundamental contradictions in the ideas and beliefs held by the intellectuals of modern Australia. On the one hand there was a desire to build a more rational social order, on the other hand there was the recognition that this social order was essentially servile and crushed individual autonomy. The source of this contradiction can be traced to a conception of evolution as a controlled and unswerving process as opposed to a spontaneous and unplanned operation created by individuals. Palmer's vision of national development had strong religious foundations and his picture of nationalism was that of a quasi-religious force being frustrated by the power of the world. In this view evolution takes on a strong element of necessity; for all his vitalist pretensions, Palmer did not provide the individual with much scope for influencing the culture.

Unfortunately, the growing disenchantment with radical nationalism which has occurred over the past twenty years has discredited not only the particular version of nationalism and culture advocated by Palmer but has also brought into question the very value of nationalism itself. The old Australian national ideas have been decried as racist, sexist and destructive of individual expression; and there is some truth in these accusations.[16] But, as Palmer rightly argued, there was also a genuine idealism.

The growing tendency to emphasise the negative aspects of the old Australian cultural ideals is related to a fundamental change amongst those who articulate the values of Australian culture. Those values, and the ideals they embody, no longer seem as compelling as they once were. Having lost their natural, inevitable quality they now appear as things arbitrary and contingent. The old evolutionary view of culture regarded the coming together of the spirit of place and the Australian people as a natural process. The historicist attack on culture has called this naturalistic idea of culture into question.

Once culture is no longer viewed as something natural and normal but as arbitrary and contingent it is not a drastic step to consider it, not as a growth but as a fiction, an artificial invention imposed on Australians by those pursuing ignoble ends. According to this view, culture and national identity do not have their roots in the real concerns of men and women but in the desire by certain groups and classes to maintain their dominance over the population at large. Culture is conceived of as a tool of domination in the hands of the few; a means of perpetuating social disunity and inequality by creating the illusion that equality and social harmony have been achieved. This can only be the case if culture is considered as something 'invented' or 'fictional', as something imposed on, rather than growing out of, the needs of the people.[17]

The foundation of this conception of culture is the idea that human beings are consumers whose needs are manipulated by those who wish to make a profit out of them. It is interesting to note that for the Servile State school of social criticism, amongst which Palmer should be counted, culture was advocated as part of an active 'production' mentality in opposition to the passive consumer mentality induced by the Servile State.[18] For the writers of the 1970s and 1980s culture can be understood only in terms of consumption. Drawing on the writings of Louis Althusser and Antonio Gramsci they came to view culture as something produced by the state in order to make people think in a certain way.[19] A corollary of this view is that if the state can be 'captured' by a group of people then it should be possible to break the hegemony of one culture and replace it by that of another. Such is the thinking, for example, behind Donald Horne's espousal of the 'clever country'.[20]

For Palmer, culture was a living positive thing, created by people to give reality to their lives. For his successors, culture is much more insubstantial, a thing which can be imposed on people by the state at will. The principal effect of this change was a devaluation of culture to something transitory, a thing waiting to be replaced by something new and better. Part of this is to be explained by the fact that a genuine discontinuity does exist between the 'culture' of Palmer and that experienced by the writers of the 1970s and 1980s. Indeed it is a central argument of this study that in calling his work *The End of Modernity*, James McAuley was bringing an era to an end – the era of modern Australia and, more generally, the era of humanism and culture.

Writing in 1974, John Docker viewed the intellectual and cultural traditions of Sydney and Melbourne not as living realities with which to argue but as things of the past to be cast off as burdens.[21] Four years later, Tim Rowse's *Australian Liberalism and National Character* attempted to demonstrate that many of the fundamental ideas held by Australian intellectuals could be reduced to a 'liberal ideology'.[22] Hence the world of ideas created in Australia could be condemned firstly as out-of-date and secondly as 'mere ideology'. In other words, Docker and Rowse recovered many of the basic important ideas of Australian intellectual life only to consign them safely to 'history', thereby demonstrating their irrelevance for the contemporary world. The growing emphasis on discontinuity in cultural analysis had its origins in a genuine feeling that a real discontinuity had taken place in the development of Australian culture. Something had broken what had earlier been perceived as the calm evolutionary flow of Australian development.

While the evolutionary nationalists had emphasised continuity, growth and unity, the new school of the 1970s and 1980s saw discontinuity, contingency, plurality and artificiality as the keys to understanding Australian culture. One immediate consequence of this position is that a distance grows up between the cultural analyst and the culture which he or she seeks to examine. The culture is reduced to data, or a series of texts, to be dealt with through the application of 'theory' – it is no longer a living bundle of ideas with which the interrogator holds a conversation.[23] But from where, it may be asked, does this 'theory' come? Why should it be considered relevant or true?

This is a serious question and can only be answered by examining the central ideas of the most popular of these works of recent cultural criticism, Richard White's *Inventing Australia*. The basis of White's argument is simple: there is no 'real' Australia as it really was.

A sense of national identity does not emerge out of the real concerns and interests of ordinary men and women; it is an 'invention' which is 'made' rather than 'grown'. It is 'artificially imposed' from without rather than from within. As it is invented so it cannot be real. Consequently, ideas concerning the 'essential Australia' are 'all intellectual constructs, neat, tidy, comprehensible – and necessarily false'. He provided no argument as to why invention and intellectual construction necessarily imply falsehood (the addition of the word 'necessarily' implies that he believes his argument to have logical force, that is, all attempts to make intellectual statements about the essential Australia are false by definition). For White, however, the crucial issue was not whether such ideas are true or false 'but what their function is'.

White isolated three main forces in explaining the function of national ideals in Australia:

1 modern ideas about nationality and the intellectual fashions underlying those ideas;
2 the role of the intelligentsia in propagating those national ideals;
3 the role of those groups who wield economic power.[24]

The general thrust is that intellectuals create those ideas which establish the hegemony or cultural dominance of those holding the economic power.

Two points are worth making. Firstly, this picture of the intelligentsia seriously underestimates the autonomy of this group and their capacity to pursue their own interests. It also masks the desire of many intellectuals to hold the reins of power in their own right. Secondly, White's three forces can be used to explain the success of his own ideas as follows: contemporary intellectual fashions plus an intelligentsia seeking bureaucratic and academic power plus the need for certain economic groups to create a more internationally oriented outlook in the 1980s led to an acceptance of White's own position.

Does this mean that White's position is therefore 'artificially imposed' and 'necessarily false'? *Inventing Australia* is, after all, an 'intellectual construct'. Unless White can establish that his work is in a different logical category to other works about Australian national identity (which he does not) then the only possible conclusion is that *Inventing Australia* is a false invention which nevertheless makes claims about Australian nationalism which it wants its readers to believe are true. The real problem facing White is that in his obsession with function he cannot distinguish between true and false statements. Why should intellectual constructs imply falsity?

At a philosophical level White's argument simply lacks coherence. He is better considered as employing a rhetorical strategy to outflank his evolutionary predecessors. Whereas they used the rhetoric of organic nature, White sought to undermine them by employing the rhetoric of the machine. By using words such as 'invention' and 'artificial' he made use of traditional distinctions between nature and artifice. Rhetorically this has value as it implies that nationalism is an historical entity rather than something inherent in human nature. But does the revelation of this historicity render nationalism 'false'? Here the limits of the nature/artifice *topos* are reached because it is a rhetorical and not a real distinction.

Invention, for example, can be considered to be a perfectly 'natural' human action. Take the case of science. Modern science is an historical creation. It could not have come into being until certain 'intellectual constructs' were 'invented'. These constructs included such ideas as law and the capacity to translate natural phenomena into mathematical terms.[25] But the 'invention' of science in no way implies that its discoveries are false; indeed, science has been remarkably successful in discovering real knowledge about the world. Scientific method does not depend for its success on the historical circumstances which brought it into the world.

Scientific discoveries are not plucked out of thin air; they cannot come into existence without past ideas and discoveries. The same is true of any invention. They are not the artificial or arbitrary creations of some hallucinated imagination but the end products of long involved processes. Historical development is not without some sort of logical structure in that journeys taken in the past help to direct us into our present and future paths. Ernest Gellner sums up this position succinctly: 'Food production, political centralisation, the division of labour, literacy, science, intellectual liberalisation, appear in a certain historic sequence. They do so because some at least of the later developments in human history seem to presuppose the earlier ones, and could not have preceded them.'[26]

Equally, it should be pointed out that the ascription of an idea or an invention to a particular group does not imply that that invention will provide benefits only for that group. It may help or it may harm other groups and individuals. The development of professional scientific medicine certainly did nothing for traditional healers but it provided more than a few benefits for the sick. Certain conclusions can be drawn. Invention is not something 'artificial' but a perfectly natural human activity rendered necessary by changing circumstances. It builds on existing traditions of thought and action. Intellectual constructs are necessarily neither true nor false. Only empirical investigation can establish their truth or falsehood. For example, the triumph of Newtonian physics and the failure of Cartesian physics can be viewed in these terms.

The situation is less clear-cut in the case of something nebulous such as 'National Character' but a similar rule applies. If someone attempted to portray Australians as drawing-room dandies who spent their days in sloth and indolence then such a portrait would be false and unable to win public support. A similar doubt hangs over Donald Horne's attempt to reconstruct Australia as the 'clever country'. Granted that there are competing visions of Australian national identity, then there is a 'real' Australia which limits the number of possible competitors. If such a 'real' Australia did not exist then it would be possible to concoct any national image and impose it. But a cursory examination of White's national images demonstrates that they are all quite similar; indeed, it is possible to read *Inventing Australia* as the evolution of ideas about Australian national identity. The fact of competing national images does not preclude the existence of a 'real Australia as it really was'.

There are serious flaws in any approach to cultural history which emphasises discontinuity, contingency and the rhetoric of invention. Quite simply it collapses into incoherence; the evidence contradicts its pre-suppositions. It is best understood as a reaction to the old idea of the evolution of the nation as a monolithic entity. Clearly the Palmer picture of a single culture evolving through a pre-determined series of stages cannot do justice to the cultural variety of Australian life. But an escape from the rigid confines of the radical nationalist model need not condemn us to some sort of mad mosaic in which fleeting images jostle each other for the attention of the consumer.

Hence, after considering both the nationalist model of cultural development and the post-modern attempts to discredit it, one is left with a profound sense of dissatisfaction. What exactly can be salvaged? Any cultural history will need to preserve the following elements. The first of these is a need to understand and appreciate continuity in the sense that ideas do not spring out of nowhere. The 'presence of the past' permeates any culture.[27] The second is a clear understanding of the meaning of culture, and the third an awareness of the diversity and complexity of human culture. Any 'culture' is, in fact, the product of a variety of cultural traditions in which individuals participate in their day-to-day lives. Every individual participates in many institutions – family, church, work, nation, voluntary organisations, political parties, etc. – which have their own norms and ideals. Blinded by notions of 'hegemony', writers like White want to ascribe primacy to a single institution – the state – and so make national identity the dominant and basic element of culture. The real world is much more complex than this. The importance of the nation and national identity cannot be denied but the significance of other cultures also needs to be recognised. The easiest way to do this is to consider the national culture as constituting one tradition amongst a large number of other traditions.

Another major problem with the White style of cultural analysis is that it divides human beings into two groups: those who, like White, are enlightened and can see that culture is merely an invention, and a great mass of manipulated fools. But why should anyone assume that the pre-occupations of the majority of human beings are mindless and foolish?

Really, we are here dealing with two conceptions of culture: one which emphasises the inherent intelligence and rationality of purposeful human activity and one which views human activity as passive and acqui-escent, the product of whim and fancy. Alain Finkielkraut has summed up the distinction neatly: 'In effect the term "culture" now has two mean-ings. The first asserts the pre-eminence of the life of thought; the second denies this: from everyday gestures to the great creations of the human spirit, is not everything culture?'[28] Alasdair MacIntyre has shown that this second conception of culture can be traced back to the eighteenth cen-tury philospher, David Hume. For Hume, he contends, 'Philosophy is a delightful avocation for those whose talents and tastes happen to be of the requisite kind, just as hunting is a delightful avocation for those whose talents and tastes are of *that* kind.'[29]

The roots of the relativism espoused by such post-modern philoso-phers as Richard Rorty can be traced back to Hume.[30] The distinction between culture as purposeful activity and culture as delightful avocation should not be confused with that between high and popular culture. High culture can surrender to the temptation of 'delightful avocations' just as popular culture, properly understood, is rooted in the belief that certain actions and forms of behaviour are superior to others. Indeed, John Carroll has recently argued that popular culture is much more able to understand and portray fundamental truths than high culture.[31]

Philosophically there is no distinction between high and popular cul-ture. Empirically the division does exist but it is less important than that which exists between culture as a living force and culture as passive con-sumption. (In recycling 'French theory' high culture follows the model of consumer capitalism.) One possible move is to salvage the valuable elements in both the Palmer and the White positions. Palmer is funda-mentally correct in pointing to a vital, living idea of culture as that which stirs the active intellect. White has probed behind the facade of Palmer's national culture to reveal its true nature as a patchwork quilt of images and ideals.

White's arguments do not deny the idea that there is an Australian cul-ture but it is not a culture in the radical nationalist sense. Rather, Australian culture at any particular point of time is the sum of those traditions in which Australians participate and which they see as possessing value. Hence Australian culture has a history in that it is composed of traditions extending over time, is real in that these traditions reflect the real concerns of ordinary men and women, and pluralistic in that it cannot be given a single definition. Pluralism is a central feature of any modern industrial society. Writes John Gray: 'We are none of us, defined by membership of a single community or form of moral life. We are "suckled on the milk of many nurses" as Fulke Greville puts it, heirs of many distinct, sometimes conflicting, intellectual and moral traditions.'[32]

These traditions grow, evolve and mutate; their progress and mutual interaction can be plotted and described. If there is such a thing as a national culture then it surely consists in locating these traditions and then describing their history over time. In this, at least, White is perfectly correct in denying the existence of fixed, essential national characteristics.

The central question is the degree to which the culture which men and women create for themselves is amenable to rational investigation. In White's view, culture has very little to do with human rationality but is rather a force imposing itself on people from without and which they accept for fundamentally irrational reasons. Human beings are essentially creatures of passion impelled by interest. This particular view of human nature clearly derives from David Hume who considered, for example, that monotheism was adopted not through consideration of its intellectual superiority but for other sentimental reasons.[33] Here are the roots of White's view that image can impel action. Peter Brown has criticised Hume's conception of religion noting that it ultimately leads to a two-tier picture of *homo religicus* – that is, the enlightened for whom rationality plays a role and the vulgar who remain prey to superstition and enthusiasm.[34] By implication, White's model only makes sense if viewed in a similar light. Its picture of the average Australian is hardly flattering. More importantly, for it to have any logical coherence it must pre-suppose two groups, the 'enlightened' who are not swayed by their passions and the ignorant, prey to their emotions and interests.

The task of the cultural historian is to unravel the threads of those traditions which constitute the flourishings of a community, plot their progress and their interactions, and explain why one should grow and prosper and another 'wither on the vine'. This is not to say that he or she should remain neutral in relation to their merits, consequences and the like; if a given tradition encourages obscene conclusions or immoral consequences the historian should say so – on this matter Hugh Stretton is absolutely correct.[35] In this context it is worthwhile recalling that cultural traditions are themselves concerned with value and judgement. They are not the whole of life but rather, bodies of ideas in which individuals participate so that they might give value and order to their lives. In a very real sense they are partial attempts by human beings to give expression to the objective, if largely unknowable, order which underlies all creation. It is now possible to make an attempt to clarify the nature of culture.

Understanding Cultural Traditions

In the first instance, culture arises out of the real needs and wants of individuals. It is a perfectly natural human activity. While the passions and prejudices do play a role in the creation of cultural traditions, these traditions also embody principles of rationality which make them amenable to systematic investigation. In other words, there is a logic in human activity which can be discerned by the observer. The problem of human action is the central element in any discussion of culture because, as Blondel correctly argues, *'l'action, dans ma vie, est un fait, le plus général et le plus constant de tous'*.[36] We cannot not act; non-action is a valid form of action. In acting we must necessarily exercise judgement in relation to possible courses of action. Culture provides the basis on which that judgement is exercised (judgement covers ethical, aesthetic, political and other forms of action). Just as action is necessary and a fact, so there is a need for some framework which makes judgement possible, both as a basis for action and as a means of evaluating acts.

Culture provides the ideal logic for human action. It defines and limits the number of repertoires available to an individual and consequently sets the parameters as to 'what is possible' in any concrete situation. Moreover, the internal logic of these repertoires makes them amenable to classification. Traditional political theory from Aristotle to Montesquieu understood this very well when it divided the possible forms of government into three – the rule of one, the rule of few, and the rule of many – and then proceeded to elaborate on the consequences of following one particular form.[37] More recently, John Gray has conceded that only certain types of flourishing are possible under particular political forms. If, as Gray suggests, the real question is 'which of the many natures latent in my nature shall I adopt as my own' then it is culture which impels a man to adopt the persona of a twentieth century intellectual rather than that of a monastic recluse or Renaissance astrologer.[38]

In a way, this is to say no more than that certain types of activity and sets of values have an elective affinity for each other, and so are usually found together. The essential point is that cultures act as limits on action such that it is impossible for any single, concrete culture to express all that is good, true and beautiful in human nature. And the truths, goods and beauties that a culture emphasises do allow for classification and do possess an internal logic which can be discerned with the passage of time. Limitation does not necessarily imply relativism; rather it should be viewed as an antidote to absolutism.

A repertoire may be identified with a tradition as consisting of a set of ideals, beliefs, or arguments considered both as actualities and potentialities, that is, its current state and the possible directions in which it could move. Traditions are, like individuals, 'matrices of possibility', but not unlimited possibilities. Within a tradition the movement of ideas is limited and thus neither contingent nor arbitrary. The enlightened as much as the vulgar must operate from within traditions. A particular cultural tradition comes to acquire its characteristics (and its matrix of possibilities) through the accumulated judgements of those who claim its mantle. Through the never-ending process of judgement, choice, action and reflection, carried out by a myriad of individuals, a cultural tradition is transmitted and transformed. Again it should be emphasised that judgements can be foolish, actions lead to dire consequences and reflections on their outcome mistaken. Culture is the product of both truth and error.

Strictly speaking, cultural history concerns itself with that element of a cultural tradition from which the real (that is, actions) has been removed so that the judgements and reflections can be evaluated. It deals with the ideal structure and inner logic of cultural traditions. Cultural traditions come into being, for the cultural historian, as particular sets of judgements and reflections on judgements as expressed within an established, continuing framework. Alasdair MacIntyre defines a tradition as follows:

> A tradition is an argument extended through time in which certain fundamental agreements are defined and re-defined in terms of two kinds of conflict: those with critics and enemies external to the tradition who reject all or at least key parts of those fundamental agreements, and those internal, interpretative debates through which the meaning and rationale of the fundamental agreements come to be expressed and by whose progress a tradition is constituted.[39]

The idea of a tradition as an argument is a useful one although one should be wary of treating a tradition purely as a formal logical system. As well as logical progressions there are quirky movements of thought, insights and inevitably errors. Equally, contradictions and confusions can occur within an argument. In this sense, Michael Oakeshott is closer to appreciating the 'messiness' of cultural traditions:

> Perhaps we may think of those components of a culture as voices, each the expression of a distinct and conditional understanding of the world and a

distinct idiom of human self-understanding, and of the culture itself as
these voices joined, as such voices could only be joined, in a conversation –
an endless unrehearsed intellectual adventure in which, in imagination
we enter into a variety of modes of understanding the world and ourselves
and are not disconcerted by the differences or dismayed by the inconclusive-
ness of it all.[40]

A cultural tradition is an argument but it is one founded on a 'partial'
and 'conditional' understanding of ourselves and the world. And yet it is
not without a logic which can be recovered if not reduced to a merely
formal structure. A culture is defined by the traditions which jostle for
recognition within its confines – even within a single individual. Each
tradition contains truths but only partial truths. Hence there is a great
foolishness in attempting to subordinate one particular tradition of culture to another. This is the essential flaw in most ideas of national culture which portray the nation as a unified closed system. On this
question Donald Horne is correct – nations are important;[41] but culture
does not stop at the borders of a nation. Rather it extends like a web
amongst nations, an overlapping series of traditions amongst which
national traditions are of great but not ultimate significance.

Culture is an overlapping and complex network of partial under-
standings sometimes in conversation, sometimes not. For this very reason
the integrity of culture is best preserved if one voice in the conversation
is not allowed to raise itself to a shout and drown out softer and more
subtle voices. By denying that cultural traditions are closed, exclusive
systems this picture of culture also avoids much of the problem of incom-
mensurability. It cannot be denied that there is much in the experience
of both individuals and communities which cannot be expressed to
outsiders. But there are also commensurate elements which are rooted in
the objective and universal experience of humanity. For example, the
creed, liturgy and organisation of a religion can be understood and
analysed by outsiders; the experiential element, which derives from particular and local experience, cannot. The one, being portable, passes
from culture to culture, the other remains at its place of origin. One consequence of this is that when the formal structure of a cultural tradition is
translated into another environment it will become a different beast from
the original. Form is commensurate, style is not; while what Oakeshott
calls the 'how to do' can be reduced to propositions, the 'what to do'
remains untouched, rooted as it is in the experience of those conducting
the conversation of that tradition.[42] In Australia, for example, under the
guise of similar formal structures to Europe, new conversations emerge
out of new experiences – often without anyone noticing the changes
which have occurred.

Hence, culture possesses an essential unity but the circles in which its conversations are conducted are various. There is the family, the world of education, of religion, of leisure activities, of politics and public affairs. In this sense culture can be intensely local as ideas, beliefs, ideologies and arguments are generated in particular circumstances and reflect the experiences of those circumstances. Even the universal ideas advocated by a group such as the university educated owe a great deal to the particular experiences involved in acquiring that education. Even if Gellner is correct in contending that one of the primary features of modernity is the creation of a universal high culture, it does not follow that any single group can claim a monopoly on that culture and its universal vision.[43]

Rather, there are the interlocking realms mentioned above, in which individuals can conduct conversations and invest in an identity; in all can be found cultural traditions embodying certain principles, ideas and arguments about those ideals. The faith in universality was a distinctive feature of modernity, simultaneously its strength and its weakness. The real problem arose when attempts were made to reduce this universality to monistic closed systems; such attempts at intellectual centralisation form one of the central themes of twentieth century Australian cultural history.

Finally, it must be recognised that cultural traditions are prey to all the changes and vicissitudes of human existence. There are whole civilisations, religions and systems of philosophy now lost to humanity; one of the saddest events of the twentieth century has been the virtual destruction of its most vital civilisation, that is, the Jewish/German civilisation of central and eastern Europe. Cultural traditions, both in themselves and in their relationship with other traditions, are always changing as a consequence of human action and human choice. Arguments are modified, circumstances change, attitudes undergo a 'sea' change, ideas from other times and places are discovered or rediscovered.

A New Direction for Cultural History

The foregoing discussion of culture was intended to establish a number of important points:

1 Cultural history is best understood in terms of traditions which form an inter-related set of arguments, beliefs and ideals which are developed over time by individuals participating in them.
2 Intellectual and cultural history are necessarily related as it is impossible to understand the general culture of a period without an understanding of the ideas which form the ideal framework against which it is evaluated.

3 Cultural traditions are best understood as dynamic entities undergoing change as a consequence of individual action and choice.
4 In any particular culture there will be a number of cultural traditions. Any single individual will participate in a number of traditions. Nevertheless, this does not prevent attempts to establish the dominance of a particular tradition and to subordinate others to it.

At the present time there is a need for a more thorough and rigorous approach to Australian cultural history. The Palmer–Ward model is too narrow, the White approach too destructive and more recent work has failed to take up the intellectual challenge posed by the notion of 'culture'. John Rickard in *Australia: A Cultural History* claims that he is dealing with culture in the anthropological sense.[44] But the picture of Australian cultural development which emerges in this work is strangely conventional, primarily because it wants to portray Australia as a single cultural entity. At the other end of the spectrum, Smith and Goldberg in their introduction to the *Australian Cultural History* collection opt for an 'anything goes' view of culture – an approach which is less than helpful.[45] Equally, in his introduction to the *Under New Heavens* collection, Neville Meaney does little to extend the discussion about the nature of culture.[46]

It is hoped that the approach discussed above charts a safe passage between the threatened anarchy of pluralism and the rigidity of viewing Australia as a single cultural entity. By viewing a culture as the product of the cultural traditions that encompass it and by considering these traditions as both arguments and as voices expressing partial Truths in the conversation of humanity, we have an approach which combines intellectual rigour and an appreciation of diversity. In many ways this conception of culture overlaps with the concerns of those seeking to understand the nature of multiculturalism in Australia.[47] There is no whole beyond the sum of the parts and yet those parts can be analysed, dissected, plotted and considered in the light of other voices and other arguments.

That then is the task of this study: to examine a particular cultural tradition in Australia, to lay bare its fundamental ideas and to plot its passage through time. The central concern of the study will be with the internal dynamics of the tradition, the immanent unfolding of ideas. As such, its approach is avowedly rationalist as it seeks to follow the argument of a conversation. It does not survey all the speakers nor all the works which have constituted it; only those who have made a significant contribution to its development. It is unashamedly a study in cultural and intellectual history. At the same time, it does not ignore the context or general framework within which this tradition developed but its major concern is with the intellectual tradition itself.

Cultural Liberalism: A Tradition of Modernity

In the previous section the theoretical foundations for this study were established and a justification made for a rationalist analysis of a particular cultural and intellectual tradition. But what exactly is the tradition under analysis? To a large extent it cannot be fully described until it has been plotted, but a rough sketch of its major features can now be provided. In his study of Frederic Eggleston, Warren Osmond referred to the aristocratic liberalism found amongst Eggleston and his Deakinite liberal friends.[48] To an extent this is an appropriate description though we are dealing here with aristocrats of the spirit. Given that the tradition is not narrowly political but concerned with wider cultural and spiritual matters, the term 'Cultural Liberalism' would seem to be closest to capturing its true nature. Its important features are:

1 An emphasis on the autonomy of the individual and his or her right to individual liberty.
2 A belief, shared with scientists, in what might be termed the 'Culture of Rationalism'. This implies an essential faith in the power of reason to understand and explain the workings of the universe.
3 The potential excesses of the 'Culture of Rationalism' are tempered by a view of human beings as essentially spiritual and ethical creatures. This is a tradition touched by Romanticism and, as we shall see, sometimes dragged off into the world of Romantic madness. To a certain extent it is a tradition looking for religious values in a world stripped of its sacred qualities. Although one is tempted to say that 'culture' becomes a secular form of religion, it is worth noting that for many in the tradition 'civilisation' is the key word.
4 A faith in evolution as a process through which the world becomes more enlightened, rational and spiritual.
5 The individuals who participated in the tradition came to it through their university education. It was through this experience that they were initiated into the world of 'culture' and came to share common values. In terms of class they were not homogeneous although many came from a clerical or professional background. It was their education which convinced them that ideas, and the people who hold them, matter.

The tradition, then, that we are seeking to describe is an amalgam of rationalism, a spiritualised humanism and liberalism – although as we shall see its liberalism was more closely related to civic humanism than to *laissez-faire*.[49] Its final characteristic was universalism, a faith that a single rational set of principles could be found both to describe the world and

create a better one. Hence in politics it abided by the universality of liberalism and in science by that of classical physics – it attempted to iron
out the rough edges so that all could be fitted into a single harmonious
whole.

John Gray claims that liberalism is the political theory of modernity.[50]
Our claims are more modest; the tradition of Cultural Liberalism, with
its faith in the capacity of the emancipated enlightened individual to
control his or her world, is appropriately considered as a tradition of
modernity. Modernity, like progress, is a problem word. Just as progress
may be described as the 'going on of what goes on', so the modern can
be considered simply as that which is the most recent.[51] Equally, there
can be confusion as to what constitutes the 'modern'; traditionally the
French Revolution has been considered as an event ushering in the
modern age, but recently Simon Schama has argued that it was essentially a reaction against the modernising tendencies at work in eighteenth century France.[52]

Nevertheless, it is possible to ascribe a meaning to the term 'modernity'. Certain aspects of the twentieth century European world mark it
out as qualitatively different from the Europe of the eighteenth century.
These differences are real and require explanation. Likewise, modernity
can be considered to constitute a particular cultural position capable of
being held during a variety of historical epochs. It is a quality of a cultural tradition; that tradition may be weak during certain periods and
more powerful during others.[53] Perhaps the use of the word 'modernity'
is unfortunate, but in a very real sense modernity constitutes itself
through intellectual and cultural traditions such as the one under discussion. Non-modern traditions continue in the modern world. In a way,
the modernity of a culture depends on the configuration assumed by the
cultural traditions which compose it.

Hence I would want to argue that there is a distinctive modern period,
both in the European world generally and in Australia in particular,
which can be described in terms of structural changes at the economic,
social and cognitive levels, and the interaction with those changes by
both cultural traditions of modernity and cultural traditions of non-
modernity. The modern age and modernity are not the same thing.
Ernest Gellner in his *Plough, Sword and Book* attempts to distinguish what
he terms the Industrial Age from the Agrarian Age which preceded it.
Gellner characterises 'Agraria' as being founded on 'dogmatic, clerisy-
ridden, thug-dominated scripturalist systems' in which the surplus was
not used to enhance the productive equipment or cognitive potential of
its members. The transition from agraria to the industrial age occurs
when 'production replaces predation as the central theme and value of
life'.[54] It is the freeing up and expansion of production, both technolog-

ical and cognitive, in the wake of the expansion of the market, which holds the key to an understanding of modernity. In other words, it is the prospect of infinity which lies at the heart of modernity. Gellner identifies two other central elements of modernity. The first is the creation of a division of labour founded on a universal high culture and a differentiation of skills within that culture.[55] The second is the replacement of Platonism (that is, ideas in this world being viewed as a reflection of another reality) by Cartesianism (that is, ideas about this world having to be justified within this world).[56] Gellner's picture of industrial society does possess a stark clarity, freed as it is from an excess of empirical detail. Nevertheless there is much to be said for its characterisation of modernity as the promise of infinity; the modern age can be defined as that epoch in which this theme became increasingly dominant and its consequences manifest.[57] As noted earlier, modernity can be described as the tradition created around this belief; the modern age slowly emerges as this tradition strengthens and reacts with other cultural traditions.

The tradition of Cultural Liberalism was a tradition of modernity; it incorporated the promise of infinity. It was concerned with understanding and working out the implications of the coming of modernity. The focus of this study is Australia, and Cultural Liberalism can be identified as an Australian tradition of modernity which reached its maturity in those years after 1900 when modernity entered its age of crisis. Its particular set of conversations and arguments can be seen both as contributing to, and reacting against, that crisis. There are European analogues to the Australian tradition of Cultural Liberalism. In particular, there are close affinities with British New Liberalism which is not surprising given the influence of T.H. Green on such figures as Francis Anderson.[58] Nevertheless, this study considers Cultural Liberalism as an essentially Australian phenomenon which is best understood within the context of the Australian experience of modernity. Comparisons with European and English parallels must await a further study.

As far as the contents of this book are concerned, the remainder of this chapter is devoted to locating Cultural Liberalism in an intellectual and social context. The following chapter considers the dominant modes of liberalism in nineteenth and twentieth century Australia – Free Trade and Protectionist Liberalism – as the background against which the distinctive features of Cultural Liberalism can be established. The rest of the book examines the dynamics of Cultural Liberalism as an intellectual tradition in Australia, focusing initially on its development at the University of Sydney prior to World War I and subsequently on a broader range of individuals in the period after the war. I have attempted to capture the 'rise and fall' of Cultural Liberalism in

Australia, its growth and flowering, its weaknesses and decline, before concluding with some reflections on its continuing relevance for Australian intellectual, cultural and political life.

The Historiography of Australian Liberalism:
Rowse, Macintyre and Roe

To understand the significance of Cultural Liberalism it is first necessary to examine those works which have attempted to deal with the liberal tradition in Australia: Tim Rowse's *Liberalism and Australian National Character*, Stuart Macintyre's *A Colonial Liberalism*, and Michael Roe's *Nine Australian Progressives*.[59]

Rowse claims that liberalism has been the 'dominant discourse by which the problems of Australian society have been discussed by intellectuals'. The essence of liberalism, he continues, has been that the 'individual owes his or her first allegiance to the state rather than to any social grouping within society'.[60] Such a definition would appear to have more to do with Communist Russia or Nazi Germany than Australia – in short, it is a very peculiar definition of liberalism. John Gray ascribes the following characteristics to the liberal tradition:

> It is *individualist*, in that it asserts the moral primacy of the person against the claims of any social collectivity; *egalitarian*, inasmuch as it confers on all men the same moral status and denies the relevance to legal or political order of differences in moral worth among human beings; *universalist*, affirming the moral unity of the human species and according a secondary importance to specific historic associations and cultural forms; and meliorist in its affirmation of the corrigibility and improvability of all social institutions and political arrangements.[61]

No mention of the state appears anywhere. Now it may well be the case that, in Australia, the state occupies a more important role in liberal thought than elsewhere. If so, this needs to be argued and explained. As it stands, Rowse's definition owes more to Machiavelli than to J.S. Mill, and is closer to civic humanism than liberalism. If Rowse's claim is true then it raises fundamental questions about the nature of liberalism in Australia. Why should Australian intellectuals have been so attracted to a civic humanist and statist variety of liberalism?

The problem is that the central aspect of liberalism is not that of allegiance to the state but of individual autonomy. The role of the state is highly problematical for liberals. According to seventeenth century liberals such as John Locke, the individual is the bearer of universal rights that carries the individual into society and upon which it is illegitimate for the state to infringe. T.H. Green, who influenced many Australian liberals, argued that individuals hold rights by virtue of their membership of associations, including the state. Alexis de Tocqueville, another major influence on Australian liberals, believed that voluntary associations, what is normally known as civil society, were necessary to counteract the growing power of the state. All three, however, sought to establish the conditions under which individuals could grow and flourish.

In other words, the issue cannot be reduced to a simple 'essence' of liberalism that dominates intellectual discourse in Australia. Liberalism is not simple but complex and one must take great care in distinguishing amongst its varieties.

Strangely, for a Marxist, Rowse makes no attempt to provide a socio-logical context for his liberals or to explain their place within Australia except to assume, with apparently no evidence, that they are ideological mouthpieces for the ruling class. Nevertheless, Rowse's book raises three issues which are central to any understanding of Cultural Liberalism. These are:

1 the acknowledged role of the state in Australia as something which marks out Australian social development;
2 the traditions of knowledge and political understanding to which the university educated in Australia have been the heirs;
3 the place of the university educated within Australian society and how this has affected the sorts of ideas they have come to hold.

In Rowse's version of the liberal tradition in Australia, Francis Anderson arrives from Britain bringing with him the torch of the New Liberalism which is then passed on to a number of liberal thinkers who then, according to Rowse, espouse 'liberalism' as the dominant ideology in Australian intellectual life.[62] What he appears not to understand is that the tradition of evolutionary liberalism is also the tradition of culture. The roots of that tradition in Australia can be traced back to the 1850s; great care must be exercised in dealing with what it meant when it advo-cated such notions as 'service to the state'. Similarly, Rowse makes no attempt to establish the relationship of its adherents to the wider Australian culture. He assumes that it acquired a hegemonic centrality whereas, as we shall see, it was essentially critical and at best, on the periphery of power. Many of its adherents became expatriates. Rowse has correctly identified a tradition of liberalism in Australia but almost completely misinterprets its significance. He wants it to assume a certain ideological function and is unwilling to explore its complexities, pre-sumably because of a basic lack of sympathy for his subject. This study, at least in part, can be read as an attempt to deal with the inadequacies of Rowse's book.

Stuart Macintyre's *A Colonial Liberalism* is much narrower in focus being a study of three nineteenth century Victorian liberals: George Higinbotham, David Syme and Charles Pearson. Nevertheless, in many ways Macintyre's approach is far more satisfying than that of Rowse. For one thing, he recognises that liberalism is concerned with the 'autonomous self-sufficient individual' and the capacity of that individual to act in a rational and moral fashion.[63] Macintyre also recognises that his three liberals form a 'lineage' and thus constitute a tradition of ideas.

Michael Roe's study consists of a set of nine mini-biographies of Australian thinkers and social activists of the early twentieth century. The figures he examines are university educated and largely Protestant, and Roe successfully demonstrates their importance in pushing for what he calls 'progressive' social reform in the early decades of this century. They were not, however, all members of the Cultural Liberal group; in fact, Roe nicely captures some of the ambiguities of his subjects who began as progressives but who, in the wake of World War I, moved closer to a form of fascism, particularly in their views on such topics as eugenics.

Roe's group consists largely of lawyers and medical men who were thoroughly convinced of the value of science as the basis of a more rational social order. With the exception of R.F. Irvine they appear to have had largely antiseptic souls and do not seem to have grasped the human implications of progressive social reforms. As such, Roe does not establish that they are Australian equivalents of the European revolt against positivism during the same period. Rather, they represent the secular equivalent of a Protestant desire to improve people through such measures as temperance, town planning, eugenics and increasing the population size by abolishing drink.[64]

Roe does demonstrate the importance of the university educated professionals in determining many of the intellectual issues of early twentieth century Australia. His 'progressivist' tradition of Protestant rationality overlaps with, but is distinct from, that liberal tradition which is the subject of this study. His subjects are equally part of a tradition of modernity and in Alvin Gouldner's terminology they are closer to constituting a technical intelligentsia than what would be normally understood as intellectuals.[65]

A New Class?

How then are we to understand the Cultural Liberal tradition and its relationship to both modernity and to other varieties of liberalism? Rowse's approach was to consider intellectuals as mouthpieces for what he believes to have been the dominant ideology, while Roe's biographical technique emphasised the role of individual thinkers. Neither is really an adequate approach. But how are we to come to terms with that very special form of cultural tradition – that of the intellectual? To begin, I should like to list a few contentions which have been made about the role of ideas and intellectuals in the modern world. Ernest Gellner argues that in the pre-industrial world the discourse of high culture was merely one discourse among many, just as the university was one of many guilds.[66] One of the consequences of modernity has been to create a high culture based on science and mathematics and to make it the dominant discourse of the modern world. John Hall and Michael Mann both contend that ideas as a means of power have been important in two periods of human history.[67] The first was when the great world religions were established. The second has been those years since the coming of industrialisation.

Alvin Gouldner has argued that intellectuals in the modern world have come to constitute a 'New Class' whose main source of power and influence lies in its ideas and culture.[68] These intellectuals do not have capital but culture, they prize their personal autonomy, favour criticism and debate over authority and have developed a critical discourse marked by its theoretical approach and its reflexivity.

There have been numerous objections to the idea of the 'New Class', many of them along the lines that the criterion of knowledge or culture is not strong enough to indicate a class. Nevertheless, there is considerable evidence to suggest that ideas, in the sense of theoretical constructions, together with the agents of those ideas, have risen in importance during the past two hundred years. The rise of the new professions attests to the growing importance of ideas. In a more limited way Roe's study of his professional progressives demonstrates how important this group of university educated professionals had become in Australia by the early twentieth century. In many ways it is extraordinary, given the amount of time devoted to the 'rise of capitalism', that so little has been given to that of the intellectuals, a point often made by New Class theorists (who, it should be pointed out, are politically both of the Left and the Right).[69]

On the one hand, there is an undeniable phenomenon, the growing importance of ideas and of those skilled in their use; on the other hand, there is the awkward term 'New Class' which many find uncomfortable and inaccurate. Eva Etzioni-Halevy suggests the term 'knowledge elite' as a way out of this difficulty.[70] Another approach, in line with our emphasis on cultural traditions, might be to refer to a 'culture of rationalism' as expressing that set of cultural values to which the New Class, considered as that group which has acquired its values through its experience of higher education, adheres. The Culture of Rationalism broadly covers all those groups who, through their adherence to the primacy of rational knowledge, helped to create that general phenomenon: modernity. Gouldner does not consider the New Class to be a homogeneous group but sees it comprising two important components: the technological intelligentsia and the more humanistically inclined intellectuals.[71] In a way this would seem to correspond to the two culture idea of C.P. Snow; it is a real distinction of great importance.

The best solution would be to say that the tradition of Cultural Liberalism is a sub-culture of the culture of rationalism and its adherents members of the intellectual sub-group of the New Class.[72] In other words, Cultural Liberalism represents one segment within the burgeoning culture of rationalism. Like the other traditions which comprised this culture its participants tended to be associated with the universities, either as teachers or as former students. They came from humanities backgrounds but they do not include all members of the humanities. They were often the children of clerics or became clerics themselves.[73] In denominational terms, Anglicanism and Liberal Protestantism predominated. What distinguished Cultural Liberalism from the other elements of the culture of rationalism was its concern with the spiritual side of human nature and the relationship of this spirituality to the dominant rational scientific spirit of the modern age. From John Woolley to Christopher Brennan to Marjorie Barnard to James McAuley this preoccupation illuminated their work. It is this 'religious' dimension – even amongst those writers and thinkers who were secularists – which marks out this group and allows us to maintain that its members constitute a distinct tradition.

If it is conceded that one of the dominant features of the modern world has been the development of a large group for whom ideas and rationality are of prime importance and that this group has created its own peculiar 'culture of rationalism', then the tradition of Cultural Liberalism represents a strand within that development, both sociologically and intellectually. As that strand was concerned very much with humanity's spiritual aspirations it often developed a critical stance both to the world around it and to many of the leading ideas of the culture of rationalism; many of its critiques were directed towards exposing the inadequacies of that mode of rationality which questioned the legitimacy of those spiritual aspirations. Equally, as it possessed that reflexivity discussed by Gouldner,[74] it could turn its critique with devastating effects back on itself. The argument of this study focuses on the dynamic of this tradition as it seeks to describe its ideal world, criticise the obstacles in its path and come to terms with its own failures and weaknesses.

If we are to avoid the problems of Rowse's somewhat abstract approach then we must provide a broader context into which this particular tradition of modernity can be placed. This can best be done by examining the cultural development of Australia during the late nineteenth and early twentieth century. The following chapter will consider the two major traditions of liberalism which developed in Australia during those years. Such a procedure will enable us to bring into relief the distinguishing characteristics of Cultural Liberalism as a particular tradition of liberalism. The rest of the study is then devoted to understanding the dynamic of Cultural Liberalism as its conversation developed in the late nineteenth and early twentieth century.

CHAPTER 2

Traditions of Modernity in Australia

Australian Modernity: Some Characteristics

Two viewpoints, not necessarily conflicting, have been expressed regarding the place of the modern in Australia. The first is that Australia was born modern;[1] it has not had to carry any of the weight of the European past but in its early years acquired all the trappings of the modern such as a capitalist economic system, a free press, parliamentary democracy and the nuclear family. The second emphasises the progressive nature of nineteenth century Australia and then is puzzled by the conservatism of the twentieth century. How did Australia change so much they ask? Why did it go to sleep after World War I? Even Roe admits that Progressivism turned somewhat nasty in the 1920s.[2] An understanding of this important cultural development is necessary if the role and place of Cultural Liberalism in Australia is to be appreciated.

If the nature of modernity in Australia and of what can properly be termed 'modern Australia' is to be understood, one factor stands out as being of crucial importance. It is that the two dominant colonies had different traditions of liberalism and that the coming of Federation saw the victory of Victorian Protectionist Liberalism over that of New South Wales Free Trade Liberalism. The changing nature of Cultural Liberalism can best be appreciated through an understanding of both varieties of liberalism. This is particularly so in the period after World War I when it must necessarily be considered in relation to the cultural developments which had taken place in Australia during the early years of the century. The most significant of these developments is what I have termed the 'protectionist mentality'. By this, I mean the state of mind which accompanied and endorsed the triumph of Protection as both an ideology and a set of public policies.[3]

In socio-economic terms late nineteenth century Australia was characterised by a number of peculiar features. Its economic system was capitalist and, by the end of the nineteenth century, it had become heavily urbanised. It possessed no established church, a secular, state-run education system and a democratically elected legislature. It did not have heavy industry or an industrial proletariat; it was, and remains, heavily dependent on the export of raw materials to earn a living. Moreover, it was a society which was 'bottom-heavy' in terms of its class origins possessing the most heavily unionised population in the world and only a small professional middle class. Equally there was not a great deal of personal wealth concentrated in the hands of individuals. Hence, Australia was primarily a society of clerks, artisans and tradesmen employed in small commercial, industrial businesses or self-employed. Its professional middle class was composed of doctors and lawyers – the demand for the new professions of engineer, scientist, architect was not great. The universities only began to grow when they developed their professional faculties, and in the humanities growth was dependent largely on the expansion of teacher training. The proletariat was rural as much as urban and the first great successes of the labour movement occurred in rural areas.[4]

By Western European standards this was a peculiar society. Outwardly it looked very modern, possessing many of the features of modernity. Yet there were other aspects of it which point to a much more complex matrix. As well as exporting commodities to England and Europe, Australia remained dependent on English capital for development. Australia was, and is, locked into world financial and trading markets. Consequently, the Australian colonies had to import from England many of their requirements and were constantly in debt to English bankers and financiers. This necessary relationship with England and the outside world could be interpreted in a variety of ways both positive and negative.

As Australia did not develop the newer intellectual professions, the older professions such as law and medicine remained relatively more important. In the mid-nineteenth century, colonial intellectual life had been dominated by lawyers and clerics; it possessed a cross between clerisy and literati rather than a new class of intellectuals.[5] Even by the twentieth century, Australian intellectuals had not been particularly 'modernised'; they often had strong clerical connections (for example, W.K. Hancock, E.H. Burgmann, V.G. Childe) and continued, in the humanities, to enjoy a broad, general and unspecialised education. For example, V.G. Childe studied Greek, Latin, philosophy, geology and mathematics during his years at the University of Sydney.[6]

Many years ago Louis Hartz proposed 'fragment theory' to explain how colonial societies came to differ from the mother country from which they were derived.[7] According to the theory migrants transplanted to a new society attempt to preserve their culture as it was when they left the home country. A society of migrants, even if they bring a progressive image of their homeland with them, will tend towards cultural rigidity. This is the 'fragment effect'. In his chapter in Hartz's collection, Rosencrance argued that Australia constituted a 'radical' fragment just as America had been a 'liberal' fragment. It is difficult to know if the values of the migrants coming to Australia can be categorised so easily. Many of the migrants coming to Australia in the nineteenth century were either lower class Englishmen or Irish peasants. They brought with them the traditional values of their class. Much as these values expressed a desire for equality and justice, they did so not so much in a liberal framework as in a traditional one.[8]

During the second half of the nineteenth century the power of the state increased in all the Australian colonies. One reason for this was the lack of genuinely wealthy Australian entrepreneurs able to bear the cost of such ventures as railways which the state built and ran. Another factor was that central authority preceded that of local self-government. In New South Wales responsible government was achieved in 1856; local government appeared in its wake and, in many areas, was only taken up at the end of the nineteenth century. Education was taken over and directed by the state during the 1870s and 1880s; central bureaucratic direction rather than local initiative became its hallmark. As we shall see, Charles Pearson believed that it was the development of this state power which was the most characteristically modern feature of the Australian colonies.[9]

So it can be said that there were three definite characteristics of Australian modernity as it emerged in the late nineteenth century:

1 modern institutions combined with many traditional values;
2 the growth of the state;
3 a dependence on the world for money and markets.

How then were the Australian colonies to react to the peculiarities of their circumstances? The most significant thing is that there was not one but two responses – two distinct and distinctive traditions of colonial liberalism emerged. These two traditions related to the different economic policies adopted by the two major colonies: Free Trade in New South Wales and Protection in Victoria. But it was more than just a difference regarding tariffs; it was a conflict between two differing value systems regarding nature, human nature and the foundations of human society. To understand Cultural Liberalism and to highlight its distinguishing characteristics, it is first necessary to analyse these two dominant modes of liberalism in Australia. In conducting this analysis our primary focus will be on the writings of the two key theorists of nineteenth century liberalism in Australia: B.R. Wise in New South Wales and C.H. Pearson in Victoria.

Liberalism as Free Trade

Free Trade in Australia has suffered over the years from being viewed through the eyes of the Protectionists who triumphed over it and who attempted to portray it as the doctrine of selfish, unprincipled men. Free Trade has been stigmatised as 'the raw capitalist ethos celebrating the business spirit, Social Darwinism and neo-Nietzschean entrepreneur–superman notions'.[10] This claim cannot be supported, especially as the author of these comments makes no attempt to examine what Free Trade did mean to its adherents for whom it was always viewed as a doctrine of co-operation which, because it was invariably underpinned by Christian morality, was the antithesis of Social Darwinism and amoral individual selfishness.

I have discussed the values of the Free Trade ideology of New South Wales during the second half of the nineteenth century elsewhere,[11] but it is worthwhile, for the sake of the argument of the study, to restate the argument briefly. The ultimate foundation of Free Trade was a belief in the power of nature to heal social wounds and to create a world of harmony and co-operation. This foundation can be summarised under the following three headings:

1 Natural Religion: the idea that God rules His universe through laws which can be known by human reason;
2 Beneficent Providence: the idea of a progressive world moving towards a pre-ordained goal;
3 Ultimate Harmony: the optimistic belief that the goal of history is a sort of Platonic universe from which conflict has been banished.

In the early 1850s this faith in Providence and the course of Nature had led to a colonial version of what Patrice Higonnet has termed 'bourgeois universalism',[12] the faith which had animated the men of 1789 in France with the hope that all was possible and that major change could be achieved without disorder and upheaval. A disillusionment did occur in the 1860s when the obvious flaws of this vision were exposed. It was the men of culture who suffered most when the illusions of bourgeois universalism, of the faith that a cultivated independent democratic society could be created, dissolved into nothing.[13]

In the 1850s and 1860s John West of the *Sydney Morning Herald* extolled a doctrine of humanity, internationalism and the brotherhood of man founded on Free Trade and the role of commerce. West believed in the common unity of mankind and argued that nationality should be subordinated to the common interests of humanity because, he argued, 'Humanity is broader than nationality, and substantial progress is not to be sacrificed to what, after all, is but a sentiment.' Hence, Free Trade was a doctrine of humanity because it developed those universal human qualities which were most noble and moral: 'The intercourse of nations strengthens the intellectual energy and purifies the opinions of the mind. Commerce created the periodical press and still sustains it.'[14] It is worth pointing out that West's ethical liberalism meant that he opposed racism, supported the rights of women and advocated co-operation between both individuals and nations.

The most significant element of Free Trade ideology was its belief in social sympathy, an idea derived originally from eighteenth century philosophers such as the Earl of Shaftesbury and Francis Hutcheson.[15] It was social sympathy which made co-operation between a variety of people and peoples possible. It was conceived to be a human characteristic which could be cultivated and developed through interaction with an ever increasing circle of human beings. Free Trade, which presupposed the free movement of ideas as well as of goods, was seen as a primary way in which social sympathy could be developed so that all members of the human race recognised their common destiny and came together in a common brotherhood. Viewed in this way Free Trade was a highly moralistic doctrine in which ideals of co-operation occupied a central place.

Free Trade in the 1890s: Wise and the
Australian Economic Association

The most systematic expression of the values of Free Trade is to be found in the writings of the Oxford-educated politician and writer, B.R. Wise.[16] In his 1892 work *Industrial Freedom: A Study in Politics*, Wise both restated the case for Free Trade and developed the liberal objections to Protection and the closed social order which that doctrine implied. Wise did not believe that Free Trade meant justifying the universal reign of competition and considered that legislation could check its worst evils. Like most of his Free Trade friends in the Australian Economic Association, including Professor Walter Scott and Andrew Garran, he believed in the virtue of co-operation as a means of checking competition. His aim in advocating Free Trade, he said, was to 'prevent the labourer sinking into the mere drudge of a machine, and to make him once again a craftsman with an artistic love and knowledge of his work'.[17]

National or protectionist economics, claimed Wise, was founded on two beliefs. The first was that every nation must be entirely self-sufficient and the second that the development of productive powers, not national wealth was the objective of wise statesmanship. In emphasising the connection between self-sufficiency and national production, Wise was describing the stationary, self-enclosed state which Protectionism necessitated. He examined the consequences of pursuing such a course of action: trade must be constricted with foreign countries and every nation must be for itself, regardless of the cost or injury to other countries. With trade thus restricted the state must then direct industry, driving individuals into this or that trade. Protection implied the development of what Pearson called State Socialism.[18]

Wise was particularly savage on the moral and psychological consequences of Protection. He argued that it helps one section of society at the expense of the majority by creating vested interests dependent on Acts of Parliament. These interests then make use of tariffs rather than enterprise and self-reliance to support their industries. Manufacturers 'lose the power of facing difficulties like practical and courageous men'.[19] Originality, ambition and enterprise are destroyed and the fibre of national life threatened. Protection threatens the self-reliance of individuals and consequently the good of society at large.

The detrimental effect on industry links up with the moral foundations of Protection: 'It rests avowedly on selfishness.' This selfishness finds its expression in a national isolation and the belief that nations should wage warfare by means of tariffs. It has devastating moral consequences; by discouraging the intercourse of nations it encourages stagnation by destroying the liberating effect of meeting other peoples and exchanging ideas with them. Instead, Protection encourages competition between nations and the cultivation of selfishness; it is the enemy of progress and social growth because 'each nation finds its own true strength in a joint and peaceful progress with neighbouring countries'. Instead of developing an expanded consciousness and moral sense, and a spirit of co-operation between nations, Protection fosters selfishness and competition.[20]

Moreover, Protection weakens national fibre because it limits the free actions of individuals. True national development can only occur if individuals are free to develop their talents consciously and are unrestricted by artificial government constraints. 'Human nature', claimed Wise, 'reaches its highest development when it consciously, and of its own free will, enjoys at all times that which is best'. Commerce encourages that free activity and Wise went so far as to distinguish between commercial and industrial nations, contending that commercial nations are in the forefront of civilisation. It is also interesting to note that Wise's Free Trade beliefs saved him from the worst racist excesses of White Australia. In his

The Commonwealth of Australia Wise argued that it was Germany and not China or Japan which was the real enemy, and that Japan possessed an ancient civilisation not necessarily inferior to that of Europe.[21] For Wise, living in Free Trade New South Wales, the shortcomings of Protection were all too obvious. As an Oxford-trained liberal he continued to espouse the hope that the souls of men could be enlarged and liberated through Free Trade and the development of social co-operation.

What is interesting is the extent to which Wise's colleagues in the Australian Economic Association viewed co-operation as the panacea to the conflicts of modern industrial society. For example, in a piece entitled 'The cash nexus', Professor Walter Scott attempted to argue that economic individualism had forced the social organism to disintegrate into its component atoms replacing the personal bonds of earlier times with those of a temporary and occasional contract governed by the cash nexus. In reply, Wise contended both that co-operation would provide a check on competition and that a higher moral sentiment was absolutely necessary. J.T. Walker argued that co-operation would provide the true solution to the conflict of capital and labour; J. Plummer advocated an increased sense of duty and responsibility, while S.A. Byrne agreed that co-operation was no doubt the best remedy.[22] This theme of co-operation and moral duty runs through many of the articles published by this association. In line with the doctrine of social sympathy, the key was perceived to be the expansion and development of humanity's moral sense so that men and women would freely choose to work together and build a better world.[23]

Liberalism as Protection

If social sympathy, nature, beneficent providence and a faith in the human capacity to develop a universal personality formed the basis of Free Trade ideology, what then of Protection? The 'founding father' of Australian Protectionism, David Syme, was a Scotsman though his roots were Tory rather than Whig and he seems to have had little time for the doctrine of social sympathy. Consider, for example, his famous condemnation of *laissez-faire*:

> I never could see any virtue in *laissez-faire*. To let things alone when they had gone wrong, to render no help when help was needed, is what no sane man would do with his private estate, and what no sound statesman would tolerate as a state policy. It is simply an excuse for incapacity or inertia in affairs of State. It is a policy of drift. It is just what the company promoter, the card sharper, the wife deserter, and the burglar would like – to be left alone. It can only lead to national disaster and social degeneration, when carried out in any community.[24]

This dour Scotsman would appear to have been the heir of John Knox rather than of the Scottish Enlightenment, and his condemnation of *laissez-faire* can be seen as an extension of the traditional Calvinist conception of community, best exemplified in seventeenth century New England, in which the whole community intervened to guarantee the virtue of its individual members.[25] Similarly, the fear of degeneration and social anarchy represents a fear of falling away from righteousness – and the consequences of that falling away. Indeed, his use of the term 'degeneration' is interesting as it implies that when things are left alone they fall into a state of chaos. But unlike the *fin-de-siècle* advocates of degeneration for whom the Second Law of Thermodynamics and entropy provided a scientific model,[26] Syme's version of degeneration had more traditional sources. It is also worth noting that whereas West and Wise thought in terms of humanity and the brotherhood of nations, Syme's model was that of a particular nation.[27]

But in a crucial way Syme was much more 'modern' than his New South Wales counterparts. In his economic analysis he drew on German economists rather than Anglo-Saxon ones. Consequently his newspaper the *Age* was critical of English economic policy and sympathetic towards that of continental Europe. 'England's manufacturing supremacy', claimed an editorial, 'has been purchased at the price of National righteousness'. State intervention, such as occurred in Germany, could prevent that happening in Victoria. The *Age* boasted that Victoria was closer to the 'Continental idea of the State as an initiator and regulator of industries' than to the 'English and American notion of leaving industry to care for itself'.[28]

John Hall has argued that Germany after 1870 attempted an alternative road to industrialisation – one based on the exploitation and creation of knowledge – to that taken by the English. Norman Stone has also contended that from the late 1870s classical liberalism was under siege in Europe, and it is often argued that from the 1880s onwards there was a fundamental change in Europe, economical, social and cultural, as it underwent a profound crisis, which may not inappropriately be called the modernist crisis.[29] H. Stuart Hughes has written of the revolt against positivism and the interest in the irrational and the unconscious which characterised the *fin de siècle* and the opening decade of this century. Karl Dietrich Bracher has also emphasised the growing irrationality of early twentieth century political thought and the way in which political ideas were transformed into ideologies.[30]

At the same time, Franklin Baumer has warned against overemphasising the revolt of what was essentially the intellectual avantgarde.[31] The great bulk of Europeans retained their faith in science and the order which it provided. This was a period which saw both the triumph of science and a revolt against its pretensions; as well, it saw attempts to integrate the irrational and non-rational into a scientific framework. Stephen Kern in his magisterial study *The Culture of Time and Space* has most effectively caught the dynamic of these changes in European culture. Kern emphasises the effects wrought by new technology on concepts of time, space, distance and form. The telephone, wireless and generally improved communication reoriented people towards space and time by shrinking distance, allowing events separated by a distance to be simultaneous in their effects, and enabling actions to be manipulated by breaking them down into their constituent elements. For example, Kern contrasts the achievement of a world time binding all countries together with the subjective sense of time emphasised by Bergson and his disciples. The apparent triumph of scientific objectivity provided the context for the growing irrationalism and subjectivity of the age. It would not be inappropriate to identify this triumph of scientific objectivity with the development of the German model of industrialisation and the emphasis it placed on the role of education and research on the one hand and the positive role of the state on the other.

The nature of the transition described by Stone and Kern can be examined in a more analytical fashion. One way of considering the issue is to take Hayek's distinction between *kosmos* and *taxis*. By *kosmos*, Hayek means a self-generating or spontaneous order grown by nature, and by *taxis* a fabricated order created by human beings.[32] Whereas Free Trade Liberalism founded itself on the idea of *kosmos*, Protectionism clearly had a model of nature based on *taxis*. Free Trade as an expression of *kosmos* emphasised that God's creation – nature – possessed an inherent rationality; man's role was to uncover and reveal that order. *Taxis* expressed the vision of a natural order from which God had departed; reason (science) was a human creation devised to impose order on a universe which had become irrational and potentially chaotic. Norman Stone has plotted the decline of classical liberalism in Europe from the 1880s; he emphasises the development of mass politics, the growth of class war and the impact of new technologies. Clearly, by the 1890s it was extremely difficult to maintain a vision of nature founded on *kosmos*; in response, most European governments from the mid-1890s began a programme of 'National Efficiency' which emphasised strong government, social welfare and the use of tariffs. Then from about 1906, these governments moved increasingly towards what Stone calls 'technocracy', involving the state in such areas as town planning. This reaction to liberalism, in which rationality and science came to be seen as tools of the state utilised to conquer the chaos of nature, also coincided with the growth of doctrines of degeneration, both social and racial. Put simply, the years after 1880 in Europe saw two things: first, the triumph of the

German model of modernity and industrialisation over the English one and second, the triumph of *taxis* over *kosmos*. This drive to create a rational, scientific order was founded on an underlying irrationalism.[33]

Considered in this light, Victorian Protectionism was an extremely interesting phenomenon, as it predated and paralleled European developments – just as Deakinite liberalism paralleled the growth of the New Liberalism in England. All the same ingredients were present; a fear of degeneration, the use of state intervention, a distrust of nature. Victoria was clearly swimming with the tide of the age whereas New South Wales remained content with more traditional English attitudes. One key could lie with the different religious composition of Sydney and Melbourne. Melbourne was the more Protestant city and, in the 1860s and 1870s, more amenable to free thought and rationalism – a fact used by Sydney writers to criticise and condemn their southern counterparts.[34] The weak sense of a sacralised nature still present in New South Wales was almost entirely absent in non-conformist, free-thinking Melbourne. Jill Roe has contrasted the fate of Theosophy in Sydney as opposed to Melbourne, and although she emphasises socio-cultural factors it is clear that a creed focusing on harmony, progress and the 'Universal Brotherhood of Humanity' would have more appeal in Sydney than in Melbourne – it is a vision of *kosmos*.[35]

Pearson, State Socialism and the Stationary World Order

If amongst Sydney intellectuals the solution to the disharmony of the world was the fostering of the spirit of co-operation, then for their Melbourne counterparts it was the growing power of the state to intervene and correct abuses. The link between the growth of state socialism and the conviction that the world was decaying into a stationary condition is expressed most fully in Charles Pearson's *National Life and Character*, written in 1892, just as he was leaving Victoria after a distinguished career as educator, publicist and Minister for Public Instruction.[36] Although Pearson wrote and published this book for European and American audiences he drew on his Victorian experiences to explain and describe what he saw as the future fate of liberalism world-wide. And this fate? A slow slide into a state of entropy as individuals degenerate and the European world enters into its old age. The source of this degeneration was the set of conditions created by liberalism. These conditions destroyed that very individualism which had been the foundation of liberalism's success. Pearson's pessimism rested on a vision of the state as an anti-vital force standing over the individual and gradually destroying his capacity for an active life. As the power of the state grew so did the individual diminish in stature.

For Pearson, the growth of state power was the consequence of the pursuit of liberal policies. Moreover, this movement towards what he described as 'state socialism' in Victoria was neither perverse nor unnatural. A 'system of State centralism', he contended, is 'what the English race naturally attempts when it is freed from the limitation of English tradition'. It is a system 'developed by the community for their own needs'. Equally, he did not perceive that the Victorian experience was in any way idiosyncratic or eccentric but indicative of the direction in which the rest of the European world was headed, 'an indication of what we may expect in the future'. State power had grown because of liberalism, and yet it was a result that was not actively pursued or wished for, 'we are tending to a state of things we did not altogether anticipate, and to results that are not absolutely desirable'. And yet, for any liberal the reforms of the nineteenth century – diffusion of education, extension of the suffrage and so on – 'were measures eminently defensible in themselves'. Vigorous young liberals had set out to reform their society but in achieving their aim had created a world quite different from their expectations.[37]

Pearson placed this dynamic of liberalism in a context of the exhaustion of European expansion and development. Just as acts of justice carried out by civilised men were leading to a society dominated by state socialism, so European expansion over the world had reached its limit as those temperate parts of the globe in which Europeans could live were filled up. The energy of the European world was running down and an active, vital civilisation was turning into a stagnant one. Limited to the temperate zone pursuing policies which, in the name of justice, gave increasing influence to the state, Europeans were being locked into a static social order. It was the effect of this fixed, stationary order on politics, individualism and character which formed the focus of Pearson's study because the character of the peoples will be 'profoundly modified, as they have to adapt themselves to a stationary condition of society'.

The most important consequence of this condition was, as has already been discussed, the growth of the state and the 'tendency . . . to adopt a very extensive system of state socialism'. The state had grown as a means of creating a more just society, a society in which ordinary people would no longer need to worry about the struggle for existence. State socialism created a higher standard of comfort, curtailed competition and allowed greater physical happiness. In this regard Pearson welcomed state socialism: 'human co-operation for political ends is yearly becoming more fruitful of good purpose, more sympathetic, and more successful in its attempts to relieve want'. There would be many other features of this stationary world. Towns would grow larger and come to dominate the surrounding countryside. In the vast cities both religious faith and family life would decay. The state would supplant the churches in providing

moral direction and families in the raising of children. As the 'old family feeling' disappeared from the cities so the religious feeling traditionally supported and transmitted by the family would slowly disappear.
Faith would decay and family-based morality would disappear; 'the old
instinctive virtue will be replaced by a calculating common-sense'. As
religion and the family declined a new relationship would emerge to
replace them – that of state and individual: 'The great possible motors of
action . . . will be the sense of duty to the State, and the self reliance of
individual character.'

European states restricted to the temperate zone would no longer be
able to expand and to send their young adventurous members in search
of new places. As 'outlets to trade and energy are closed' state socialism
would expand to support the growing population of the cities.
Increasingly, science would be used to solve the problems of urban living, the indebtedness of the state would increase and great armies would
need to be maintained. Most significantly, claimed Pearson, this would
lead to the creation of closed societies which would have less and less to
do with other societies. Free Trade, the vision of 'inspired Manchester
men', had not accomplished its goal: 'Trade is no freer than it was, and
war is a more pervading presence.' State Socialism had erected, and
would continue to erect, protective tariffs thereby reducing interchange
between nations and preventing the emulation of one country by
another. As state socialism expanded, the standard of work in industry
would decline as workers ceased to face the stimulus of competition, and
the barriers between nations would affect political liberty. Pearson contended that the state would attempt to prevent its members holding public meetings. Men of a different nationality would be less tolerated and
when individuals opposed their government they would discover that no
other country would give them refuge: 'The inevitable result of all this
must be to impose silence upon the men who are inclined to take up
arms against abuses in politics or in the social system.'

A more orderly and stationary world, argued Pearson, means less freedom of opinion and a greatly diminished capacity for the individual to
be original. The individual, considered in his relationship to the state,
dwindles in importance becoming 'a very small part of a very vast
machine'. Offering the individual a reasonable standard of comfort, in
return the state demands order and regularity – the order of a world
grown old. In these circumstances there would be no place for men of
originality and brilliance. Hitherto, deep religious feeling and exalted
intellectual energy had moulded character; now this was being replaced
by love of country and reverence for the state – hardly a principle,
claimed Pearson, that would strengthen initiative or encourage self-
reliance. A more prosaic and sober world was coming into being; poetry

and science were losing much of their power. In their place history and criticism, products of the 'orderly faculty' of the modern world, were becoming the literary forms of an advanced society.

For Pearson, the age of individual genius was being replaced by the age of orderly criticism and specialist investigation. The themes of great literature had been exhausted; all that was left was to produce criticism and comment on that great literature. The age of prose would be matched by an ageing population; conservatism would become much more influential leading to 'increased stability of political order, increased efficiency of exact thought'. This growth of order and stability was associated by Pearson with a 'decay of energy' and the growth of a less energetic world, a world no longer capable of reform.

This portrait of a world running down is hardly inspiring. Its power derives from the metaphor of human ageing; as individuals age their activity and ability to change the world declines. Pearson's final bleak picture resembles that of human old age 'when we shall ask nothing from the day but to live, nor from the future but that we may not deteriorate'. But Pearson's picture of the state cannot be reduced merely to a metaphor about human ageing. His vision of future historical and social development was firmly rooted in his experience of Victorian politics. Hence in his analysis of the rise of the state and the individual following on the decline of family and church he was extrapolating from what he believed was occurring in Australia. Likewise, his emphasis on comfort as the gift of the modern state and its effect on individual self-expression was a logical extension of developments already under way.[38]

The rest of this chapter can now be devoted to sketching the intellectual triumph of Protectionism and the implications of that triumph. It does not pretend to provide an exhaustive and comprehensive account of the victory of Protectionism but rather it seeks to establish, through the analysis of a number of key figures and works, the crucial values of Protection and its accompanying 'protectionist mentality'. In this way the wider context in which Cultural Liberalism developed can be appreciated.

The Triumph of Protectionist Ideology

It was in the *Bulletin*, founded and edited by an expatriate Victorian, that the advocacy of Protection, expressed as fear of the wider world, found its fullest expression. The *Bulletin* was a brilliant commercial success because it expressed, reflected and refined the values of a large section of the Australian population – and those values were often Protectionist. Claiming that its fruits were better hours, better wages and an improved standard of living, the *Bulletin* carried the message of Protection around the continent.[39] Moreover, it based its justification of

Protection on a social Darwinist vision of the world. To give one example, in an article published in 1888 it described human existence as a struggle for survival: 'Nature teaches us one stern law of existence, "Eat or be eaten" . . . [Commerce is like] warfare, there is no mercy, the weakest go to the shambles . . . By commerce or by war, nation seeks to destroy nation; race to subjugate and triumph over race.'

Under modern conditions, continued the article, the struggle for existence is conducted by communities rather than individuals. The article proceeded to attack explicitly the religiously founded optimism of Free Trade, describing the laws of nature as founded on materialism – as 'non-moral and remorseless'. Against this cruel, amoral nature, social man sets about achieving his moral aspirations, increasing 'the sum of human happiness' and abolishing 'misery and wrong, suffering and want'. Protection is the key both to providing national strength and allowing the aspirations of 'moral man' to be achieved. By closing off Australia to both foreigners and the products of their labour, it allows the country to build up a strong, skilful workforce capable of competing against other nations. Protection is thus more than an economic policy, it is 'a necessity to national existence. It is the national talisman of potency by which is maintained the dominance of the race'. The article concluded with a plea for national development to occur on a rational scientific basis so as to bring out the full qualities of the race.[40]

This theme of the nation as a self-reliant individual warring against other individuals, easily led to the concept of the nation as an organic entity requiring the intervention of science and the state to keep it healthy. For example, in a paper delivered at the 1895 AAAS conference, future High Court judge, Samuel Griffith compared the state with the human body and argued that it was necessary to understand the conditions of its health and to ensure the adequate flow of nutriments to every part of it. For Griffith, the statesman was a '*medicus rei publicae*, knowing the laws of national health, and capable of diagnosing the causes of disorder and of prescribing the appropriate remedy'.[41] This vision of the state as protector and regulator appealed both to intellectuals and scientists seeking a more active role for their talents and to supporters of the labour movement who sought to use the state to alleviate social evils. The 'social laboratory' of the first decade of the twentieth century was the outcome of this particular vision of the role of human reason as a means of taming nature. It was an Australian equivalent of European 'national efficiency' and 'technocracy' and was quickly adopted as an ideal by many Australian intellectuals. Moreover it was clearly founded on principles of *taxis* and the German model of industrial development.

The Australia that emerged as the new Commonwealth after 1901 effectively adopted protectionist values. These values found expression in what were to become the 'settled policies' of the new nation: Immigration Restriction, the New Protectionism, Industrial Arbitration, State Paternalism and Imperial Benevolence – what Paul Kelly has termed 'The Australian Settlement'.[42] The two key groups who sponsored those values were the scientists and progressivist social reformers described by Michael Roe, and the popular adherents of Protection, particularly in the labour movement. The forces of Free Trade were routed despite the fact that George Reid's 1894 Free Trade government in New South Wales had dealt with the problems of the Depression far more effectively than its Protectionist counterpart in Victoria.[43] The vision of *kosmos* could not sustain itself against the combination of the desire of interventionist intellectuals for ideological power and a paranoia pervading the Australian community. Evidence for this paranoia can be found in the Immigration Restriction debates of the first national parliament in which the Chinese and Japanese were accused of a whole range of sins, from carrying diseases to working too hard, and in which successive speakers attempted to outdo each other in their defence of racial purity.[44] The roots of the paranoia lay in feelings of helplessness created by a number of factors including social and economic dislocation, the relative decline of Great Britain as a great power, a growing international instability and the feeling of relative powerlessness which came with being an imperial dependency. The economic realities were that Australia was dependent on world markets to sell her commodities and that colonial governments had borrowed heavily from England.

With the settled policies of the New Commonwealth – (White Australia, Protection and Arbitration) – Protectionism, in the shape of Deakinite liberalism, triumphed as the dominant form of liberalism in Australia. It was nothing if not corporatist and dirigiste (advocating state control) in its outlook; it sought to create a happier, healthier white population able to defend itself and do battle in the commercial warfare of the world. Moreover, these and other protectionist policies were designed to prevent racial and social degeneration and to maintain the health of the body of the nation. Yet it would be wrong to deny a moral dimension to these policies. They contained a strong element of idealism and a genuine liberal desire to strengthen the powers of the individual. It was this mingling of xenophobia and idealism that led to their success.

The Role of the Scientists and Progressivists

For the progressivist intellectuals the need to preserve the health of the nation meant that their role would become increasingly important. For his *medicus rei publicae* Griffith had in mind the university man, trained to think accurately and logically; indeed, as he states elsewhere, democracy 'desires to be led by its best men'.[45] In his 1899 work *The New Democracy*

Jethro Brown expressed similar sentiments. Equating democracy with a society governed by the goal of equality of opportunity, Brown asserted that 'Nature has not made one man's judgement as good as another's'. 'The stern dilemma of the future', he contended, 'is the qualified and controlled leadership of the few, or the decline of the many'. Brown clearly envisaged a role for the educated in the future Australian nation, as a sort of substitute or 'true' aristocracy: democracy was to mean the rule of the gold over the silver and the bronze. Federation, he believed, would provide bonds of a non-utilitarian nature – 'national ideals' – which would bind the nation together and give it the strength it needed to meet the demands of progress. These ideals would conquer the endemic provinciality of Australians, 'broaden their sympathies and . . . refine and elevate the whole tone of their political life'. The intellectual leadership of this educated elite could establish a model of nobility for lesser mortals to emulate. George Cockburn Henderson also argued that in a democracy 'the great man was bound to rule', and later stated that a democratic government was controlled by the people but directed by the *aristoi*, 'the best men available'.[46]

For many of these scientific and progressivist intellectuals, as for David Syme, the model was not old-fashioned *laissez-faire* England but modern dynamic Germany in which, it was perceived, industry had forged an alliance with the universities to create an industrial system based on the scientific exploitation of knowledge. The model also incorporated 'progressivist' America in which the German model had been fused with the principles of democracy. Nowhere was this view better illustrated than in the inaugural ceremony of the University of Queensland in which the cause of science and industrial research was defended on the grounds of international industrial rivalry – specifically against the Germans who, it was noted, had become powerful because of their emphasis on education. German progress, claimed James Barrett, elsewhere, was the result of the 'application of character and ordered intelligence to the common problems of daily life'.[47]

The university was central to this model of industrial development; there were three key ways in which it sought to make the German/American model a reality in Australia. First, it emphasised scientific rationality as the basis of social progress and development. As Edgeworth David put it: 'Pursuit of pure science means research, research means discovery, and discovery leads to important new applications of science which makes for a nation's prosperity'. To this end the university must become 'truly national by association with the life's work of the people' as one government report put it.[48] For, as Professor Bragg asserted, the scientific research work of the country was growing and the 'country's welfare demands that we should grapple with it boldly and with enthusiasm'.[49]

Secondly, science and scholarship were conceived as a form of co-operative enterprise which could serve as a model for the wider democratic community. Edgeworth David was not alone in viewing the brotherhood of science as a panacea for the conflict between labour and capital. The third element was the traditional university belief that its role was to produce cultured men and women who would leaven the whole community. The university was an institution devoted to 'the great cause of citizen making'.[50] The new ideals of scientific efficiency were grafted on to the traditional civic humanist conception of the university.

Discussing the aims and ideals of Australasian science, David concluded that science wanted man 'to learn well that he may live well; to learn by experiment rather than wholly through the experience of others, so that he may be self-reliant and think for himself. Thinking of this kind brings discovery, and the discoveries of science uplift humanity'.[51] Science and civic humanism were natural allies.

All of this fitted into a general evolutionist framework – the triumph of reason was to be also the victory of the active citizen, and the creation of a society founded on the co-operative activity of these citizens working together harmoniously. At one level this desire to create a more efficient and rational social order was concerned with purely materialist measures which would raise the quality of life of every man. Hence the interest in town planning, pure food, baby health centres, eugenics and education. If the role of the university researchers was to provide a constant stream of new discoveries then the place of 'sociology' was to organise these discoveries so that they could be put to maximum social advantage. 'Our business' claimed James Barrett, 'is to make human life on the globe healthier, better and more complete'.[52]

The desire by the scientists and the universities for the educated to intervene and create a more rational and regulated world found a resonance in the wider community. C.E.W. Bean, writing in the wake of ANZAC successes in World War I, argued in favour of increased scientific research and advocated that universities should 'work on research into every single thing that is useful for the country to know'. The *Bulletin*'s literary critic A.G. Stephens supported the cause of utilitarian education and the training of technical specialists, of 'fighters in every field of national progress'.[53]

Labour and Protectionism

At the same time, some of the more articulate supporters of the labour movement came to support policies that would help create a strong, self-reliant and healthy state. In *Australia's Awakening*, the union organiser and Labor politician W.G. Spence argued that the opportunity existed for Australians 'to become an enlightened people'. Spence identified the Labor Party as the only true Australian party motivated by 'one common aim – one grand ideal'. Labor believed in using the state for the good of the people to create a population independent in moral character and a nation self-reliant in defence. All of this is apparently very estimable except for one problem: justice is racial and Spence believed in 'racial purity and racial efficiency': 'True patriotism should be racial'. The 1908 Labor platform expressed its faith in the 'maintenance of racial purity and the development in Australia of an enlightened and self-reliant community'. Expressed in economic terms White Australia meant autarchy. Spence claimed that Labor had stopped the borrowing 'craze' and had encouraged industries which would make Australia independent. His aim was an autonomous community which did not need to import any of its requirements. But despite the eagerness of Labor leaders like Spence and J.D. Watson to give the party of progress priority in the formulation of racial doctrine, the party of resistance also freely gave its assent to these extreme nationalist ideals. 'To be a really "White Australia"', claimed liberal leader Joseph Cook in 1914, 'we ought also to be a free, fair, federal and just Australia'.[54]

In his 1907 piece 'The limits of state interference', the future prime minister William Morris Hughes used an organic conception of the state based on the idea 'that there is a general consciousness as well as an individual consciousness, a national as well as individual life'. The modern state, he continued:

> considered as an organism, exhibits those marks which invariably accompany higher development. It responds more readily to stimuli, it specialises functions, and it has evolved new organs, or, what is the same thing, rudimentary organs have developed until they perform functions entirely new, or formerly very imperfectly performed by the individual.

Hughes identified the growth of the state with the progress of civilisation, and the evolution of humanity towards a higher stage of development. Consequently, he justified state interference in any area where it could promote the welfare and secure the happiness of its citizens, including 'the physical and mental health of the citizens' to ensure 'that production should proceed in orderly and effective fashion'. While Pearson viewed the growth of state socialism as a symptom of degeneration, for Hughes state intervention was a sign of higher development. Hughes identified degeneration with nature and the forces of competition; like the *Bulletin* he pitted moral society against 'the exercise of mere brute strength or cunning' inherent in nature. 'Were it not for State interference', claimed Hughes, 'the race would inevitably degenerate under private enterprise'. State interference improves the lot of the individual and helps to create a moral order lacking in the natural world. This is almost the complete inversion of the world picture of earlier liberals who had pitted a beneficent nature against a corrupt society.[55]

But the major attempt to use the state and the law to create a new moral system and combat the degeneration inherent in the natural order was the creation of the arbitration system. In particular, the ideology of arbitration bears the imprint of H.B. Higgins who was the Federal Arbitration Court judge from 1907–1921. Like Hughes and the *Bulletin* he identified nature with disorder and chaos, and law with order and morality. Higgins appears to have had a great fear of the possibilities of change as sources of disorder and chaos. For example, in discussing the vitality and 'intense intellectual and moral ferment' of Shakespeare's age, he expressed his disquiet at a society adrift from its moorings and losing its fixed principles – and he criticised the profligacy of that Shakespearian age.[56] He considered the nineteenth century also to have been an age in which fixed principles had been destroyed, ideals shattered and creeds broken up. It was an age of doubt and pessimism; again the villain was competition and commerce – what Higgins termed the 'bourgeois principle', and he saw his role as the restorer of order and law.[57]

Consequently, he compared the role of the arbitration court in relation to industrial matters to that of the King's Peace as a means of creating law and order and suppressing anarchy. The common good was, in Higgins's eyes, the triumph of the ideal, as expressed through law, over the chaos created by individuals pursuing selfish and sectional interests. Higgins referred to the arbitration system as the 'reign of justice as against violence . . . of right as against might' and as the subjugation of 'Prussianism in industrial matters'. If the common good and an order founded on law and justice could be achieved then two things would follow. First, the deterioration and degeneration of human beings in industry could be prevented and second, the higher powers of human beings could be developed: 'you release infinite stores of human energy for higher efforts, for nobler ideals'.[58]

Hence, the key to the development of a social order able to unleash the nobler side of human nature lay in the regulation of industrial activities. Positive human law could provide that order, while scientific research could be used to guide the formulation of that law. The inherent contradiction in both Hughes's and Higgins's account of the benefits of regulation was the belief that such regulation would encourage individual exertion and a desire for higher things. In turn, this error rested on a misconception of the collective state as a living entity greater than, and independent of, the individuals who compose it. In the event it appears that Pearson's vision of state socialism was more accurate than that of Hughes. There was an obvious contradiction between the ideal of a humanity released for higher efforts and the reality of a state seeking to protect and regulate the actions of its members.

Two things clearly stand out in this vision of Australia as a self-enclosed unit pursuing its ideal of social justice. The first is that from a Free Trade point of view, the idea was ethically unsound because it placed self-interest ahead of the interests of humanity. The notion of justice was exclusive and sought to protect a small country from the rest of the world. The second is that this political and social doctrine helped to create what is best described as the 'protectionist mentality', an inward looking and self-interested cast of mind which had devastating psychological consequences. As we noted earlier, Free Trade, building on eighteenth century doctrines of the sociability of man and social sympathy, had elaborated the belief in the development of human nature through the expansion of its social self. The first consequence of Protectionism was to restrict the social self to a specific group and to inhibit its growth. It encouraged a morbid pre-occupation with self. The best analogy might be with William James's distinction between healthy minded and unhealthy minded religion.[59] Whereas healthy minded religion allows the individual to develop freely and easily, unhealthy minded religion leads to crisis and problems. The protectionist mentality was like unhealthy minded religion – it restricted and narrowed the vision and horizons of those who participated in it.

This is not to accuse men such as Higgins of being ignoble in their aims or ignorant of the value of culture. Higgins saw regulation as the road to culture. Rather, it is a comment on the unpredictability of the consequences of human action. The intention of Higgins was to liberate human beings from insecurity and want as a prelude to a life devoted to the higher things. But the effect of regulation was to strengthen those elements in the Australian culture conducive to the protectionist mentality.

The Triumph of the Protectionist Mentality

It is often conceded that a peculiar transformation of Australian culture occurred in the wake of World War I. According to Ronald Conway, 'Something seemed to go wrong in the National Spirit in the 1920s'. It would not be incorrect to attribute this, at least in part, to the war and the sixty-thousand war dead.[60] But it is possible to argue that the condition existed before the war; White Australia and Protection were the first instalments in the victory of a mentality which the losses of the war helped to consummate. Patrick Morgan has argued that 'the traditions of the South Seas paradise and of "getting away from it" run in tandem throughout our history', but in the nineteenth century the impact of these traditions had been balanced by such ideals as that of Free Trade.[61] The victory of Protection destroyed that balance and made Protectionism the dominant cultural tradition in Australia.

The triumph of Protection coincided with the narrowing of cultural contacts which Australia had developed with other nations, with the result that England became the dominating influence on high culture in a way that it had not been before 1914. Prior to the war Australia had received cultural influences from a number of sources as well as England, especially America, Scotland and Germany. We have already seen the significance of German and American models for the progressivist reformers of the early twentieth century. Post-graduate students were sent to both of these countries in the 1890s and the first decade of this century. Many of Australia's leading academics of this period, including Francis Anderson, William Mitchell, Mungo MacCallum and Henry Laurie, were expatriate Scots.[62]

The war saw the end of the German influence as German *Kultur* was reviled as a source of barbarism. Equally, one of the consequences of the war was an attack on American influence in the name of high culture; America was to be seen increasingly as a source of low culture, superficiality and poor taste. Finally, Scottish culture in the 1920s underwent a major crisis from which it does not appear to have recovered.[63] John Anderson was the last great gift of Scotland to Australian culture – and his career would seem to indicate how out of step the critical spirit of Scotland had become in Australia. Quite simply, the war broke that international network of cultural interchanges in which Australians previously had participated.

What replaced it was a much more direct relationship with England. Morgan contends that 'Hughes's splitting of the Labor Party in 1917 inaugurated a fifty-year period of Anglo-Australian feeling' during which 'there was deference to things English'.[64] He identifies this desire for Anglo-Saxon security with the impulse to withdraw into the comfortable world of suburbia – in other words, the protectionist mentality. But as ideas of national character do change (as late as the eighteenth century the English were believed to be a violent and lawless people), it is worth asking what is meant by the term 'English'. In Mrs Gaskell's terms it is clearly 'South' rather than 'North'; Martin Wiener has argued that the image of England created in the early years of this century was one of the rural south – a land dotted by villages in which lived happy, decent chaps: Ratty, Mole and Badger.[65] Australian suburbia can easily be viewed as a reflection of this English rural ideal; the protectionist mentality and the intensifying of the Anglicising of Australia were complementary.

The effect of this Anglicisation of Australian culture on intellectual life can be discerned in the autobiographies of W.K. Hancock and Manning

Clark.[66] Both went to study at Balliol College, Oxford and were forced to come to terms with their Australian–English identity. There is no doubt that Hancock was seduced by the traditions of Oxford while Clark found the experience less satisfying. But in both accounts the central cultural factor was the Anglo-Australian axis and the necessity of dealing with the feeling of inferiority which their colonial origins seemed to impose on them. Another Oxford graduate, Percy Stephensen, attempted to deal with the situation by advocating an extreme Australian nationalism.[67] The 'English question' came to dominate in a way that it had not for an earlier generation.

Another effect of the growth of the protectionist mentality and of Anglicisation was the idealisation of the 1890s as a period of liveliness and vigour which had been followed by the gradual loss of that vitality. Vance Palmer's *Legend of the Nineties* is but one of the last expressions of a belief which is also found in such works as Lloyd Ross's *William Lane and the Australian Labor Movement*.[68] The final piece of evidence for the profound effect of the 'protectionist mentality' on the Australian psyche and Australian culture is to be found in the pages of D.H. Lawrence's *Kangaroo*. Lawrence was in Australia in 1922 and he sensed an inward disintegration in the personalities of the people he described. Consider, for example, the following passages:

> They just blankly don't care about anything, and they live in defiance, a sort of slovenly defiance of care of any sort, human or inhuman, good or bad. If they've got one belief left, now the war's safely over, it's a dull, rock-bottom belief in obstinately not caring, not caring about anything.

> They're marvellous and manly and independent and all that, outside. But inside, they are not. When they're quite alone, they don't exist.

> The profound Australian indifference, which still is not really apathy. The disintegration of the social mankind back to its elements. . . . But it felt like a clock that was running down. It had been wound up in Europe, and was running down, running right down, here in Australia. Men were mining, farming, making roads, shouting politics. But all with that basic indifference which dare not acknowledge how indifferent it is, lest it should drop everything and lapse into a blank.[69]

This theme of indifference, lack of inwardness and inability to care pervades Lawrence's descriptions of Australians. He implicitly linked it with degeneration and the loss of the soul brought by Australians from Europe. He also associated it with freedom – freedom not to care, to get away from the problems of the wider world. The pre-conditions for that freedom were the fences created by White Australia and Protection (and the British Navy) and the guarantees of security provided by Protection and Arbitration. A modest comfort could be pursued behind a wall with a sign 'Keep Out' erected on it – and this in a country dependent on foreign trade for its prosperity.

Lawrence's diagnosis presented a culture composed of personalities looking inwards and seeking the vacancy of a life freed from larger interests and responsibilities. It is by no means an uncontroversial analysis; Australians of an Anglophiliac disposition have often found it distasteful. Others, perhaps possessing less of an investment in England, have found it a remarkably incisive picture of the Australian personality. These range from V. Gordon Childe to John Douglas Pringle to Ronald Conway.[70] Lawrence's picture of Australia corresponds to the description of the Australian personality made by F.W. Eggleston in which he referred to the 'self-contained' man, and to Bernard Smith's account of the 'isolationism' of Australian painters during the inter-war years. Writing in 1930 G.V. Portus described Australians as a 'self-centred folk turning our faces inward'.[71] Most importantly, for the argument advanced by this study, Lawrence's depiction corroborates the fact that the 'protectionist mentality' after World War I had become the dominant feature of Australian culture. And, most significantly, the malaise detected by Lawrence was the consequence not of the thwarting of the ideals of the first decade of the century but of their consummation.

Australia at the Turn of the Century: A Summary

The argument presented regarding the general cultural development of Australia (and the fate of its competing liberal traditions) during the early decades of this century can be summarised as follows:

1 In nineteenth century Australia two distinct patterns of liberalism developed which can be labelled according to the system of political economy to which they adhered: Free Trade and Protection. But these two patterns, or cultural traditions, were concerned with much more than just economics; they had completely different attitudes to nature (which may be described as *kosmos* versus *taxis*) and different conceptions of human nature. The colonies of pre-World War I Australia participated in a wide ranging series of cultural networks ranging from America to England to Scotland to Germany. Overall, nineteenth century or colonial Australia was relatively pluralistic and open to a variety of cultural influences.

2 The dominant feature of the New Commonwealth was the victory of Protectionism as summed up in the three key policies of the decade before 1910: White Australia, New Protection, Arbitration and Conciliation. Modern Australia was born in a mood which sought to repudiate various elements of modernity and, following Jeffrey Herf,

I have suggested that the term reactionary modernism would not be
an inappropriate term to describe it.[72] This Protectionist cultural tendency was reinforced by World War I when the cultural networks linking Australia to non-English cultures were broken and the dominant
cultural influence on Australia became an England seeking to remake
itself on a southern, rural pattern. The cosy shire and the cosy suburb
neatly complemented each other.

3 Australian intellectuals in general assisted in this transformation, not
   because they endorsed a protectionist mentality, but rather because
   they were products of institutions and universities which emphasised
   the need for people like them to intervene if a rational world was to be
   created. Thus, although the universities saw themselves as allowing
   their products to develop their powers, much as in the fashion of Free
   Trade, they also encouraged a view of the world founded on *taxis* in
   which the educated man intervened in order to correct the errors of
   the unenlightened. (This theme is explored more fully in the next
   chapter.) Consequently the ideas of H.B. Higgins had an elective affinity with those of the inward looking Protectionists – both worked
   towards creating the Australia Lawrence discovered in 1922.

4 By the 1920s the rather fluid and pluralistic cultural condition of nineteenth century Australia had congealed into a set protectionist mould
   which was to dominate Australian culture until the 1960s. The other
   traditions did not die but merely became minority tastes existing on
   the fringe of the mainstream culture. The consequences of this hard-
   ening were less than pleasant for Australian intellectuals, even though
   many of them were, at least in part, responsible for it.

How then does the tradition of Cultural Liberalism fit into this overall
pattern of development? That will be the theme of the remainder of this
study.

CHAPTER 3

Ethos and Myth:
The Dynamics of Cultural Liberalism

Elements of a Tradition

For the university educated in late nineteenth and early twentieth century Australia, there were three traditions or tendencies which were of the utmost significance. The first was *civic humanism* which was essentially the tradition of citizenship and service as expressed in the ideal of the university man as a leader of his community. University education was believed to create a virtuous individual capable of acting dispassionately, free from bias and prejudice. This was also related to the belief that the university produced individuals able to look beyond self and interest and see things 'as they really are'. Education led to disinterestedness and the capacity for cool, rational thought; once shown the road to truth and virtue any individual would choose it as a matter of course. The second was *culture*, closely related to civic humanism as educated individuals were believed to have cultivated both their capacity for disinterestedness and their powers of spiritual discernment. Culture enabled the individual not only to see things 'as they really are' but also to see them in a higher spiritual way, to pierce the illusions of sense and look into the heart of things. The third significant tradition was that of *scientism and utility*, which followed from the belief that there was an objective, rational order in the universe which could be known and understood by the educated who could then make use of this knowledge to improve the lot of their fellow human beings. A better world was therefore defined as a more rational one – one in which scientific principles formed the basis of human action.

These three strands can be found in varying degrees amongst all the university educated men and women of this period. To an extent they correspond to John Carroll's characterisation of the humanist university as being founded on the ideals of civilisation, the gentlemen and utility.[1]

Carroll accuses this liberal humanism of a facile optimism which he believes to have been its undoing. To an extent this is true, but Carroll ignores the self-reflective capacities of rationality and the ability of at least some of its practitioners to probe its weaknesses and deficiencies. A tradition which has produced Manning Clark and James McAuley can hardly be accused of superficiality.

The Cultural Liberals comprise that group for whom the second element was pre-dominant; those who valued culture and its attendant spiritual vision of humanity more highly than either civic humanism or science – although elements of both of those other strands were invariably present in their thought. More often it was the civic humanist implications of culture which concerned them. It was this priority accorded to culture in their interests which marks out the Cultural Liberals; for them science and civic humanism were to be made to conform with humanity's wider and deeper nature.

The purpose of this chapter is to explore the dynamics of this tradition in the years leading up to World War I. To say that the tradition was dynamic is not the same thing as saying that it was 'progressive'. Most certainly it possessed its own peculiar pattern of development but this pattern is best viewed as a series of recurring themes. Themes elaborated in the writings of John Woolley can be found in the works of later figures such as Christopher Brennan. In any tradition only a number of set repertoires or arguments are generally available, although as circumstances change an increasingly large set of variations on these becomes possible. Alasdair MacIntyre identifies two dimensions to any exploration of a cultural and intellectual tradition:[2] its internal development through the elaboration of its arguments and its reaction to external threats. Using the terms 'ethos' and 'myth', the internal dynamics of Cultural Liberalism in the late nineteenth and early twentieth centuries can be elucidated. An examination of the 'battle for culture' waged against the humanities by the sciences and social sciences will enable us to consider how Cultural Liberalism was affected by external challenges.

In the nineteenth century, the tradition of Cultural Liberalism was to be found primarily in Sydney, and, in particular, was centred around the University of Sydney. This is not to say that it did not exist elsewhere but that its purest manifestation was to be found in Sydney. Already, in the 1850s a vision of Cultural Liberalism had been developed by members of the Stenhouse Circle such as Daniel Deniehy. The rational spirituality inspired by the American transcendentalists, Channing and Emerson, had transformed itself into a Romantic angst whose heroes were Poe and Thomas de Quincey. Indeed there is a continuous Romantic/Gnostic tradition in Sydney leading from Woolley and Kendall down to Patrick White, a tradition chronicled in part by John Docker.[3]

As Warren Osmond has pointed out, Cultural Liberalism in Melbourne belongs to the later generation of Deakin, Murdoch and Eggleston;[4] it shared many of the spiritual aspirations of its Sydney counterpart, though it seems to have been less prone to Romantic excess. By the first decade of the twentieth century it is possible to speak of a Cultural Liberalism existing amongst the educated classes of Australia, though with subtle differences from State to State. Hence, while this and the following chapters will concentrate primarily on Sydney as possessing the longest tradition of Cultural Liberalism, later chapters will broaden their focus to include such figures as Mayo, Eggleston and Hancock.

Platonism, Gnosticism and Romanticism: A Digression

To appreciate the significance of ethos and myth in the development of Cultural Liberalism in Australia it is first necessary to make a detour to antiquity and to consider the full meaning of one of the most enduring images of European civilisation – the allegory of the cave which appears in Plato's *Republic*.[5] In it Socrates traces the passage of individual enlightenment from the intimations of truth provided by the shadows to the complete knowledge of the world which exists only under the sun's full glare. But, as Socrates continues, if the individual were then to return to the darkness of the cave he would find it difficult to compete with those whose eyes were accustomed to the cave's shadows. Nor would they only merely laugh at him, they might also attempt to kill him as a reward for trying to set them free. In gaining wisdom one acquires the desire to pass it on to those who are still trapped in the shadows. But by leaving those shadows one also becomes different from those who remain; to them the message of wisdom is both incomprehensible and threatening.

Both Plato and the neo-Platonists of the Roman Empire, such as Plotinus, viewed the passage to truth and enlightenment as the outcome of the cultivation of the faculty of reason. There is, however, a variation on this Platonic allegory which denies the capacity of reason to bridge the gap between man and truth (or God). The Gnostics faced a hidden God who was not even creator of this world; an inferior God (sometimes identified with Jehovah) had captured divine sparks within earthly vessels. Consequently, this world was believed to be totally corrupt and knowledge of it useless in the soul's task of escaping the world and returning to the heavens. Secret knowledge, in the form of incantations and the manipulation of symbols, rather than reason, permitted the soul safe passage through the various heavens beyond which was located the throne of the unknowable God.

In his study of Gnosticism, Hans Jonas compares the feeling of hopelessness experienced by the Gnostics in the face of a God beyond reach, to that of modern existentialism and its doctrine of *dasein*.[6] In fact, Gnosticism reappeared in modern European thought in the movement which pre-figures many of the themes of Existentialism, that is, Romanticism. One of the key motifs of Romanticism is that of the 'lost vision',[7] the momentary experience which grants to the poet a vision of the divine, but which he cannot bring back with him into the realm of everyday life. The very experience of the vision marks the poet out as different from everyman, while its continuing absence ensures that he cannot remain satisfied with the necessary compromises of day-to-day existence. By denying the efficacy of reason and locking himself into a private quest for the absolute, the Romantic/Gnostic renounces any interest in, or capacity to, change the world.

There is a variety of reactions to this position. A very large school from Nietzsche and Croce to the present day views this variety of Romanticism with distaste, the *mal du siècle* of 'womanish, sentimental, incoherent, voluble spirits who egged themselves on to multiply doubts and difficulties which they were then unable to master, and courted perils which then they succumbed to'.[8] The objections to these 'womanish souls' are many, but ultimately most of them come down to a suspicion of their otherworldliness and the belief that inwardness and an apparent hatred of 'reality' are inadequate as an orientation towards the world.

In her study of English Romanticism, Marilyn Butler contrasts starkly those Romantics who clung to the traditions of the Enlightenment (the principles of rationality and social and political reform) with those who allowed their alienation to lead their art to become 'the subjective expression of men in private rooms'. Likewise, when Lucien Goldmann defined *'l'esprit romantique par l'inadéquation radicale de l'homme au monde et par le fait que l'homme place les valeurs substantielles – l'essence – dans une réalité extramondaine'*, he did so in the expectation that in a socialist world subject and object would be reconciled and a new classicism forged.[9] The central fact of Romanticism is alienation; for the classically minded, alienation is a disease waiting to be cured. For them, the only good Romantics are those who, in the face of all obstacles, cling to a faith in reason and to the belief that there is order in the universe.

Others would disagree. Morse Peckham believes that Romanticism emerged when all of those traditional explanatory schemes – Platonic Christian idealism, Baconian empiricism, scepticism – which had been founded on the assumption that a connection exists between our thoughts and the world, broke down. Alienated and isolated from the world the Romantic realises that words and thought tell him not about the world but about himself. The individual cannot authenticate himself in the world – his ideas are merely things imposed by him on the world, a radical cleavage has opened up between the true self and its outward manifestation. With his soul imprisoned in an alien hostile world, the Romantic, who has reached the highest cultural level of the modern world, is placed in the same condition as the ancient Gnostic. Peckham sees the creation of a series of anti-roles as the Romantic response to this modern dilemma of the need to create authenticity.[10] Geoffrey Thurley argues, in a similar way, that Romanticism is not a form of escapism but a facing up to the central issue of the age – alienation. Thurley is particularly hard on those modernist critics of Romanticism who found refuge in the safe harbour of Catholic Classicism.[11] Well might it be asked, who is really the escapist?

The problem of Romanticism is complex and there is no single approach to understanding it; how one reacts to Romanticism is one fundamental dividing line for intellectuals in the modern world. But Butler, Peckham and Thurley all agree that Romanticism is best understood as a process in which the central theme is a coming to terms with a universe that is no longer fixed and simple. As David Morse puts it:

> In Romantic discourse there is no longer a positing of fixed entities. Language is plural and perspectival; consciousness is dissolved into multiplicity; science confronts not essence so much as relations. The signature of God is withdrawn as guarantor of stable and univocal correspondences and man confronts a shifting and unstable world, in which there is no longer any one place to begin.[12]

If Romanticism is a process then ethos and myth constitute two moments of that process. The passage from Platonism to Gnosticism is a central element in the renunciation of reason and in the dynamics of the Romantic sensibility. The problem of reason must be crucial to any discussion of Romanticism, and in many ways Australia has been a test of reason and of its capacity to order a new world. It is no accident that Romanticism first emerged in Australia in Sydney during the late 1850s and early 1860s in the wake of the failure, perceived by many thinkers, of the coming of democracy to create a more rational and refined world – in other words, the failure of a form of Cultural Liberalism to take root and create a political order led by men of culture and reason.[13] Moving in an everyday world of corrupt politics and social relationships they found that their 'authentic' selves had been separated from their everyday selves. But this Romanticism, like the Cultural Liberalism which had preceded it, was a minority taste and the 1860s had also ushered in a period of prosperity and complacency. Amidst the cultural wreckage of the 1850s the University of Sydney almost alone survived, and then only by virtue of its institutional inertia. And to that wreckage clung the remnants of the Cultural Liberals, men such as William Forster, Bede Dalley and Charles Nicholson. In it they invested the vestiges of their hope that a refined, cultured society could be built in the colony.

Like the English universities from which it derived its spirit, if not its substance, the University of Sydney was very much dominated by the allegory of the cave. The nineteenth century university became increasingly Platonic in inspiration. Young men passed through it on their way to becoming guardians of the state. It was meant to be both an intellectual and a spiritual institution. Rigorous mental training was supposed to provide these young men with the ability to penetrate behind surface appearances, to be free of the tyranny of sense and to grasp the underlying principles of knowledge. The university stood for the permanence of truth, a fortress 'of the higher life of the nation' as against the sophistry and mere opinion of the democratic masses. In a word, those with a university education acquired 'culture'.[14] Now this culture was not just the training of the mind. As an antidote against the illusions of the phenomenal world it enabled its possessors to 'see things as they really are'.

But this training was spiritual as well as intellectual; 'Truth' was believed to contain an element of that type of knowledge which does not submit to lawful regularity and is normally associated with intuition, a non-rational type of knowledge which, following Robert Musil, we may term the 'other'.[15] The roots of this idea that rational training is a preparation for an entry into pure, intuitive knowledge are in Plotinus rather than in Plato. Plotinus cultivated philosophy in a quest for the mystic vision of unity with God which, Porphyry informs us, he achieved four times while Porphyry was with him.[16]

This ideal of the university raises a number of important issues. The first is that the seeds of the mythology of the educated lie in this account of the source of their knowledge. They have been to the mountain (or out of the cave) but by definition, on return, what they tell the people who have remained behind must be unintelligible to them. It makes no sense in the darkness. Secondly, the doctrine is simultaneously democratic and aristocratic. It is democratic in so far as the knowledge is meant for all; it is not the secret or esoteric doctrine of a religious sect. Similarly, in theory, there are no restrictions on who may leave the cave and gaze upon the sun. The doctrine is also aristocratic because in practice only a few are able to make the journey out of the cave. These must bear the burden and the responsibility of what they have seen. Thirdly, will the ordinary people who cannot understand what is being said, and yet must benefit by it, listen? D.H. Lawrence noted in *Kangaroo* that, in the Australian context, this really came down to the problem of authority.[17] In Australia, he perceived, there was no authority, no distinction within society between its responsible and its irresponsible members; ministers, he wrote, were but 'the merest instruments' of the proletariat. In England there could be obedience without understanding; in democratic Australia everyone was entitled to their darkness. Finally, the

curious mixture of Romanticism and Aristotelianism which underpinned this view had a place for both non-rational and dynamic ideals of
knowledge, for poetry as well as reason. It had little to do with the naive
positivism usually associated with nineteenth century thought.

So we arrive at two sets of dualities – between rationality and poetry,
democracy and aristocracy – which define this ideal of knowledge and
which are necessary to maintain the belief that university education per-
forms both a religious and a civic function. To understand the dynamics
of this cultural ideal the terms ethos and myth can be used, both of
which must now be examined a little more closely.

Ethos

Ethos, in its English usage, is a peculiarly Oxford word in its origins and
derives from the 1830s, the decade when the Oxford Movement and its
influence was at its height. The first two principals of the University of
Sydney, John Woolley and Charles Badham, were products of the Oxford
of the 1830s, and Badham makes a brief appearance in Dean Church's
study of the Oxford Movement, discussing Coleridge with Charles
Marriott, soon to become a leading member of the Movement.[18] The
ideal of ethos was an outcome of that decade and was used to give
expression to the belief that Oxford was both an educational and a religious institution. It is best summed up in Stephen Prickett's description
of it as 'a metaphysical reality; a platonic vision where holiness and learning met in eternal dialectic'. But Oxford was more than just the home of
lost causes and muddied Romanticism. It was also the English home of
Aristotle and of a rigorous logical approach to the world. An Oxford
man acquired, as David Newsome puts it: 'an attitude of mind; at least a
fastidiousness in exposition and in setting out the limit of one's enquiry
. . . a striving for definition or settling the meaning of one's words, combined with a sensitivity for every conceivable qualification'.[19]

The Oxford of the 1830s set about grafting this new Romantic sensibility on to the sturdy old tree of Aristotle and Bishop Butler, combining
a feeling for spiritual realities with the pedantry of logical distinction.
For those who have wrestled with the Romantic excesses of John
Woolley's prose it comes as somewhat of a surprise to read that Sir
Samuel Griffith recalled Woolley primarily as an advocate of the Greek
concept of *spoudaios*, of being earnest and thorough.[20]

The word 'ethos' can be appropriated to describe the democratic and
rational elements of the ideal of the University, its Platonic pretensions.
Simultaneously the University was to build a more rational and a more
spiritual world. In this context it is necessary to understand the religious
pretensions of the University of Sydney, and its desired role as the centre

of a non-dogmatic religious and civic ideal which could provide the basis of social cohesion in a world threatened by disorder and dissolution.

In the eighteenth century the doctrine of civic humanism emerged as an essentially secular account of the means through which a virtuous and stable social order could be achieved and maintained. But even Rousseau had argued for the necessity of a civic religion, and the Jacobins of 1793 realised that the new republican order could not hope to survive without some sort of religious foundation.[21] The distance separating Rousseau and John Adams from Coleridge and Arnold, or even T.H. Green, is not as great as it is sometimes made out to be. What did change during the Romantic period was that, in the wake of the French Revolution, religion was discovered to be central to any understanding of how the social and political order functions. For Montesquieu, Hume and Ferguson the religious issue was peripheral to their speculative accounts of the nature of human society; for Fustel de Coulange and the nineteenth century Scottish school of philosophical historians, from Robertson Smith to Frazer and the founders of sociology such as Durkheim and Weber, religion was the central element of the social order.[22] From Burke onwards, English political thinkers placed the problem of the Church, and of religion generally, at the centre of their agenda. Equally, there is a trajectory amongst significant English writers, including Coleridge and F.D. Maurice, leading from Unitarianism to Anglicanism. This is not to say that these thinkers ceased to find the concerns of civic humanism relevant, but merely to establish that their concentration on the religious problem added a new dimension which eighteenth century political thought had lacked. This changed emphasis resulted in a theory of the University in which, as the repository of permanent truths, it would provide a rational basis for the 'general will'. As both a religious and a civic institution the University was to be the New Church guaranteeing social order in a world threatened by anarchy.

The development of this line of thought can be seen most clearly in the writings of Coleridge and Arnold. In 'On the Constitution of the Church and State', Coleridge stated that 'in relation to the National Church, Christianity, or the Church of Christ is a blessed accident, a providential boon'. Coleridge's idea of a national church was conceived as something quite distinct from the existing English religious institution. Its scope would be broader and more secular; its role 'to secure and improve that civilization, without which the nation could be neither permanent nor progressive'. Anything which strengthens and preserves 'Nationality' falls within the province of the Church and so it must be composed of everyone employed in that task, be they scholars advancing knowledge within the universities or parsons and schoolmasters in the local parishes producing the future 'citizens of the country, free subjects of the realm'. Theology has a place in this scheme of things as 'the shaping and informing spirit' but it is by no means clear whether this theology would be Christian or dogmatic.[23]

What is clear is the essentially Platonic origin of Coleridge's ideal of education. The clerks of the Church, the clerisy, are not merely to diffuse knowledge and to instruct their charges; their task is the spiritual cultivation of men to enable them to take their place as citizens of the state. This idea of the Church is religious but not essentially Christian, and fills the role of Rousseauian civil religion. Like Rousseau, Coleridge was concerned with the question of citizenship and for him, the Church played a crucial role in ensuring that the forces of civilisation did not dissipate themselves in chaos. His concern that the division of labour and commerce undermined one's capacity to exercise citizenship is an extension, rather than a repudiation, of Enlightenment values in the light of the changing circumstances of the early nineteenth century. The Church counters these potentially destructive developments by providing those elements of permanency without which the individual citizen is deprived of the capacity to exercise reason and rational citizenship, to recognise the common good. The University, as the New Church, can guarantee citizenship by initiating its members into the mysteries of oneness. It can provide the necessary religious foundations of civic morality. The ideal of 'culture' became a necessary component of this theory of the University because 'culture' was a quasi-secular version of civil religion which, it was hoped, could provide both the spiritual bonds of social unity and a model of rational behaviour. Now we must examine more closely what Arnold meant by culture.

Arnold defined culture as making reason and the will of God prevail so that the best that has been thought and known in the world will be currently available to all. Culture implies an objective set of principles, of 'right reason', which will become the focus of social harmony and unity in an age threatened not only by class conflict but also by rampant individualism and mere opinion. But culture is not only a set of ideas about the world; it is also a state of being, through which the individual attains an attitude of harmony. By throwing off his partial self and disinterestedly pursuing culture the individual reaches a rational or universal self. 'Sweetness and light' is the necessary outcome of this pursuit of perfection. A society composed of men of culture would be a universal society – they are 'the true apostles of equality'.[24]

From this it should be clear why Arnold emphasised the role of the state as an embodiment of right reason; through the state the citizen expresses his universal self, his self brought to the True, the Good and the Beautiful through culture, his soul rendered harmonious by reason. But Arnold not only looked back to Rousseau but also forward to

T.H. Green. Green's ideal of the 'higher morality' as 'morality of the character' governed by 'disinterested motives', that is, by interest in some form of 'human perfection' sounds suspiciously like culture.[25] Both desired the creation of a universal self and to discover a model of citizenship which would bind all elements of society together in a harmonious whole. Culture for Arnold was the key to social harmony, as the process which turns factious, quarrelling classes and individuals into harmonious entities who then pursue a common set of goals. Rooted in the English tradition of 'concrete reason' and serving the dual purpose of theory of knowledge and state of being, culture, with its powerful spiritual and aesthetic elements, is the opposite of the tradition of 'cold' abstract reason usually associated with positivism (and dissenting Protestants). In this sense it was perfect for a university claiming to play a civic, moral and religious role; in this form culture really does come to embody the full meaning of 'ethos'.

Myth

'Myth', on the other hand, represents the aristocratic and poetic side of the coin. Indeed, in New South Wales it was a case of 'Beware those bearing the gift of Greek'. Simone Weil may well have been right when she asserted that Greek poetry is more easily understood by the working people than by the middle classes. The only problem is that they will not read it because it has become tainted as a result of its association with the bourgeoisie. The bringers of 'sweetness and light' must mix with those who would kill them if they proclaimed their message. Having seen the sun they move back into the cave only to discover that they are both part of that world and at variance with it. Their precious gift of Reason is, almost by definition, potentially subversive.

In the Platonic vision it is clear that Plato was here alluding to the death of Socrates. A central issue is the power of a democratic community to dispose of those whom it cannot bear to hear. The problem of Socrates is very much the problem of democracy and of the place of the rational intellect within it. This issue can be illuminated by examining what Alexis de Tocqueville said about the role of ideas in a democracy. Tocqueville was, of course, discussing America but much of what he said could apply equally to Australia. In his account of the place of ideas in democratic America, de Tocqueville highlighted a few characteristics which are of particular interest:

1 the power of public opinion in democratic society;
2 a taste for general ideas in the sense of 'rules' which can be applied so that there is no need to consider particular cases;

3 a taste for the tangible, the real and the practical;
4 a tendency to exclude the supernatural and to deny anything that cannot be understood by ordinary men.

Tocqueville concluded his remarks by advocating that there was a real need in America to cultivate the theoretical as the practical could well look after itself.[26]

In other words, de Tocqueville was arguing that democracy encourages men to penetrate only to the outer shell of knowledge and to remain satisfied with phenomena and the illusions of sense. Curiously this argument is not so far removed from the diagnosis that the Antipodean Tocqueville, D.H. Lawrence, made of the Australian psyche. According to Lawrence, Australians lacked depth and seemed to consist only of the outer kernel. Egalitarianism, he correctly perceived, was as much a spiritual problem as a political issue. Equality might be a need of the human soul but, as Simone Weil has pointed out, so are hierarchy and obedience.[27]

Tocqueville mentioned the implications of democracy for rational knowledge, and Lawrence explored the impact of this attitude at a spiritual and psychological level. Egalitarianism denies authority and hierarchy not only at a political level but also in the realm of the spirit. If Australia is the most democratic country in the world, it is also the realm of the outer man and practical knowledge which rarely penetrates beneath the surface of things. It is the natural home of sophistry and opinion: of *doxa*. Because of this it is much more likely to be hostile, or indifferent, to the pretensions of the *pouvoir spirituel* of the university, to an institution devoted to the cultivation of theory. In this sense, the ethos/myth dichotomy developed much more fully in nineteenth century New South Wales than elsewhere in the European world because this was a democratic country. Socrates is truly an icon for Australian intellectuals – he was the original 'tall poppy'.

Myth, then, expresses the separateness of the men of knowledge who have been out to look at the sun but who lack the intrinsic authority to make their fellow citizens take their vision seriously. It is what remains as comfort when the dream of a cultured society fades from view. Myth can take many forms. There is the Romantic despair of John Woolley renouncing reason for poetry, the Bohemianism of the legal/literary elite which expressed itself in the cafe society of late nineteenth century Sydney, and finally there is the cult of personality, the myth of the heroic man of letters battling manfully against the philistines.

Ethos and Myth: the University of Sydney

It is now possible to develop this theme of ethos and myth in relation to the development of the intellectual life of the University of Sydney. From its foundations the university defined its role in terms of a desacralised religious ideal – it was to be the centre of a spiritual force which would temper the potentially destructive effects of the growth of commerce and democracy. 'Material advancement,' explained Charles Nicholson, first Chancellor of the university, 'without a corresponding progression in the moral and intellectual condition of a community, is of small avail in promoting its real happiness or ultimate greatness'.[28] Unlike the Free Traders who believed that the general operation of Nature's Laws as embodied in commerce and the diffusion of knowledge could achieve this end, Nicholson believed that only the permanent spiritual presence of a university could guarantee progress.

The role of the university was to provide access to the light outside the cave, to become a religious and spiritual centre upholding the values of civic humanism. John Woolley conceived his role as that of aiding the creation of a world in which spiritual and moral values controlled the course of man's material progress, to bring God 'back to Earth again, not in distorted and fantastic symbols, but in His own pure Majesty'. Woolley considered his own age to be an age of 'luxuriant civilization', an age in which spiritual values were threatened by the 'refinements and comforts of life, with the attendant diffusion of information, with its desultory superficialism'. Science, he believed, awakens man's consciousness of his spiritual nature and increases his desire both to satisfy his spiritual longings and to enter into spiritual relationships. In other words, the way to the 'good life' lay in escaping the superficial world of the phenomena of the cave into the solid permanent world of spirituality, illuminated by the sun's glare. For Woolley, the university preserved spiritual values and science by teaching those disciplines which 'conduce to mental vigour and selfrelying thought'. In a society subject to the corrupting influences of rapid progress, the university remains a repository of permanent spiritual values, a true *pouvoir spirituel*, a 'monument to endure throughout all generations' which 'guides and regulates' to ensure that progress moves at the correct pace and in the right direction. One concrete way in which it could achieve this aim was by producing statesmen whose 'practice of life may be regulated by fixed and eternal principles'.[29]

In paying tribute to his former teacher, Samuel Griffith, founding father of Federation and High Court judge, diagnosed that the 'want of accuracy in thought, a carelessness of thought' was a great defect in Australian life. Griffith went on to say that democracy 'desires to be led by its best men' and that graduates should endeavour 'by their conduct in life' to convince the public that a university education had made them 'fitter men for conducting the affairs of the country'. Whereas Griffith signifies the rational, Aristotelian side of Woolley's ideas, it was another former student, William Windeyer, who captured Woolley's mystical,

Romantic side. As an undergraduate, under Woolley's influence, he attacked the utilitarian spirit of philosophy and wrote of the earnest seeker 'with his soul intent upon the ideal' who 'imperceptibly grows into harmony with the good'. Later in life Windeyer was to involve himself in spiritualism just as Woolley's widow was to become a leading Theosophist. Amongst the circles of the 'thinking classes', late nineteenth century Sydney was awash with Gnostic and Romantic quests for spiritual illumination – a parallel with Deakin's spiritualist experiences in Melbourne.[30]

Ethos and Myth: Charles Badham

The tale of Woolley's descent into the pit of despair and his entry into the myth of Romanticism has been chronicled elsewhere.[31] The theme of ethos and myth can be developed more fully through a discussion of Woolley's successor, Charles Badham. Badham arrived in Sydney in 1867 at the age of fifty-four and continued as principal until his death in 1883. His 1867 commemoration speech marks him out as an heir of Coleridge, averring as he did that 'To give civil society its dignity and its permanence is the peculiar function of a university.' The university was to assume the role of the Church in colonial society. Badham continued:

> Although industry and the spirit of adventure may bring civilization to unknown shores – as in this particular instance it was brought here – the spirit of industry and the spirit of adventure cannot create civilization; neither can they arrest its inevitable decay if the conditions of its existence are not carefully maintained. By the same arts, by the same studies, by the same devotion to the higher principles and faculties in man which created it, must it always and for ever be maintained.[32]

As a fortress of permanence and an antidote to superficiality the university was a guarantee that the fruits of civilisation would not be lost. Badham accepted the fact of democracy in the colonies and expected that with time they would become even more democratic. The task was to temper its worst excesses. In particular, Badham was not impressed by the pretensions of colonial mercantile civilisation. To European eyes, he asserted, it exhibited some 'strange phenomena'. There was an enormous amount of wealth in the hands of illiterate men, a lack of learning to be found amongst the learned professions, including the Church, and a low standard of intellectual and literary taste amongst the mercantile classes.

Moreover, according to Badham, there were dangerous currents operating in modern society; it was an age 'of nobility without grandeur, of wealth without public spirit, of ambition without statesmanship, of science without culture and refinements', an age which believed that

'education is the mere training of the mind', an age threatened by char-
latans and social impostors 'whose politics are a contradiction of history,
whose language is a burlesque upon language, whose arguments slap
logic in the face'. What the uncultivated colonists needed was a source of
authority which could provide them with guidance in an age of confusion, an 'object which shall claim their reverence, and so habituate
them to self-control. That object cannot be birth or title, and heaven for-
bid that it should be money.' Culture was to be that thing, a guarantee
that amidst the flux and disorder of a democratic society people would
keep to 'fixed principles and laws'. Wrote Badham: 'When we see the
same feelings, aims, affections, anxious doubts, and topics of consolation
in the literature of bygone times, the thought of our permanent humanity and of the ineffaceable identity between the soul of the past and the
soul of the present, makes us thoughtful, reverent, social, patriotic.'

To this state of affairs Badham attached the word 'culture'. Culture
was, for him, a quasi-religious ideal which would guarantee social order
by providing the spiritual foundation of a living civic humanism. The
university was to create a class of men possessing both the virtues
described above and a 'trained and tried intellect'; men who would
determine the standards of culture and become the measure of it in the
community. Such a group would not remain locked up within its ivory
tower; its place was out in the wider world – a small nucleus setting the
tone for society and diffusing the 'blessings of civilization around them'.
Badham believed that his students would become beacons of light in the
community providing that element of co-operation and virtue necessary
to combat materialism and selfishness, and to bind society together into
a harmonious whole. In such a way would the university remedy the
defects of democracy and usher in the reign of harmonious reason.

For Badham the path to culture lay in the study of classical languages.
In particular, he believed that the mental exertion called forth by the
analysis of grammar and language produced a person marked by clear
logical thought. Textual emendation was, for him, the ultimate educational source of social reform: the restoration of pure language must
lead to a more pure way of thinking and acting. Trained in these techniques the university man was possessed of a clear consciousness 'full of
reverence, refinement and clear-headedness . . . by the very conditions
of his discipline temperate in opinion, temperate in measures, temperate in demeanour'.[33]

This is very much the Oxford man reborn in a new world. It is important to realise that the humanist ideal of 'culture' grounded in grammar
is just as, if not more, rigorous than any scientific form of training.
Nineteenth century 'liberal education' was highly rationalistic and thorough – what made it 'liberal' was its belief that this training was not an

end in itself. It was the passage through which the mind must pass on its way to the True, the Good and the Beautiful. Culture and the training of thought produce a rational being but such is the nature of reason that its possessors will absorb the higher truths of morality. Education is both the training of the mind and an entry into higher truths – the possession of 'sweetness and light' being what distinguishes the university man from the auto-didact of the lower orders.

This dualistic conception of the educational process in which rational training has as its end an awareness of the eternal and the immutable is best summed up in a passage Badham wrote on Dante:

> As to the influence of his love for Beatrice he owed the exaltation of his reli-gious convictions, so to Virgil he owed the power of learned observation and wise dealing with human life and character. Indeed, Virgil was to him the type of human learning and trained understanding; and, therefore, as Beatrice was the power which superintended and commanded his whole journey, Virgil was the watchful and edifying companion of his footsteps.[34]

University men required a 'trained understanding' but such could only be a prelude for 'Reason' – they must have both their Beatrice and their Virgil. Badham believed that poetry was one of the major instruments for educating mankind into a state of civilisation. For him the beautiful was that which rescues man from the vulgar adoration of wealth and power, and from vulgar motives and standards as to the social position of others. Absolute Beauty, beauty 'in and for itself, and capable of holding the soul in beatific contemplation and never-ending rapture' is the inspiration guiding man's sense of morality and harmony. Beauty alone prevents phi-losophy from becoming 'barren and self-bewildering logic' and turns its attention to 'moral and practical enquiries'.[35]

If the works of the classical authors were the 'texts' of culture then Badham was its 'saint', the living embodiment or incarnation of all those qualities which the books merely described. W.J. Gardner points out that all of the antipodean universities had a 'cult of the founder' although, in the case of the University of Sydney, the cult attached itself to Badham rather than to Woolley.[36] Out of this need to possess a living symbol of scholarship in a society devoted primarily to the twin pursuits of getting and spending, emerged the myth of Badham.

The fullest expression of the myth is to be found in A.B. Piddington's *Worshipful Masters* in which Badham appears not only rich in culture and the greatest Greek scholar of his age but also as a sage, pundit and Bohemian – a gossip and an eminently clubbable man, a 'sceptic though a clergyman'. Robert Garran recounted that Badham was a jealous lover of the humanities who had come to Australia partly because of difficulties with the Thirty Nine Articles. Recalling the physical impact of Badham on him as a young man, Garran wrote that he believed him to have been a reincarnation of Demosthenes. Judge Backhouse likewise attested to Badham's personal influence on his students but also noted his ability to make enemies. A.G. Stephens and the poet, Christopher Brennan, kept alive this myth of Badham well into the twentieth century.[37]

Badham's power of oratory, his claim to represent culture, his Bohemianism and ambiguous position in colonial society impressed his students greatly, particularly as a cafe society and its accompanying Bohemianism emerged in Sydney in the 1880s and 1890s. Badham's reputation as a sort of antipodean 'Miss Jean Brodie' developed as a consequence of the ambiguous place of the university educated within colonial society. He was the symbol of the aristocratic university in a world without aristocrats – except those of the spirit. Badham's disciples, from Barton and Backhouse to Piddington, came not from the gentry but the petty bourgeoisie, and from the university their career paths invariably led to the Bar. These 'aristocrats of the spirit' claimed to represent Reason, and to uphold the values of culture in a society not interested in such things. They lacked the social prestige which would have given their utterances authority, and they were a tiny minority. Truly had they to face the perils of the cave. The 'myth' of Badham was a response to their feeling of separateness, to their claim to be a cultural aristocracy devoted to the common good. Like the Bohemianism with which they flirted, and the cafes they attended to escape the philistines, the 'myth' of Badham expressed their uneasiness in a world to which they owed their success and which they knew full well fell far short of the ideals they had imbibed at university.

Other professors at colonial universities had expressed sentiments not dissimilar to those of Badham. At Melbourne, H.A. Strong told his classics students that he hoped that some of them would become Members of Parliament and so bring the fruits of their education to bear on the government of their country.[38] His successor, T.G. Tucker, elaborated on the value of culture, claiming that without it the full harmonious development of the senses, heart and intellect could not occur. A society governed by men of a liberal education, he declared, would be better governed, nobler and happier as it would possess the best ideal of man. And what provided the clearest route to culture? Perfect culture, he believed, would include science and literary studies. But, in an imperfect world, it was impossible to study everything. Literature in general, and classics in particular, provided the surest means of attaining culture; they 'alone possess each of the soul perfecting elements' (conduct, knowledge, beauty, manners) which mark out the cultured gentleman. Tucker, however, was already fighting a rearguard action, with his eyes cast worriedly in the direction of the sciences. His name now appears blackened as an arch-philistine while that of Badham still rides high as a defender of culture and the true ideal of the university.[39]

The Challenge of the Sciences

Badham had resisted the intrusion of the sciences into the university curriculum. With his death the old 'aristocratic' ideal of the university was forced to come to terms with the forces of the age. Not only was the status of the sciences upgraded and medicine and engineering admitted to the cloisters, but the scope of the humanities was broadened with the introduction of history, philosophy and modern languages. These changes were only apparently radical. The great English apostle of science, Thomas Huxley, who had been a friend of Badham, once described universities as citadels of the higher learning. His concern had been to establish that science, as well as the humanities, could provide a path to culture, that the book of nature as much as works of literature could be used as a text of culture.[40]

Badham's successor, Walter Scott, welcomed the alliance of the sciences and the humanities fighting for the cause of progress against the 'unnatural union of material wealth with intellectual barbarism'. Both, he argued, were founded on scientific principles and so had something to learn from the other. In the university, he claimed: 'the study of literature and natural science, of the spirit of man revealed in thought and action, and the laws of the material world, should both find a place, and work harmoniously side by side'. Scott, who, it should be noted, was a product of Balliol College, Oxford, is now remembered primarily as the editor of the *Corpus Hermeticum*. But, as befitted a man committed to spreading the light in the modern world, his major impact on Australia was as an amateur economist. He attacked the 'cash nexus' basis of modern industrial society, and, as President of the Economics Section of the 1895 meeting of the AAAS, opposed *laissez-faire* and argued that the government should take a lead by fixing a minimum wage for its employees.[41] The scope of the man of culture had widened considerably.

At the same time, J.T. Wilson, Professor of Anatomy, continued to propagate many of Badham's ideas and to uphold the 'religious' nature of the university. With the decline of the influence of the Church on the more educated classes, claimed Wilson, 'the universities have become, more than ever, guardians of the intellectual interests of humanity at the present time'.[42] The basis of the general ideal of the university was culture and character, and the 'promotion of many of the higher manifestations of rational activity upon which social progress is based, and upon which ultimately social equilibrium depends'. Unlike the cultural and social critic, Francis Adams, the scientists did not challenge the attempt by the universities to appropriate culture to themselves as their own particular possession.[43] Rather they demanded a share of it as part of their reward for having attained university status. It distinguished them from the technical schools over which they claimed superiority. 'Culture' marked out a professional from a technician; he had 'education' not merely 'training'. But ultimately this attempt to 'steal' culture by the scientists involved a transformation of its meaning – the spiritual dimension was lost and culture came to mean, by and large, the same thing as theoretical knowledge. Between 1880 and 1914 there was a series of 'battles' over culture in the Australian universities in which the major participants were the new sciences, the new social sciences and the humanities. It was a mini-version of the science/culture debate of the old world, and it was a direct consequence of the need by the university to assimilate the variety of new disciplines created by an increasingly complex society.

Both the scientists and the social scientists emphasised the new ideal of research: the belief that university scholars 'make' as well as transmit knowledge. For John Woolley, such a suggestion would have been blasphemy: men did not create knowledge but merely uncovered that which God had made. But for the spokesmen of the new ideal of the university, research was its key element. It was what William Mitchell, James Barrett and R.F. Irvine emphasised after visiting American universities, often implying that Australian universities were only the equivalent of American colleges.[44] The conception of 'making knowledge' derives from Romantic notions of the creative self and the power of the will to remake the world in its own image. Potentially, at least, it has Gnostic overtones. It has clear affinities with pragmatism and the idea that knowledge can be constructed to meet changing circumstances. In particular, such a conception of knowledge is attractive in a new society such as America or Australia, in which institutions have been made rather than merely inherited from the past. It has been pointed out that the idea that law can be 'made', as opposed to the belief that it is founded upon unalterable principles of reason and revelation, is a modern one.[45]

Such a conception of law and knowledge represents a victory of *taxis* over *kosmos*: real knowledge is that which men and women have made in society. As mentioned earlier, such a view of knowledge rests on an opposition between society and nature in which the moral order has retreated to society which then becomes the defence of humanity against a hostile and amoral nature. Nature is stripped of its divine quality and becomes an inert substance on which human will exerts itself. Hence there exists a genuine affinity between Protectionism and the new idea of the university which emerged during the first decade of this century.

The arrival of new disciplines in the university, in the humanities as well as in the sciences and the social sciences, raised, as we have seen, the whole question as to the meaning and role of culture. Our task is to explore how this question was handled and its implications for the tradition of Cultural Liberalism. It was argued earlier that the tradition of Cultural Liberalism owed its particular configuration to the relationship existing and balance established amongst, at any given time, the three constituent elements of the humanist university: civic humanism, science/scientific rationality and spiritual growth. During these years two distinct trends occurred amongst those to whom the label Cultural Liberal can be attached. On the one hand, there was a tendency to emphasise civic humanism and scientific rationality in terms of creating a more efficient and democratic society composed of an active, rational citizenry; and on the other hand, there was an intensification of a desire for spiritual growth and the possibility of creative self-expression both at the personal and the collective level. This expressed itself specifically, in continuing outbreaks of Romanticism.

These two trends were best summed up in the two writers who were seen to provide the intellectual foundations for the 'New Education' then being introduced into Australia: Johann Friedrich Herbart and Friedrich Froebel.[46] Whereas Herbart emphasised character building as the foundation of citizenship, Froebel saw the child as an organism which developed through creative self-activity according to natural laws. It was no accident that the leading Australian educational theorist of those years, P.R. Cole, should have attempted a synthesis of Herbart and Froebel.[47]

The rest of this chapter will be devoted to the first of these trends, and, in particular, the effect of the development of the sciences and social sciences on the idea of culture.

Science and Civic Humanism

This new ideal of science as culture is best described by Edgeworth David, Professor of Geology and sometime Antarctic hero. The special function of a university, he contended, is to confer culture upon its alumni – science is an integral part of that culture. The essence of culture is criticism of life and the fully cultured individual must be 'acquainted with the great scientific truths revealed in Nature's Laws'. Science was an important source of culture, and scientific work, especially research, contended David, 'strengthens the character, and entails self-denial, and the correct interpretation of experiments strengthens the reasoning power'. Modern science teaching leads the student both to live well and to think correctly. For David the university and its culture were a source of social harmony; in troubled times when class was pitted against class, labour against capital the university was needed 'to level up in a noble, common brotherhood'.[48]

Using similar arguments, Anderson Stuart, Professor of Medicine at the University of Sydney, asserted that technical education can train the mind and that the culture of any man was determined by the 'method in which he approaches knowledge'. Often stigmatised by humanists as being utilitarian, science was viewed by its proponents as a bulwark against utilitarianism. Orme Masson argued that the discovery of new Truths, and not general utility, was the true role of science, a view endorsed by George Knibbs, who claimed that the liberal element of a scientific education was needed to keep the utilitarian tendencies of modern technology under control.[49]

It was James Barrett, however, who most rigorously argued the case against the classical ideal of culture and in favour of the value of science and utility as sources of culture. Barrett believed that culture could be just as readily obtained from a study of agriculture, engineering or chemistry as from literature. A good classical training was, he claimed, essentially scientific in nature. Culture was simply the attitude of an educated man and included the capacity to deal with problems from an impersonal and detached viewpoint (disinterestedness) and the disposition to indulge in the sympathetic treatment of other people. Barrett believed that any systematic education could produce men possessing those attributes normally believed to be the possession only of the classically educated. A thoroughly utilitarian education would still produce cultured men. The cultured man was also the efficient man – and the ethical man. The man who spent his life at the pitch of the greatest efficiency would be, on the average, the one from whom the greatest amount of human happiness is extracted. Taken together, Barrett's statements on 'culture' constitute an ideology of the educated who are considered to be superior both intellectually and ethically.[50]

This use of the term 'culture' as a general attribute of the educated was quite common during these years. Generally it was associated with an ideal of citizenship; the cultured individual would make a model citizen whom lesser mortals could emulate. Even as staunch a defender of the humanities as Mungo MacCallum agreed that colonial universities should teach practical subjects – but in such a way that they provided the 'liberal aspect in education'. (MacCallum did contend, though, that without literary subjects the university would be a glorified technical school.) It is worth noting that many of the key players in this debate, including MacCallum himself, were the products of Scottish universities and thus sympathetic to ideas of utility. They found the civic humanist and democratic vision of the university congenial; for example, Professor Naylor believed that the main function of the university was to turn out the best type of citizen and he affirmed the 'Scotch' idea that even a ploughman should learn Latin.[51]

The general movement, despite rearguard actions by figures such as Tucker, was towards admitting new and useful subjects into the inner sanctuary of culture. The objective was to make utility into something liberal by providing 'useful subjects' with a powerful theoretical foundation. The Report of the Royal Commission on the University of Melbourne claimed that there was no necessary divorce between utilitarian and liberal studies and that the highest utility may be combined with, and is hardly attainable without, a high culture.[52]

It was this desire to be considered cultured and its affirmation of civic humanist values which saved science from degenerating into scientism. The Melbourne Report went on to advocate both the training of students and research as ways in which the university could 'be truly national by association with the life's work of the people'. Similarly, the most important scientific researcher of this period working in Australia, Professor W.H. Bragg, advocated that the universities and science should be more in contact with the daily life and tasks of the people. He claimed: 'If the State university is to live its full life, it must not separate itself into the wilderness, like the hermit of old; but must mingle with the people and draw strength and inspiration from the attempt to minister to their needs.'[53] Science and scientists had civic obligations because as men of culture they were capable of disinterested enquiry into national problems and of thus serving the people. That extraordinary polymath of Australian science, George Knibbs, summed up in 1923 the hopes of this vision of science: 'We shall need to gird ourselves for the task, and create for ourselves a world where our sons . . . will excel in the art of using to the full the heritage our nation has given us. Then indeed will science have rendered noble service to the sons of Australasia.'[54] Scientists could easily assimilate the civic humanist dimension of culture but they could not use the spiritual dimension. The effect was both to broaden the conception of culture but also to narrow its meaning so that it became almost purely cognitive – a body of intellectual theory. It is this insensitivity to an important aspect of human existence which lies at the core of the division of scientists and humanists into two cultures. Consequently, during these years there remained a resentment between scientists and humanists simmering under the surface of university life.

Griffith Taylor, geographer and controversial advocate of unpopular causes, can be used to illustrate the last point.[55] As a young man he admitted to 'not going in for culture' and he became a spokesman for those who wished to use scientific research to solve Australia's national problems claiming that: 'This is the age of co-ordination and co-operation. The independent worker must ultimately give place to the vastly more economic amalgamation or trust. And this is true of science no less than of industry.' Taylor attacked a number of the pressing problems facing Australia in the 1920s only to be rewarded with vilification and the banning of one of his books by the University of Western Australia.[56] On the one front, Taylor had to battle all of those who found his scientific theories distasteful. On another front, he took on the traditional advocates of culture. In a piece written in 1928 Taylor argued that geography was crucial in the education of young Australians as it taught them to appreciate their own position in relation to the world around them. More geography meant less Latin – and it did not imply less culture: 'True culture implies a love of beauty . . . It promotes a sympathy with the concerns and ideals of other individuals and peoples . . . these ideals will rather be promoted by the study of the human environment of to-day than by the study of a language of twenty centuries ago.'[57]

This article led to a rather acrimonious exchange of letters with the Professor of Latin at Sydney, Frederick Augustus Todd. Todd argued for Latin in terms of its beneficial effects on human reasoning powers, while Taylor discussed the relationship between geography and contemporary Australian problems. There was no resolution of the argument. Later that year Taylor left Australia for a position in Canada, frustrated in his attempts to establish geography at Sydney. Months later, Edgeworth David wrote to him saying that the Arts side of the university was attempting to wipe out the School of Geography.[58] And yet neither the advocates of culture nor those of utility truly won the day. In the same letter David referred to the inertia of the university. Writing in the 1930s, G.V. Portus characterised Australian universities as professional schools turning out doctors, engineers, lawyers, dentists and teachers.[59] Arts courses were essentially seen as teacher training courses; neither culture nor utility in the service of the people seemed to have conquered the 'practical' nature of the university.

If the sciences had an impact on the idea of culture then this was paralleled by the social sciences as they sought to establish themselves as members of the Academy. James Barrett advocated sociology as the bridge between the scientific discoveries made in the national universities and the practical application of these discoveries in the wider society.[60] Many such pleas for sociology were made during these years and yet the discipline failed to take root in Australia until after World War II.[61] Social psychology, despite the brilliance of such men as Elton Mayo and Bernard Muscio, suffered a similar fate. Economics and public administration, being 'practical', gained a foothold. But the real success story of these years was education. As education was professionalised, new teacher training colleges were established and a body of theory developed to justify this professionalisation. By and large this theory was derived from the New

Education and came from England and America, but it paralleled more general ideas about culture and its role in society. To see how the social sciences affected ideas of culture and the tradition of Cultural Liberalism, I propose firstly to examine the ideas of two educationalists, Peter Board and P.R. Cole, and secondly to consider the position developed by the most brilliant of the advocates of social science, R.F. Irvine.

The Influence of Education: Board

Peter Board was one of the great educational reformers of Australia, a practical man who was Director General of Education in New South Wales but who, in his scattered writings, has left us with a rationale for this reforming work. Board was Australian-born of Scottish parentage, an heir of the Scottish tradition of civic humanism which emphasised both citizenship and the use of education as a means of creating a more democratic social order.[62] Indeed, it is the possibility that a universal education system provides for the democratisation of the social system which dominates much of Board's thought about education and culture. Consequently, Board could say that the 'American University is the biggest expression of the American ideal of democracy' anticipating that reform of Australian education would create a similar situation in Australia.[63]

In a paper written after his retirement Board stated his case succinctly: 'It is to Education that we must look for the creator of the soul of the nation' for, as he continued, 'the sum total of the results produced by all teachers on all the children is that which determines the character, the outlook, the tastes, the spiritual standards of the community and the nation'.[64]

How then did Board view the soul of the Australian nation? As has been mentioned previously, the two keys to this were democracy and citizenship. Delivering his address at the 1909 meeting of the AAAS, Board spoke optimistically of the 'Renaissance of the twentieth century. . . . In every department of human activity there is a deep consciousness that there is something better to be gained, and that every step onward is a step upward.' Board believed that this Renaissance followed closely on the democratising of education in the second half of the nineteenth century. He argued that: 'Literature, science, industry, social development, politics, religion, all owe their vitality, their dynamic restlessness, to the wide diffusion of intellectual power that has followed upon popular education.'[65]

Board linked this democratisation of education with a number of other trends. Firstly, he argued that 'utilitarian' was no longer a term of reproach but meant simply a form of education which 'equips the individual for rendering service to society'.[66] Board himself was attracted to that element in the writings of the educational philosopher, Herbart, which emphasised character and citizenship and he believed that 'the highest education is . . . that which best enables him [the citizen] to render service by doing something that other people want done'. In other words, Board wanted to link an expanded notion of utility with ideals of citizenship so that the usefully educated individual would become the citizen of a democratic society. Moreover, Board wanted to connect public education with both 'the fulfilment of distinctly national purposes' and the needs of industry: 'The school will become the adjunct of the workshop, and the workshop a class-room of the school'. Board wanted students to study practical subjects which dealt with the real and immediate world around them as opposed to the abstract mental gymnastics involved in classical training. He could advocate history on the grounds that 'it introduces us to a laboratory, where the actions and reactions of human passions, ambitions, ideas, and ideals have played their part in the crucible of time'.[67] Board's conception of knowledge as useful and dealing with the real and the tangible, like his advocacy of national purposes, is not far removed from that of Griffith Taylor and the scientists. Education must deal with the real and the practical.

All of this sounds depressingly like views expressed by bureaucrats in more recent Ministries of Education except that Board is saved from such philistinism by his ideal of citizenship and his appreciation of the spiritual nature of humanity. In a paper entitled 'Australian citizenship', Board argued that authority now passes upwards from the people to those who govern. He claimed that the modern state only works properly when every individual recognises the mutual obligations existing amongst all members of the community, the obligations owed by individuals to the community as a whole, and the obligations owed by groups to the community as a whole. This requires a new and democratic conception of citizenship. Such a conception of citizenship, Board believed, involved a curtailment both of liberty and of personal selfishness. If the individual was to practise good citizenship by considering the greater good of the whole community, then he or she needed to look beyond narrow individual or occupational interests to those of the whole. In a similar fashion to Elton Mayo, Board contended: 'Thinking that is dominated by the ideas of the social or occupational group to which the individual belongs cannot contribute to the common good'.[68]

To counter this narrowness Board advocated education through discussion – a solution not dissimilar to that advocated by the Workers Educational Association liberals. Like them, Board also looked beyond Australia and considered that an enhanced sense of citizenship implied a greater willingness to participate in the international order. In an address on 'History and Australian history', he argued that the Australian nation had grown up in isolation such that Australia possessed 'qualities of national character and modes of thinking and personal habits which differentiate it from what is purely British'. Australia had matured as a nation, a maturity consummated on 25 April 1915; on that date 'history and Australian History were fused'. As a mature nation Australia must become part of the world community and make its voice heard by that community. Clearly it was the task of the education system, and Board spoke of an Australian national education system, to express this nationality and create 'the soul of the nation'.[69]

In the writings of his retirement he again took up the issue of the importance of education, only at this point, just as in his citizenship piece, he concerned himself with the problem of social division and unrest. Education was the key to overcoming social unrest; it would ensure that men and women became more than just cogs in the social mechanism. Thus, in his retirement, Board went beyond a concern with citizenship and utility to a consideration of the spiritual nature of humanity. In terms of the educational philosophies of the day he turned from Herbart to Froebel and came to recognise the three elements on which the tradition of Cultural Liberalism rests: science, spirituality and citizenship.

First Board argued that 'the interests of society as a whole . . . demand that man should be educated as a spiritually endowed organism and not a mere mechanical worker . . . that will enable him to feel superior to the mechanism he works . . . he will be not merely a worker but a man'.[70] He then argued the case for science and the part it 'plays in the welfare of the race' and the value of education as a motor of progress. Again pleading the cause of utility, he stated the case for bringing education into 'closer relationship with the everyday realities of human life'. Finally, Board provided a picture of his ideal education as a process in which science, citizenship and spirituality are welded together in a single splendid vision:

On the other hand, from every teacher who sees in every subject he teaches an open door through which he leads his pupils into a spiritual world, a world that calls for wonder, admiration and worship, a world where the imagination is stimulated, where the image of Duty and Service beckons with an attractive hand, where the soul of the pupil is fed by a contemplation of the beautiful and the true, it is from such a teacher that there comes into the social life of the State that stream of young life which will make the nation realise the highest aims to which any national life may tend.[71]

Board certainly had broadened the conception of culture, but unlike the scientists, he remained true to the spiritual conception of human

beings, and his final position is very much an affirmation of the principal tenets of Cultural Liberalism. The essential unity of civic humanism,
scientific rationality and spiritual growth could be maintained in an
almost Utopian vision of the power of education.

Cole: Two Roads to Culture

Similar concerns can be found in the writings of P.R. Cole, perhaps
Australia's leading educational theorist of this period, who also sought
to address the problem of the connection between culture and utility.[72]
In his early work, Cole attempted a synthesis between the two key
philosophers who inspired the New Education: Froebel and Herbart.
Cole argued that in a democracy the curriculum would be formulated
with the aim of adjusting individuals to social ideals and would reflect
the progressive and evolving nature of democratic social life. The curriculum would consist of two elements: a Herbartian tendency which
would emphasise the humanities as being essentially intellectual and
aristocratic; and a Froebelian bias (democratic in nature) towards science, industries and processes. The aristocratic humanities are summed
up as culture; the democratic sciences as nature. Cole saw that the synthesis of Herbart and Froebel would unify culture and nature, the
humanities and the sciences, aristocracy and democracy. He believed
that the humanities could become practical and the manual arts human,
and in this way the cultural and occupational sides of the curriculum
could be unified. The aim of the teacher must be to 'humanise science
and to idealise nature'; in this way a practical utilitarian education can
become a rigorous cultural education.[73]

Cole returned to this theme in the last chapter of his *History of
Educational Thought* entitled 'British and American Paths to Culture',
arguing that the 'national individuality' of America is 'reflected in the
character of their colleges and schools'. He identified the British 'path
to culture' as knowledge for its own sake, the possession of an aristocratic leisured gentleman pursuing a liberal education in the tradition
of the Greek philosophers. America, on the other hand, possessed a
'practical and progressive culture' which expected to 'find culture everywhere, in industry as well as in literature, in commerce as well as in logic,
in transportation as well as in the fine arts'. Whereas English culture
sought to produce 'highly trained leaders', America satisfied itself with a
'well-educated proletariat'. This is the Herbart/Froebel distinction
restated. But are these two versions of culture irreconcilable? Where
does Australia fit into the model? Cole noted that the American system
was an 'experiment' made only by America, Scotland and some of the
British dominions. Peter Board emphasised powerfully the relationship

between the culture of a country and its educational system. Should not then the 'soul' of Australia be matched by its education system?[74]

Cole discussed the question of the 'Australian Social Type' in a paper delivered for the Royal Australian Historical Society. He asserted that the 'Australian type is still in the making' and went on to describe the record of progress which had gone into that making. Cole praised both the 'hereditary equipment' which white settlers had brought with them to Australia and the beneficial effect which the environment had worked on that 'equipment'. Like Board, he saw the greatest danger to Australian development in insularity and remoteness from the rest of the world. The cure for narrow provincialism: 'an enlightened system of education, supplemented by the encouragement of travel and the facilitation of other means of international intercourse'.

Education was thus crucial to Australian social development. Australians had shown themselves to be 'decidedly enterprising, self-reliant and inventive' and had created the world's political laboratory in which 'unparalleled experiments are being conducted in the development of democratic and social institutions'. Only in art, literature and religion (which, of course, was where the aristocratic humanities were of the greatest importance) had Australians been imitative and lacking in great achievements. In those Froebelian, democratic areas of life, Australia had progressed remarkably and the public education system had been a major factor in this progress: 'To the public schools maintained under this department children of all classes thronged, and from them has spread a democratic, unifying, sincere and benevolent spirit which has had no little effect upon the development of the Australian social type.'[75]

So Cole, like Board, ultimately came down in favour of the democratic, civic humanist and practical notion of culture although neither was unsympathetic to the aristocratic cultural ideal. For Cole, the good life was grounded in efficiency and guided by habits that were informed by intelligence and reason. In striving for good character one would also attain a kind of beauty of the soul.[76] Although both men professed themselves as democrats seeking an enlightened citizenry, they also believed that democracy would produce an educated elite based on merit rather than social status. Democracy meant equality of opportunity as expressed in the 'Exhibitions' for study at university established by Board. Similarly, Cole distinguished between the professional who gained satisfaction from the actual performance of his work and the tradesman who derived satisfaction from something outside his work.[77] Of course, in practice, pupils at schools like Sydney Boys and Sydney Girls High Schools accepted the notions of public service but continued to aspire for honours in Latin and Greek. Only the less able studied 'practical' subjects such as geography and commerce. Just as Griffith Taylor emigrated, so the progressivist conception of culture remained an ideal – America did not triumph over Britain. 'Democracy' and 'culture' were very much connected with the creation of an elite and the way in which that elite could justify its place in the world. Culture belonged to those who had proved their ability to possess it; the aristocracy of a democratic social order.

So it can be discerned that even in committed democrats such as Board and Cole, the old tension between democracy and aristocracy as elements of culture re-emerged and remained unresolved. The same was true of those who advocated sociology and the social sciences as the road to a better future; in this case the new aristocrat was the scientific expert who is also cultured and spiritually aware.

Irvine: the Social Sciences as Culture

In the years before 1914 there were many 'pleas', from people such as Barrett and Francis Anderson, for the introduction of sociology into Australian universities. This was perceived principally as a democratic measure and the Scottish–American connection mentioned by Cole was very much in evidence. The model most commonly used was the American state university, and Wisconsin in particular, although Barrett was also a great admirer of German education and its 'practical' contribution to the development of German industry. It is in the unfortunately scattered writings of R.F. Irvine that the most cogent and interesting case for the social sciences is to be found. Irvine was raised in New Zealand and arrived in Sydney in the early 1890s. He worked as a schoolmaster and public servant before becoming a lecturer at the University of Sydney where he established foundation commerce courses. In 1912 he became Professor of Economics, a post he held until 1922. Like Francis Anderson, he was both academic and social reformer.[78]

It is clear that Irvine sought to take the crown of culture away from the traditional humanists and appropriate it for the social scientists. While the humanities were wedded to obsolete ideas, sociology was able to unify applied science and the spirit of the humanities. In other words, sociology could provide a new basis for culture in which scientific rationalism, civic humanism and human spirituality would continue to work together for the cause of human betterment. In a piece entitled 'The new humanism', Irvine contended that two things were needed: a new educational 'discipline' capable of giving unity to the fragmentary life and thought of the modern world, and a new inspiration to impel men and women to thought and action. This inspiration involved both the appreciation of the beautiful and of the creative spirit of art and a 'New

Humanism'; 'a science of man, a faith and a worship, a religion of great expectation'.[79]

Furthermore, Irvine saw that this 'New Humanism' would not be brought into being by 'respectable mediocrities' but by the 'soul-transforming power of great, creative personalities'. Creativity is essential because without it, men and women become practical and mechanical – 'weary of life' – they degenerate such that 'the finger of fate has written their doom'. But by 'creative personalities', Irvine did not have in mind Romantic poets and artists but rather the new specialists and professionals being produced by the universities, professionals who had been educated to escape from the 'narrow mentality' of their scientific training and were capable of seeing life as a whole.[80]

Although opposed to the values of the established middle classes, Irvine saw the hope for the future in a new middle class composed of technical experts serving the community and inspired by an idealistic vision. The age of the amateur was over and that of the expert had begun; the need was to create a new unity in which science, citizenship and spirituality were reconciled – this was to be the role of sociology. In Irvine's advocacy of sociology is to be found a new vitalist conception of culture as an antidote to the threat of degeneration in a rapidly changing world.

Like Barrett and the Progressives, Irvine wholeheartedly supported the rational scientific approach to social problems. Like them, he also looked to Wisconsin and its 'utilitarian idealism' seeking to make 'culture an active force in the community'. He saw the role of Wisconsin as a 'Department of Research for the whole State' providing expertise and service for the whole community. It trains its students for action, and by inference, service, thereby leading to a breakdown in the distinction between the scholar and the man of affairs. Irvine followed the 'American' position, arguing that all good education is utilitarian enabling individuals to become better citizens, and, through their actions, making culture an active force in the community.[81]

Utility is not opposed to culture, but is part of the road leading to culture. Irvine saw the university as the place where experts could be trained in rigorous scientific techniques, 'trained to observe quickly and accurately' and with a critical eye so that they could then go out into the world and work for social progress. This was the role he envisaged for his own university School of Economics. Likewise he advocated a bureau of research for municipal administration which would provide a storehouse of expertise for administrators. He envisaged this bureau as a 'true People's University dedicated to social service and to the continuing study of how the community may realise itself in noble ends'. In the same way, Irvine wrote in support of 'National Efficiency' as a means of organising the community in the most effective way thereby realising common goals and objectives.[82]

This cult of experts and expertise was supported by civic humanism and a desire to create a more beautiful world. 'We are all under a sacred obligation', claimed Irvine, 'to develop a true social interest and public spirit'. Science must be accompanied by a disinterested desire for truth, a 'civic spirit, faculty of co-operation, love of the best'. Equally, it must take account of creativity and imagination and seek to build a more beautiful world. In his writings on town planning he insisted that buildings should combine utility and beauty and that architecture should express creatively the ideals of human imagination.[83]

Irvine seems to have wanted the whole – efficiency, beauty, individualism, rational order, social co-operation, service to the community. But surely this was contradictory except in some world in which harmony was miraculously achieved? Indeed, Irvine's vision only makes sense if it is seen as the product of all individuals willing to co-operate and work together freely for the cause of social progress. Hence, while Irvine supported state intervention as a way of expanding the scope of liberty, he remained essentially suspicious of the state and in favour of the reconstructed individual, considered as expert, active citizen and seeker of ideals as the primary motor of social reform.

An early piece entitled 'Patriotism and nationalism' provides a clue to Irvine's position. In this essay Irvine attacked both cosmopolitanism and English liberalism as effete and decadent. He also disparaged unselfishness and the brotherhood of man, arguing in favour of 'eternal conflict' and 'the will to power'. Claiming Nietzsche as his guide, Irvine wanted to view individual struggle and suffering as the road to true greatness. It is all a matter of maintaining individual and collective vitality in a world threatened by soft, sentimental and enervating tendencies. In opposition to England, Irvine praised Germany as a model of vitality; through social reform, education and protection, Bismarck had built up a powerful and united Empire. Irvine concluded that for a democracy to be successful 'it must educate itself in a way that will make it practically efficient; . . . it must sacrifice itself for the nation'.[84]

In his opposition to British 'decadence', Irvine preached a strange mixture of individual assertiveness and national efficiency as a means of maintaining vigour and virility. These ideas are not far removed from those found in the *Bulletin* – also in a context of masculine self-assertion. Irvine's programme makes sense as one designed to escape the threat of disintegration and decadence. The state was a potential source of that decadence. Consequently, Irvine made a clear distinction between state and community; the community was the source of spontaneity and creativity, the place where spiritual values were created. The community evolved beyond the control of the state and the state existed to maintain and develop the essential system of rights and obligations created by the community – an argument extended by Elton Mayo.[85]

The state was necessary; state intervention in the community had produced favourable consequences. But, Irvine continued, there were real dangers in the excessive development of state power:

> A highly regulated people is apt to lose breadth of vision. Its mind becomes bourgeois, immersed in petty business. It never lifts its eyes to the eternal hills and even loses the power to plan and conduct the big business, for the really big business requires imagination and a strain of idealism.

The solution: 'a society so enlightened that it can be trusted to make free choices and not injure itself'.[86] It is not bourgeois individualism – the service of *laissez-faire*, which Irvine advocated, but the individualism of man combining expertise, duty and creativity. It is the professional expert transformed once by the vision of democratic man inspired by the American poet, Walt Whitman, and a second time by the Nietzschean ideal of the superman creating higher values. Such individuals can escape the danger of decadence and create the vision necessary for society to follow the path of social progress. Again it is a reworked image of the educated or cultured individual leading the masses into an age of Enlightenment.

Irvine, Board and Cole may have been impatient with the older humanistic conception of culture as advocated by Badham, but they did not reject its essential values. Rather they attempted to create a New Humanism, a new ideal of culture, which could be reconciled with utilitarianism and whose home would be in the New Humanities – the Social Sciences.

CHAPTER 4

Ethos and Myth:
The Humanities Strike Back

Changing Conceptions of Knowledge

In the previous chapter some of the routes which the tradition of
Cultural Liberalism took during its various conversations in the late
nineteenth and early twentieth centuries were explored. In particular,
two dimensions of these conversations were explored. The first was the
dialectic of ethos and myth, of the democratic and aristocratic implications of the ideal of culture. The second was the three-pronged nature of
culture: rationality, civic humanism and spiritual growth. In this way the
dynamics of the conversation of Cultural Liberalism were investigated,
firstly in terms of the establishment of colonial universities, and secondly
in the light of the growth of the physical sciences, the professions and
the social sciences. The conversation moved in different directions;
while the scientists adopted a position in which the primary emphasis
was on rationality and civic humanism, social scientists such as Irvine set
themselves up as the new guardians of culture.

Amongst the scientists the tendency was to reaffirm ethos in a modified form – more rational and virtually without a spiritual dimension.
The social scientists and educationalists were strongly attracted to ethos,
which is to say that they found Herbartian 'character' more compelling
than Froebelian 'self-expression', although it is clear that Board and
Cole appreciated the spiritual dimension of human experience. Irvine
is more interesting; on the one hand, he was a spokesman for ethos in
the new, progressive and scientific sense, on the other hand, he possessed an individualistic Nietzschean and Bohemian streak which drove
him into the arms of Romanticism. This rebellious streak, for which he
was eventually to become a martyr to philistinism, is a reminder of the
potentially subversive quality of culture.[1]

81

The task now is to return to the conversation of the humanities themselves as they sought to cope with the challenges of the new disciplines
and come to terms with the new progressive idea of knowledge.
Although John Woolley believed in progressive revelation he also saw
knowledge as something absolute which God revealed to man. Likewise,
Charles Badham had viewed his task as the transmission of those eternal
verities which the classical texts contained. The importance of change
and the role of human agency in the creation of knowledge became
much more urgent questions as the humanities faced up to the implications of the scientific conception of culture with its emphasis on efficiency, research and the utility of knowledge.

One major consequence of this development was the opening up of a
classical/progressive or culture/utility dichotomy within the university
which, as we have seen, was not clear-cut, but which can still be considered
as providing the 'ideal types' of these two conceptions of knowledge. Both
positions started from the problem of change and the assumption that the
world is in a state of flux. The classical position argued that behind the surface world of phenomena there is a set of eternal verities. The progressive
view is that knowledge consists of a body of theory but that body is constantly changing as new discoveries are made and new problems emerge.
As the world changes so the university must conduct research and develop
new theories to deal with that world. The knowledge so created can be put
into practice to solve the world's problems because such problems are
amenable to rationalist solutions. It is tempting to treat this classical/pro-
gressive division sociologically, as a cleavage within the 'culture class'
between the traditional academic and legal elite and the parvenu doctors,
engineers and social scientists. There is some truth in this but the case of
A.B. Piddington, progressive reformer and propagator of the Badham
myth, is an indication that the real situation was more complex.[2]

How was the True to be reconciled with a dynamic conception of knowledge? The torch of the humanities passed out of the hands of the classi-
cists after Walter Scott and T.G. Tucker and the conversation came to be
conducted by the exponents of the New Humanities: Modern Languages,
Philosophy and History. In the early 1890s the University of Sydney established Chairs in these three areas. As Professors, two graduates of Glasgow
University, Mungo MacCallum and Francis Anderson, and one from
Balliol College, Oxford, George Arnold Wood, were chosen. At Glasgow,
both MacCallum and Anderson had been students of Edward Caird, who
was to succeed Jowett as Master of Balliol College. Caird, Idealist philosopher, disciple of Hegel, and civic reformer in such areas as housing, education and women's suffrage, was a central figure in that Glasgow which
served as a 'model Christian municipality' based on a tradition of volun-
tarism dating back to the early nineteenth century theologian and

preacher, Thomas Chalmers, and a devotion to civic ideals and practical reform.[3] From this Glasgow heritage both Anderson and MacCallum received a powerful idealism in which religion and civic humanism were fused, an idealism which shaped their view of the role of the university. Wood received a similar idealism from his non-conformist roots and his Balliol education. All three brought their idealism to bear on the problem of the humanities and the role of knowledge in the world.

MacCallum: A Dry-as-dust Idealist

Considering that Mungo MacCallum is remembered today for establishing a dry-as-dust school of literary criticism and keeping the study of English in New South Wales in a state of advanced mummification, his writings of the 1890s are surprisingly vital and idealistic. Perhaps, unlike Brennan, in the conflict between scholarship and life MacCallum chose scholarship, just as he chose Empire over Justice. Yet it has been claimed that MacCallum was sympathetic to the Labour cause because it offered the hope of idealism.[4] The travails of the spirit are many, and it is unfair, as Manning Clark did, to condemn MacCallum as merely a representative of British philistinism.[5]

In a sense he was, like Brennan, caught between the demands of the authority of culture and the desire to search for the ideal – between classicism and progressivism. His literary criticism of the 1890s reveals the initial strength of his idealist vision derived from the philosophy of Hegel. In his book on the Arthurian Legend, delivered initially as lectures at Sydney during the early 1890s, MacCallum gave a symbolic reading of Tennyson's 'Idylls of the King'. For MacCallum, Arthur was the spiritual principle in conflict with the operations of sense. This spiritual principle is the ideal which governs the lives of men, the eternal pattern which they seek to realise in time; but as it is infinite and divine it can never be realised within time. The inevitable result is imperfection and an order that rises, flourishes but ultimately passes away. Hence the Ideal is the true Reality and is far more important than the world it creates. But there is no clear-cut and easy relationship between the Ideal and the world. On the one hand, if it is not to remain a shadow the Ideal must affect the real world, on the other hand, its union with sense can never be perfect and without reserve. It was this imperfection, MacCallum believed, which lay at the root of modern pessimism.[6]

The 'Idylls of the King' are then to be read as a symbolic rendering of the fate of the Ideal in the world. Camelot is representative of the gradual accretion of human belief, culture and institutions, much of which has become unsound and may be overthrown. Arthur is the spiritual principle; as the Emissary of the Lady of the Lake, or the spiritual essence lying at the heart of all there is, he is the Ideal revealed under the limitations of time. Lancelot is compared to the Imagination and those poets who are given the first glimpse of the Ideal but are more at home in the 'serene sport of art' than in the 'practical conflicts of life'. Merlin is the Intellect and typifies the assistance which every new principle receives from the intellect as it 'pays homage to the ideal and labours on behalf of the highest'. Does this imply that the Ideal is beyond Reason and the rational intellect? MacCallum's conception of Arthur as the Ideal does seem to be pushing it into the realm of the supra-rational and, in a sense, the non-rational. He does seem to be moving beyond the position that the ideal, or intuitive knowledge, does have a relationship to discursive reason. Part of the problem is that by making the Ideal historical, MacCallum also made it somewhat arbitrary because it was no longer part of a fixed eternal order.[7]

As the embodiment of the new spiritual principle, Arthur enters the world at a time of confusion and anarchy when the old order is passing but also 'when no new order or principle has arisen to meet the wants of the age'. Once the new principle is revealed it shines 'with all the authority of a divine message'. Endowed with a clear insight into the nature of things, it proceeds to build a new order including all the warring elements from the time of confusion which have now been subdued by this new principle. Founded on the needs of human nature the new Ideal dominates the age; it is both the 'ought' setting out mankind's goal and the 'is'. At one with the innermost nature of things, it is 'the only eternal, all-inclusive reality'. Although in conflict with what is, or perhaps what appears to be, the Ideal is Reality, that which is behind the phenomenal show. Allying itself with its opposite it fulfils itself in sense even though this union can never be perfected; the ultimate consummation of this union between the Ideal and the World must remain a 'matter of faith and hope'. Even so, men must continue to try to make themselves at one with the Ideal, recognising that this aim can only ever be fulfilled in 'rare intervals of spiritual exaltation'.[8]

The Ideal comes, completes its task and then ultimately passes away until the time comes when a new Ideal must emerge to carry out its divinely appointed mission to the world. Helped by the power of the poet and the thinker a new phase of the Ideal emerges, one suiting 'the wants of the time' which 'furthers the spiritual liberation of men'. Those who feel its influence discover that 'their common efforts form a kind of ecclesia which both anticipates and repeats the true life of the world, and in which they feel at one with the inmost nature of things'.[9]

Two relevant points emerge from MacCallum's Hegelian reading of Tennyson's poem. In his emphasis on the non-realisation of the Ideal and its essentially historical qualities MacCallum reveals a Romantic outlook which threatens the rationality of his Hegelianism. The Ideal is doomed never to succeed and even when it is at the height of its influence only the few can ever rise above themselves to penetrate it, and then only for an instant. There can be no ultimate victory of the Ideal, no escape from the ceaseless movement of the world – Reality and its worldly emanation, the Ideal, lie trapped beyond human hands. Hence, MacCallum's philosophical aesthetics demonstrate their strong Romantic flavour. This is comparable to the theme of many Romantic poems of the 'lost vision' which the poet is unable to bring back with him to the world. The second point relates to his view that those who feel the touch of the Ideal 'form a kind of ecclesia' which is similar to his vision of the university as a 'Civitas Dei', a 'Platonic Republic' forming a society more perfect than almost any other that can be named. Like Coleridge, MacCallum appears to have conceived of the university as an 'Idea', a pattern towards which other human societies would slowly move. Those who have been touched by this Idea 'go forth as graduates to do their part in perfecting the State, the Commonwealth, the Empire of fact, in which they work'. For MacCallum, the university is the protector of the things of the spirit, 'a witness to the totality of civilised man's view of the world' which alone can guarantee true greatness. The university keeps the Ideal alive in the world in preparation for its next revelation; its graduates are like Arthur's knights in support of the Ideal.[10]

There appears to be quite a distance between Badham's confident vision of the capacity of the university man to scale the heights and gaze upon beauty, and MacCallum's resignation that one must rest content with the occasional glimpse. Both agreed that the university was a concrete embodiment of the Ideal, and that its ethos provided a spiritual direction that was lacking in ordinary society. MacCallum's idealistic vision appears to have been tempered with time; by 1910 he was stating that it was enough for university men merely to aim at living honest and worthy lives in their private, professional and domestic capacities.[11]

Wood: The Spiritually Active Individual

A similar idealism can be found in the writings and lectures left by George Arnold Wood – they contain an exposition of the spiritual principle, at once religious and political, which provides a guide to the noble and virtuous life. Wood developed his picture of the virtuous, spiritually active man through studies of figures he admired and who could be held up as models for his contemporaries, in particular John Milton, St Francis of Assisi, Savonarola and Tennyson. As a non-conformist, John Milton appears to have been a favourite of Wood and one of his few published works is an exposition of the Miltonian Ideal.[12]

For Wood, the Miltonian Ideal was that of liberty and it was this faith in liberty which sustained Milton during his life. But what did this 'liberty' mean? Wood made a number of points which help to define Milton's conception of liberty. Firstly, liberty does not depend on circumstances but on the individual himself. This self-dependence was related to the possession of virtue, a virtue which had as its primary elements piety, wisdom, temperance, justice, frugality, abstinence, magnanimity and courage. The virtuous man seeks to educate himself in liberty, to pursue a spiritually active life in which he reaches out towards an independence founded on his own spiritual strength. Hence Wood upheld the active life in which men are encouraged to act and think for themselves, as a natural corollary of the Miltonian Ideal. This principle of activity meant that the worship of God should be 'a spiritual activity, the direct spiritual communion of each man with his God'.[13] A society composed of such sturdy spiritual souls is one devoted to citizenship, of men acting together in the pursuit of liberty. Milton's ideal political society is thus a 'democratic commonwealth, and chiefly for the reason that this is the form of government that recognises the Christian valuation of man, and that does most to stir men up to undertake the duties of "patriotic piety"'.[14] It is clear that Wood shared this vision of the 'spiritually active man' seeking to perfect his liberty and virtue. It was the vitalism of the Miltonian Ideal, the emphasis on liberty and virtue as active ways of life, which Wood found most satisfying. It also helps to explain his other enthusiasms.

Wood discovered a similar spiritual activity in St Francis of Assisi; a man whose teaching was that of the heart, a man who 'in reckless scorn of consequence, sacrificed the whole world that he might in perfect liberty possess his own soul'.[15] He was also attracted to Savonarola whom he depicted as a cultured man of the Renaissance, an original thinker but above all a religious man dedicated to the reformation of the Church. Like St Francis, his teaching was simple, a spiritual religion founded on the gospels and appealing to the heart. And like Milton, Savonarola sought the ideal of a 'Christian democracy' in which every man was educated and able to carry out his duties to the commonwealth and to his fellows.[16]

Coming closer to his own time Wood considered Tennyson to be the modern equivalent of Shakespeare and Milton. As a poet he was the representative of his age. Wood believed that poets were 'men who have realised the spiritual life', men driven by a passion for righteousness to study and understand other men. Poetry is the 'passionate expression of the passionate exertions of human souls striving at the good'.[17] Tennyson, for Wood, exemplified the 'spiritually active man' whose poetry was an illustration both of the spiritual principle and of the English ideal of life. What attracted Wood to Tennyson's poetry was its living religious quality and its capacity to express religion as something alive and vital founded not on reasoning and logic but on the facts of the whole spiritual nature.[18]

Wood viewed religion as essentially vitalistic, as the expression of individual souls in search of purity and virtue. Discussing the Bible, he commented that the real significance of Jesus's life was that it was a 'life of spiritual growth'.[19] The ideal society is one composed of those spiritually active souls who come together to will the good collectively. Consequently, Wood could write enthusiastically of the last sixty years of English history as a time in which a true ideal had made itself more and more evident in all departments of national activity, in religion, politics, society, literature. This ideal was the belief:

> that everyone, man or woman, should be all that his nature, under favourable circumstances, would allow him to become; that all that is good in him should be educated and developed, and that all that is bad should be extirpated; so that he may live what the Greeks called 'the good life'. Our ideal is that man should be fully man, that woman should be fully woman; that our English nation should be a nation of men and women striving to attain perfection of life and help one another to attain it; and lastly that our nation should do what it can to help other nations to do the same.[20]

During the nineteenth century Englishmen had tried to make their own lives, and the lives of the people, better. And they had largely succeeded: 'They have to a large extent reformed themselves.'[21] The spiritual ideal had become active and worked towards the good. Wood may not have been a 'progressive' but he was a believer in knowledge as the practical expression of a vital spirituality in search of virtue and liberty.

Anderson: In Search of a Universal Brotherhood

And so we move on to the third member of the trio, Francis Anderson, Professor of Philosophy at the University of Sydney from 1890–1920.[22] In some ways, Anderson is the pivotal figure of this study because in his ideas are to be found the central tenets of Cultural Liberalism as it came to express itself in Australia, and because of his influence on other Cultural Liberals such as Burgmann, Cole and Childe. Anderson left behind no major work but it is possible to reconstruct, through an examination of his scattered works and of lecture notes taken by one of his students, much of his philosophical position.[23]

Francis Anderson's philosophy was motivated by both spiritual and religious objectives. 'Philosophy' he claimed, 'differs from poetry and not so much in inspiration and insight as in method and system'.[24] Anderson was in search of the 'Real' by which he seems to have meant the totality of existence. To know God, he preached, is not the same thing as to have an idea of Him.[25] While the latter was a concept in the mind, the former was a concrete perception, a living act, and a merely intellectual view is necessarily inferior to one which is known. Knowing is the expression of the whole man in search of the whole Truth. Anderson argued that in accurate thinking the image corresponded to the object as it is in reality, while bad thinking involved the 'substitution of the abstraction for the reality'. Like Badham and Woolley, Anderson opposed an organic and concrete view of human thought to that of cold abstract reason; in education, he contended that 'word, image and thing, expression and impression, be connected in the life and thinking of the pupil'.[26]

But the Real was for Anderson, as it was for MacCallum and Woolley, beyond human vision. Philosophy merely turns inspired gleams of insight into reality, into verbal or logical constructs; the metaphysician 'seeks contact with reality in the mystic vision'. But to try to encapsulate this vision in some doctrine or other is 'a perversion of the truth' and 'a libel on reality'.[27] As a transcendental ideal, the ethical is never definitely realised and escapes us at the moment of attainment. All we can hope for are occasional flashes of inspiration, that is to say we must live by the truth and attempt to bring the world into accord with it but we know that such perfection is ultimately beyond human hands. The vision dies when we bring it back into the world and turn it into something verbal because reality is something living and embodied in action. Even so we must carry the truth into the world in an attempt to re-enchant it and so ensure that our political and social activities are guided by more than self-interest.

The ethical ideal is like the Kingdom of God, an animating spirit in the hearts of men guiding humanity as it strives to realise it. The goal of human knowledge is not a vast system of abstract theory but the realisation of ideals as substantial and concrete elements in the lives of individuals. Society, he claimed in 1890, was 'reconstructing itself in the enlightened hearts and consciences of its citizens'.[28] Or, as he put it nearly thirty years later: 'The world is simply another name for Humanity, slowly organising itself, by means of the powers divinely bestowed upon it, into a kingdom of justice.'[29]

Referring to T.H. Green as a 'practical philosopher', Anderson saw clearly that philosophy's role was to make real those ideas which originally had existed only in the realm of thought.[30] The universe, he argued, was in constant evolution, a never-ending progressive unfolding towards a higher stage of development. Human history is a great adventure in which 'man sets out to discover himself and the secret of his personality'.[31] Again, for Anderson this is not an abstract conceptual scheme of human development but a real empirical process. In the political arena Anderson opposed the abstract theoretical socialism of Marx but lauded the practical form of state socialism he saw emerging in Australia.[32]

Anderson's philosophy led him to an historical view of man as a dynamic subject seeking self-realisation. In an early article on 'The poetry of Matthew Arnold' Anderson discussed the stages of Arnold's development, claiming that in Arnold the spiritual history of his own time could be read. Arnold had passed through three stages. The first had been a Greek period during which he had found peace in his devotion to Nature and art. But, according to Anderson, Arnold had discovered that Nature was not enough and had been forced in upon himself during his second, or stoic, period. This inward retreat provided little comfort, leading only to moral atrophy, and so Arnold entered his third, or Christian, period in which he came to recognise that 'wisdom and goodness they are God'.[33]

For Anderson, Arnold's development was an illustration both of personal growth and of the general historical progress of mankind. Anderson's educational ideas were also founded on this premise; the stages of the development of the individual were equivalent to the stages of development of humanity. The human soul was a unity but the mental life could be viewed under three separate aspects: knowing, willing and feeling. As education is the 'continuous and harmonious development of the child' all three elements of the mental life must be trained. They are three sisters who are inseparable: knowing requires wisdom just as willing must have goodness and feeling beauty. Stoicism with its emphasis on reason, Epicureanism stressing feeling, and Puritanism the will, were tendencies to be found both in individuals and communities. But in both the individual and the nation they must be unified and harmonised. 'We mutilate our nature when we try to sever the activities of the soul', claimed Anderson concluding with Emerson's words: 'All our progress is an unfolding.'[34]

Through education the individual moves towards reason and reality, unfolding into a higher state and a more harmonious personality. The human spirit, Anderson told his students, seeks unity, a central point of view. The whole man must seek to harmonise his intellect with his feeling and his will because this unity makes for human sanity and progress. Unity in knowledge implies unity in life; knowledge can only become effective if it is used to guide action 'in a shaping or creative way'.[35]

Discussing the nature of religion, Anderson placed a similar emphasis on its reality which, he believed, was ultimately to be found in the hearts of men. 'The progress of religion,' he contended, 'consists in the freeing of man's spirit from the bondage of the external and the material'. In primitive times this externality had expressed itself in rite, myth and magic; more recently, spiritual values had taken form in symbolism. Anderson believed that man's essential religiosity was intuitive and non-dogmatic, a form of religious sentiment that was poetic in character. Religious doubts and disputes arose only when the rationalising intellect was set to work on this fundamental human religiosity. Just as practical socialism is superior to Marxism so real religion is more important than the abstract religion of dogmatic theology. In other words, the practical realisation of religious values in the world finds its surest foundations in man's simple intuitive religious sense.[36]

Religious progress, for Anderson, was the unfolding of human powers on to a higher plane – it was the progress of man's movement towards a more pure form of religion and a more practical expression of that religiosity. It was a progression towards the Real. Hence, in his discussion of T.H. Green, Anderson described religion as a 'living stream of energy in the actual present of here and to-day, making for righteousness as well as culture, conduct as well as creed, inspiring men to nobler deeds, and showing them how to create a higher manhood and a purer society'.[37]

Likewise, Anderson viewed science and religion not as being in conflict but as two different and complementary activities of the human spirit. In its own domain, the realm of objects, science was supreme. Religion is not science but a 'form of life' with its roots in a reality beyond scientific demonstration; its essential function is not to disclose truth about the world but to bring into being a universal human brotherhood.[38] The road to that brotherhood lay through history, the tale of the progressive unfolding of humanity and the development of its powers and moral capacity. In his 1922 work *Liberty, Equality and Fraternity*, he gave one account of the rise of humanity as the cumulative work of four revolutions: 'the moral revolution known as Buddhism, the religious revolution known as Christianity, the political revolution of which France was the standard bearer, and the economic revolution in the midst of which we are struggling, and the end of which is not yet'.[39]

The first revolution had taught man to look towards the world within which he would find the moral law before which all souls were equal. Socially, however, Buddhism had been ineffective because it had proven unable to translate the inward into terms of the outward. The second revolution – Christianity – was a spiritual revolution founded on the principle of personality, a principle bringing both the message of salvation and the means of civilising humanity. The negation of the Christian principle, claimed Anderson, was the spirit of egotism and Mammon. By appealing to those moral and spiritual forces which 'alone can save a nation from degeneration and death', Anderson was clearly claiming the Coleridgean inheritance, as discussed in the previous chapter. This appeal to spiritual forces as the basis of the civilising principle also implied the growing unity and harmony of the individual and society: man is civilised by being bound more closely to his fellow man and co-operating with him.[40]

But Christianity could not achieve the emancipation of humanity: 'its promises of a new liberty, equality, fraternity, are still promises and possibilities, rather than performances'. It remained for France, the inheritor and transmitter of Latin civilisation to the modern world, to have its Revolution, a great outburst of religious fervour to make that possibility into something approaching a reality. The revolutionary gospel of liberty, equality and fraternity, however, was formal and abstract, lacking positive principles of social construction; it required the Christian principle of personality for its consummation, to provide it with living spiritual significance. The centre and source of all true liberty, argued Anderson, was the civilising principle of personality.[41]

Anderson believed that history was the record of man's efforts to discover himself, as he moved towards a realisation of his personality, a realisation that could not be completely defined, only striven towards. Humanity is constantly on the move towards the infinite because it cannot rest content with the imperfections of the finite world; man wishes to 'rise above his limitations, and enter into the life which is infinite and eternal'. He must move ever closer to reality. By promoting personality, humanity approaches the goal of the 'full and free development of the activities of man – as a moral and spiritual being'. The enemy is materialism and the spirit of Mammon which 'defiles the springs of life'. 'Materialism can breed nothing but materialism' – one could almost be listening to John Woolley seventy years earlier.[42]

In his philosophy lectures at the University of Sydney, Anderson gave a somewhat different, though related, account of the rise of humanity towards 'Personality'. A set of lecture notes taken by a student attending his courses in 1910 and 1911 survives and is useful in locating the sources of Anderson's philosophy. These enable us to have a much fuller picture of Anderson's evolutionary description of human development. Defining philosophy as an attempt to 'understand the universe of experience as a whole', Anderson described the history of philosophy as an 'account of the successive and complementary attempts to arrive at a full definition of reality, and of the human mind itself'. Like Hegel, Anderson began his history of philosophy in China, where man's thoughts had been put to sleep, and then moved westward towards Greece. He clearly distinguished between the East, founded on principles of love, mystery, the temper of acquiescence and a lack of liberty, and the West, in which were to be found justice, liberty and scientific enquiry. Philosophy began with the Greeks whose energies were stimulated by their physical environment; the Persians, also an Indo-European race, had exhibited progressive civilising tendencies but had been 'unable to resist the enervating influence of climate, and the corruption of surrounding nations'.[43]

Along with this contrast between East and West, a distinction expressed in similar terms by Anderson's student, V. Gordon Childe, in the preface to the first edition of *The Dawn of European Civilization*,[44] Anderson also discussed the evolution of humanity from the primitive state to the civilised. He characterised primitive (or revealingly) uncultured peoples in terms similar to those used by Frederic Eggleston, a fellow evolutionary theorist.[45] Such peoples follow stereotyped rules of conduct, criticism is absent and individuals display a psychological similarity. The individual submits to the collective. Primitive man is limited by the particularity of his vision, by the 'primitive quantitative way of regarding life, as a kind of sum of moments or of pleasures'. The story of humanity is the story of progress, of the liberation of the individual from the collective and of the growth of social morality from coercive forms to free subordination. It is the movement from particular to universal: 'only line by line do child and race learn to look beyond the moment and particular to a larger life and wider interests'.[46]

In his lectures on ethics, Anderson also provided a speculative account of the evolution of such institutions as the family and social classes.[47] His reading list for his lectures on the family is particularly interesting as it includes not only Frazer's *Golden Bough* and Robertson Smith's *Kinship in Arabia* but also Morgan's *Ancient Society*. In the course of the lectures he also discussed Frederick Engels's views on the family.[48] When he came to examine the development of social classes he stated that the 'main factor was the division of labour as human needs grew more numerous and complex' and plotted the progress of humanity from savagery to barbarism to agricultural life. The first class division he attributed to the keeping of prisoners of war as slaves.

Like Eggleston, Anderson viewed humanity's subsequent development in terms of the model developed by the nineteenth century historian, Sir Henry Maine, of the transition from status to contract.[49] Modern society was a new phase of social consciousness linked to the rise of free labour. 'There is a gradual reconstruction of society along economic lines' claimed Anderson, in which the distance separating classes was being diminished and a regime of forced co-operation was being replaced by one of free co-operation. Man was being transformed from a 'thing' to a being of 'personal worth and dignity'. Again, what Anderson was looking for in the modern world was the possible realisation of 'personality', free men seeking to realise their individuality through the pursuit of social solidarity.

How then did Anderson view the process of social evolution? It is to be considered as a series of stages, epochs or ages in which:

- the material of the preceding stages is utilised;
- each stage is a movement of differentiation through adaptation to partial ends;
- each stage has a unity of composition created by a directing or controlling idea, and
- the whole being of the stage can be understood once it has arrived at its mature state.

The dominating factor for the present age, Anderson contended, was the rise of the workers. Although he did consider that the state does have a legitimate role in legislating to protect labour, he was essentially interested in the development of a society composed of free, moral individuals: 'The guardianship of the state of the individual [sic] is only morally permissible in as far as it is subservient to a higher concept – the ideal of the development of personality.'

A similar picture of progress as a movement towards the creation of the free responsible individual is also found in Anderson's picture of the growth of the moral sentiment. For the individual, the pattern of development is one in which respect for elders leads to respect for custom which leads in turn to the demand for reason, while for society the institutional development is as follows: leaders, priests, elders are succeeded by common traditions embodied in laws and institutions which results in the moral sentiment becoming one of love and reverence for truth. The ultimate goal of progress is the free, autonomous individual who willingly seeks social solidarity as an expression of a higher moral order: 'The ethical end is a consciously willed harmony of the elements of the social whole.'

For Anderson, the 'difficulty of the future is a moral problem'. Elsewhere he argued that social and political questions could not be solved by mere mechanical rearrangements. Real solutions could only be found when the principle of personality was transformed from a promise and a possibility into a living reality. Consequently Anderson, like Irvine, was ambiguous in his attitudes to the state. He rejected the limited liberal conception of the state and recognised that it had played a progressive role by making itself an agent of justice for society. State action was necessary to maintain the common good by undertaking services in which there was a common interest and through the preservation and increase of spiritual goods such as education. At one stage he referred to the state as a form of moral person.

Anderson also insisted on the distinction between the state and civil society. In an unpublished paper entitled 'The state and the professions', Anderson contended that the new collectivism had led to the doctrine of the omnipotence of the state and the negation of individual interests. Progress could only occur if the distinction between society and state was recognised because it was within society that new needs were felt; the role of the state was to gather in and register these new elements within the sphere of law. Society was 'a living system of rights and duties, all derived from the fundamental fact of human personality, and from the actual obligations arising from human association', the place where free movement, manifold activities and spontaneous forms of self-organisation occur. The state was concerned with common goods, 'the sovereign will of the people as embodied in laws and institutions'. The establishment of the sovereign will and promotion of the common good was intended to harmonise the various sections of society, not abolish them under the rule of an absolutist state.[50]

Anderson placed his faith in a future society founded on co-operation; the various classes and sections of society would develop a 'sympathetic social understanding' and come to co-operate in the general interest. The state would do no more than represent the common good. Anderson was also ambivalent towards notions of social solidarity viewing it as a lesser moral good waiting to 'find its justification in a higher moral order; and the principle of Brotherhood contains this in relating us to God as Father'.[51]

All of which returns us yet again to 'Personality' as that which wills both solidarity and the common good without surrendering individuality. For Anderson, Personality was individuality introduced to reason and order so that its acts refer to a definite ideal. Through Personality, the antinomies existing between the two forces of human history, the quest for personal salvation and the ideal of social service, are resolved. Through seeking spiritual and social progress as a personal obligation, as a duty simultaneously to oneself and to society, the individual brings together both the personal and the social: 'To find self is to find self in others.' Equally, through Personality, society and state are unified as the particular or sectional self meets the universal self. But Personality is not a final unchanging goal; as the world evolves and changes each new generation must rediscover it and remould it in the light of the needs of the age. For this reason, the absorption of society by the state will produce a rigid order and stunt the growth of Personality. The final goal of moral life for Anderson was the ideal of Humanity, a spiritual quality shared by human beings by virtue of their common moral nature. Humanity requires that men and women look beyond the borders of their nation.

Anderson supported the increase of economic relations between nations and the interchange of scientific ideas as a means of promoting the spirit of Brotherhood. In other words, Anderson held true to the traditional ethical Free Trade position. Protection may sometimes be possible for 'special reasons' but 'Only through free commercial exchange are higher more civilized forms of life possible.'[52]

Anderson remained resolutely the optimist. Even in the wake of the disappointments of World War I he continued to believe in the possibility of Progress arguing that the only way was forward, an 'advance to a further and higher phase of development, under the guidance of the spirit of Truth'. This process of reform and evolution can only occur if lower standards of goodness are replaced by higher ones, if inadequate conceptions of God are replaced by less inadequate ones and external authority replaced by internal authority. This is the way to the Real.[53]

For Anderson, man's spiritual progress and his attempts to discover a more rational and just world were intimately related. They were part of humanity's never-ending quest to turn the abstract ideals of religion into the living elements of everyday existence and to move the human heart towards a greater purity.

Romanticism: The Case for 'Ethos' Restated

Anderson still spoke the language of 'ethos' or culture, of the faith that a more rational and spiritual society could be created. There were, however, powerful Romantic streaks which threatened his vision with the despair that follows the recognition that the ideal is unattainable. Amongst the students at Sydney during these years there was an attempt to restate the case for 'ethos', notably in *Hermes*, the student magazine of the university. For example, a 1904 editorial claimed the mantle of Woolley and Badham in arguing that the university should equip men 'with a breadth of mind that would make of them able citizens'.[54] Another piece, written a year later, probably by H.M. Green, argued that the business of an undergraduate education was to train students to think so that new knowledge becomes 'no longer mere knowledge, but part of the personality, a developed character and an extended point of view'.[55] Similarly, the Idealist philosopher, Henry Jones, who visited Australia in 1908, delivered a series of lectures in which he concluded that at the final stage of the development of freedom the individual discovers something of his debt to society and sees that he is fulfilling his own purposes by serving the state.[56] Much of this advocacy of 'ethos' however, took the form of special pleading brought about by the fact that the university was not fulfilling its public role. 'Have we a

University?' asked one *Hermes* editorial which bemoaned the lack of a genuine intellectual community, while other articles sought to defend the place of the university in the community.[57]

This quest for 'ethos' was matched by the Romanticism expressed primarily in the poetry of many of those associated with the university. In the decade before the war, *Hermes* was full of high-blown Romantic poetry with such titles as 'To the Absolute Beauty', 'Ideal' or devoted to classical themes. A sample will illustrate the flavour:

> Oh soul seek thou the truest gold,
> And thou shalt have some day a boundless store.
> For all that thou hast ever known, or thought,
> Or dreamed of Beauty – yea, even that above
> The purest passion of music and of love –
> Shall be thine own, for know, Oh man, that naught
> Shall be eternal – but God,
> And thine own soul, and Beauty.[58]

Pre-eminent amongst these Romantics, the author of a doctoral dissertation on Shelley and of a strange mock-classical work, *Gods and Wood-Things*, was L.H. Allen.[59] Allen was a fully fledged Romantic who contended that 'all artists everywhere find themselves impelled to the great basic forms which guide and enclose the spirit in the search for the absolute' and that essential art embodied the attempt to express eternal beauty, 'beauty that is one and indivisible'.[60] Likewise, the search for a higher spiritual world helped to spur on the poetic quest of Christopher Brennan's friend, John Le Gay Brereton. Brereton's outlook on the world is captured beautifully in a letter he wrote to another idealist and one-time poet Duncan Hall, who devoted his life's energies to international co-operation:

> A man's voice will carry far, if only in mysteriously waffled whispers if the divine breath of imagination carries it. The wider his sympathy, the further his influence will circle. And you, with your strength of conviction and force of will and desire to the mission of love in a form that men of all races and creeds could understand and appreciate have a voice of which the resonance will not easily be silenced by the heavy fogs of apathy.[61]

This Romanticism could be reconciled with the demands of 'ethos' and, for most individuals brought within the precincts of culture, the occasional outpouring of lofty poetry did not impede the pursuit of a legal or political career. But as we noted in the case of John Woolley, this tradition of rational spirituality contains within it powerful Gnostic and Romantic elements which can easily break through and destroy the fragile union between the spiritual inner man and the rational citizen.

Brennan: The Romantic Poet

Christopher Brennan – poet, philosopher of symbolism and Professor of Modern Languages at the University of Sydney until his unfortunate dismissal in 1925 – was clearly caught up in the tensions of this tradition and his place lies at the end of one of the trajectories thrown out by it.[62] His fate is that of pure 'myth', an exaltation of the quest of the individual for spiritual redemption in the privacy of his study rather than on the battleground of history. He seems to have harboured a grudge against Plato's *Republic* and this is reflected by his rejection of the Platonic reason in favour of the Hermetic quest.[63] By taking intuition as his road to the Real, Brennan broke the fragile web which bound rationality and the 'other' together.

While Anderson believed that the religious impulse would find its consummation in a more rational social order, Brennan, his former student, preferred instead to seek universal harmony through purely individualist means – the esoteric conjuring of Gnosticism. Having lost his original Roman Catholic faith in 1890 after an encounter with the works of Herbert Spencer, Brennan continued to crave the Absolute. This powerful aesthetic sense was his dominating passion and it drove him away from the cold abstractions of philosophy and politics towards the sensuality of poetry. Paradoxically, he pursued beauty in books rather than life, spending the late 1890s, like Dr Faustus, poring over books of magical lore. Perhaps that is why, ultimately, Brennan is much more interesting as a philosopher than as a poet.

Brennan's objective was unmediated experience of the 'Absolute' and the logic of his quest can be discerned in his 1898 paper 'Fact and idea'. Like Anderson, Brennan operated with a dualistic conception of knowledge. 'Idea' he defined as the intellectual apprehension of something, as it was grasped abstractly by discursive reason. A 'fact' was knowledge acquired in a direct and intuitive fashion and so known by the whole self, not just the intellectual part of it. The natural progression of humanity was from 'idea' to 'fact', from image to reality. But for Brennan this progression did not have a political or social dimension. Reality, he continued, 'depends on man and his search for it'. In approaching the essential unity of reality, man breaks it down into ideas according to a variety of interests, forming concepts which represent a particular standpoint and so impoverish reality considered as a totality. This breakdown of reality into concepts is a need of the intellect responding to the requirements of physical self-preservation and of intellectual unity.

But with this work of analysis there recommences the road back towards unity and the real. At any particular stage of this quest truth, which Brennan defined as the perfect accord of our concepts, can be ascertained by discovering if our assumptions and concepts work well, if they are justified by practice. The first concept is the beginning of an infinite journey, the end of which is some greater synthesis in which man will humanise the universe and attain complete knowledge of himself, moving ever towards the goal of the unity of world and human, fact and idea. For Brennan the ultimate goal was the Ideal, the great synthesis of all human endeavour. 'Every human attempt at humanization of the Universe has hitherto shaped its Ideal,' claimed Brennan, 'and by the satisfaction which this afforded – not necessarily to the mass – has justified itself'.[64]

It is not difficult to recognise the Hegelian roots of Brennan's philosophy – but with the difference that for Brennan there was apparently no final synthesis and the process itself did not appear to be rational: 'We are all following the Chimaera.' Equally, the stages of the quest were defined pragmatically by 'interest' rather than as historical stages of the growth of reason. For Brennan, unlike MacCallum and Anderson, the quest was neither social nor rational. It was the quest of an individual for the Real in a world no longer offering a stable intellectual framework – Brennan's Hegelianism is that of Nietzsche. Brennan developed and elaborated on these ideas more fully in his later works on aesthetics and symbolism as he delved more deeply into the workings of the Gnostic imagination. He appropriated the Gnostic view that man had been driven from Eden, his divine spark trapped in the material world; harmony had been destroyed as had man's intuitive knowledge of that harmony. The goal of the evolutionary process, for Brennan, was the restoration of harmony or Eden. But how was that to be achieved? Human beings have ideas which do not describe the universe as it really is but provide a symbolic picture of it. Moreover this symbolic picture is created as a response to human needs; men try out postulates on the world: if they work they retain them; if they do not then they discard them. Brennan's conception of knowledge was a form of pragmatism; for example, he supported the view that atomic theory did not imply that there were real things called atoms – it was merely a symbolic account of the world answering certain human needs.

It is not difficult to see how Brennan's pragmatism links up with his Gnosticism. 'Ideas' are purely human products answering to human needs; even successful ideas do not tell us anything about the real world. In other words, there is no necessary relationship between human reason and a world whose reality is beyond reason, a world which remains alien to a humanity driven from Eden. Discursive reason, as a merely human product, cannot lead man back to that harmony after which he hankers, it cannot probe the Real. 'Intellectual dealings with things,' claimed Brennan, 'are based on abstraction and that abstraction on practical needs'. 'Intellectual dealings' are doomed to remain within the boundaries of the human and the practical life. 'To attain to reality and truth,' Brennan continued, 'the philosopher must close his mouth and stop thinking'. Thinking is not enough; the passage to harmony and the real requires the engagement of the whole self; it needs a total act of knowing capable of bringing together every element of the human personality, both conscious and unconscious. The goal of evolution is to go beyond the abstraction of the sciences and attain self-consciousness, the 'sum of all perfected experience'. This will be achieved when man has taken up into himself the whole world, both outside and inside. The objective is to escape from the division, disunion and death of our discursive mind by finding something which will present us to our self 'as a total energy' and unify the three forces of the human personality: thought (the shaper), emotion (the soul), sense (the body).

Poetry, for Brennan, was that something; it fused these three forces and embodied 'the total attitude of the self' thereby communicating 'the real and vital' and enabling the 'meeting of our divided life with our full, perfect self'. It could take us out of this broken, imperfect world into the perfect, harmonious world, that which was true and real – the world of 'fact'. Brennan conceded that in the perfection that exists at the end of the 'time process', there would be no need for philosophy or poetry as the 'whole potency of the self shall have been realized and made explicit, and the world shall be pervaded through and through with mind'. But, in the meantime, it was poetry which would provide insights into this world of harmony. Symbolism is a means of expressing concrete spiritual facts; the law of correspondences on which it is founded simultaneously charges the outer world with meaning and awakens meaning within. The perception of correspondences arouses ecstasy and so allows us to know the world as 'fact'. As the goal is the fusion of fact and idea it is through this apprehension of the 'facts' of reality that we grow and develop: 'the reading of this world in the light of our true self will make ever more plain to us what our true self is'.

Brennan's ideal of spiritual evolution saw the mind trying out new postulates and techniques so as to discover their adequacy as routes to harmony. The 'law of correspondences' and symbolism have proven to be successful 'experiments' – they yield real, empirical results, in the shape of greater harmony and spiritual truth.[65] Symbolism points the way to man's final perfection. Through the visionary power of the poet, the whole of consciousness is brought together in symbols and man can receive intimations of a reality beyond words. Poetry becomes a form of religion as it assumes the role of man's route to spiritual reality. At the same time, symbolism is a scientific exposition of the technique required to pass from the imperfect everyday world to that of perfect harmony.

But there is a trap, one which has its origins in the Romanticism on which Brennan drew. Only occasionally can poetry pierce reality; there is a cycle in which a rare mood of spiritual ecstasy is followed by days, weeks or months of imperfection during which the memory of perfection continues to haunt whoever has experienced it. Existence comes to consist of occasional tastes of harmony and long cold nights and days dominated by the absence of that taste. Despite Brennan's concern with explaining the logic of the non-rational vision, his fusion of symbolism and pragmatism appears only to have led to a private quest which was essentially irrational in nature. The road to harmony and unity is the poetic vision; for some four years Brennan embarked on this search and then proceeded to live off his intellectual capital for the rest of his life.

To whom was Brennan to deliver this Gnostic revelation? Was he not equally like Socrates bringing back a message that none could understand? And of what use was the message anyway? Now we know from examining the works of Anderson and MacCallum that the environment of the University of Sydney was sympathetic to Brennan's aspirations. But that, by and large, was the limit of his audience – he was locked into that academic/legal establishment which saw itself as the measure of culture in Sydney society. An examination of the list of subscribers to his 'Poems 1913' confirms this; arranged in strict hierarchy, it is a list of the New South Wales legal and cultural establishment (though one truly wonders what Sir George Reid made of these poems).[66]

As a member of that small elite, Brennan was bound by the dialectic of his environment and that dialectic was one of ethos and myth. On the one hand, this was a group sympathetic to cultural enlightenment and spiritual things; on the other hand, it was devoted to maintaining standards of culture or classicism. Brennan was caught in the middle of this trap: was he to defend the classical ideal of learning as in his emendations of Aeschylus, or was he to expand the horizons of literature into new terrain? The elite to which Brennan belonged consisted of a group of practical men engaged in law and politics for whom culture was a delightful avocation pursued at night in smoke-filled clubs and accompanied by a glass of wine. Despite the best of intentions such men could never really understand Brennan's message.

In this environment Brennan's fate was to become a myth, a rebel in a cage in which he had to remain if anyone was to listen. His scholarship, his Bohemianism, his Romantic poetry were all to be glorified and tolerated – at least until less tolerant times set in – because they represented the aristocratic longings of a social group uneasy with its own place in the world. In the many writings which were produced by his students and admirers, from A.G. Stephens to A.R. Chisholm, this element of myth remained as Brennan became for many people in the humanities an icon of the heroic scholar in a philistine and materialist world.[67] He was the symbol of their frustration. Brennan himself had helped to foster the Badham myth via the entry which he wrote on Badham for the *Australian Encyclopaedia.*[68] A.G. Stephens consciously linked Badham and Brennan as great scholars assailed by the forces of philistinism.[69] Even as the icon of Brennan the Scholar was replaced by that of Brennan the Poet, the myth came to dominate the man and he became a symbol of the travails of culture in a philistine and materialist world.

Summary

The task of the first part of this study has been to examine the dynamics of the tradition of Cultural Liberalism in Australia up to the years of World War I. As with any tradition, Cultural Liberalism was not a fixed formation but an ongoing conversation which changed constantly as circumstances and the individuals taking part in the conversation changed. Three components of the tradition, civic humanism, scientific rationality and spiritual evolution, have been identified and the fluctuating relationship between them plotted. As well, the dynamics of the relationship between ethos and myth were explored as a way of understanding the peculiar pattern of development of this tradition. The slide from ethos to myth, from a faith in cultural regeneration to a refuge in Romanticism, reflected the ambiguous nature of the relationship between Cultural Liberalism and the wider community.

Cultural Liberalism also came to embody a particular ideal of the sacred through its notion of culture. It sought to re-enchant a world which it believed had become devoid of spirituality. The supporters of Free Trade Liberalism had seen Nature as essentially good and beneficent. In their eyes Nature retained a weak sense of the sacred; Nature's laws were the model of truth and morality against which human conduct could be evaluated.

At the heart of Protectionist Liberalism was the belief that Nature and Nature's laws are amoral and indifferent to the fate of humanity. What is sacred is to be found in the human heart and in society, considered as the association of individuals embodying the sacred. Thomas Molnar has pointed out that this is very much the Protestant view of the sacred, a view which in the modern world has found expression in the writings of Kant and his successors.[70] A key element of Protection was the desire of individuals carrying the spark of the sacred within, and constituted as 'society', to impose order on an amoral universe racked by conflict and strife. Moral society could then make use of Nature for honourable purposes.

The Cultural Liberals shared elements in common with both forms of liberalism. They adhered to Free Trade's conception of human psychology; individuals grow and develop outwards towards a greater social sympathy and awareness of the harmony of the universe. But, like Protectionist Liberals, they did not look to Nature as the source of that harmony. Morality was something immanent within human beings waiting to be generated by education and culture. Thus, for the Cultural Liberals, the university, considered as a body of individuals who had been initiated into culture, became the bearer of the sacred. It was the new Church whose members would seek to diffuse the light, into whose presence they had been brought, throughout the darker regions of the world. Despite the obvious symbolism of the university buildings constructed in Australia (in particular the Great Hall of the University of Sydney), culture was conceived as something found essentially in the hearts of men and women. It was no accident that the chief English exponent of a liberal university education, John Henry Newman, should also have been a harsh critic of the argument from design.[71]

. Cultural Liberalism was a distinctive tradition nourished by its association with the university and its spiritual pretensions. The second half of this study will examine its fate in the wake of the traumatic effects of World War I.

CHAPTER 5

Liberalism and Its Critics: The Realists

Introduction: Looking Inwards

It has widely been held that World War I marks a watershed in Australian cultural and intellectual development. Michael Roe contrasts the vitality and forward looking attitude of the 'progressives' in the years before the war with their somewhat reactionary attitudes after it. Similarly, David Walker divides his study between the dream of the early years of the century and the disillusion of the post-war years. Something appears to have gone desperately wrong in Australia during the war years but no one seems to be able to pinpoint exactly what it was.[1]

The war is likewise a great divide for the tradition of Cultural Liberalism. Up to and during the war, the works produced by the exponents of the tradition concentrated largely on what needed to be done and how to do it. This is reflected in the sort of literature that they produced: lectures, short articles and other varieties of fragmentary and occasional writing. One reason for this is that the culture of the university and the thinking classes of those years was predominantly oral. Culture required the inspired teacher and was transmitted more through personal contact than published works.

After the war the atmosphere and the tone had changed. For one thing, the word 'culture' was no longer used as freely as it had been. No doubt this was related to the discrediting of the German *kultur*; in its place 'civilisation' appears as the preferred term to describe the higher activities of society.[2] Secondly, the literature became critical and concerned primarily with what had gone wrong. As such, larger and more detailed studies appeared over the next few decades including some of the great classics of Australian political and social thought. The Owl of Minerva certainly does fly at dusk because the intellect stirs itself most when analysis comes to replace action. But this late flowering could not have occurred without the exertions of the preceding generations, without the stock of ideas, ideals and hopes which they had built up. So, as Cultural Liberalism turned its attention in upon itself, as it moved from action to analysis, it made use of the conversation which had been developing, and turned it to new purposes. In so doing, it built up a body of social and political thought peculiar to Australia because it adapted a universal conversation and made it speak with a native accent about local and universal matters.

If Cultural Liberalism had looked forward to a future which was harmonious and rational, one in which the universal qualities of humanity would prevail, then the war dispelled all of these illusions. Its two chief cultural effects were to intensify the protectionist mentality and to make social conflict and division the dominant theme of Australian life. The war opened up and exacerbated class and religious differences in Australia; it encouraged xenophobic attitudes and intensified the 'Britishness' of Australia.[3] The two themes of conflict and closure are closely related because, as was noted in the earlier discussion of Protection, it was the growing perception of the world as amoral and conflict-ridden which encouraged the growth of Protection.

The Cultural Liberals had cautiously favoured state intervention in social matters but their ultimate faith was in the capacity of an enlightened active citizenry to transform the world. They failed to achieve the latter goal while the former succeeded all too well. It is difficult to explain loss of cultural vitality; no doubt sixty-thousand war dead played its part, as did the self-defeating nature of protectionist policies. Another crucial factor was the narrowing of cultural horizons. Germany was no longer held up as a model, America was increasingly condemned as a source of low culture and superficiality, and Scotland was in cultural crisis. No longer were Australians sent to Germany or Harvard or Columbia to study the humanities. London and Oxbridge became the destinations of young Australians in search of culture, in particular the much favoured Balliol College.[4]

The cultural effect of this narrowing of horizons was pernicious. As we have already seen, young Australian intellectuals were either seduced by the glories of Oxford, as in the case of Keith Hancock, hurt by being treated as colonials, as in the case of Manning Clark, or turned into wild colonial boys, like P.R. Stephensen. The most interesting case is that of Elton Mayo who was lauded at Harvard but failed to make any impact on the English. Mayo never got the English post he so wanted but remained such an Anglophile that he sent his daughters to be educated in England, with unhappy consequences.[5] In general, the effect of this on the intellectual elite was an unhealthy pre-occupation with the Anglo-Australian relationship; it tended to warp and distort their vision of the world.

Still there can be no doubt that Anglo-Saxonism dominated Australia after the war; but, as was argued earlier, it was an Anglo-Saxonism of the 'South', of rural counties, public schools and Oxbridge. The 1920s began the heyday of the Australian private school modelled on the English public school. These schools enthusiastically adopted the ANZAC ideal and, as Geoff Sherington argues, continued to emulate the public school model at the same time as many were turning away from it in Britain. Likewise, R.G. Menzies could continue to see the role of the university in Oxbridge terms, as the home of pure culture and learning, just as he looked to English models as a way of organising Australian art.[6]

Indeed, it could be argued that just as many in that generation accepted as Australian art only the landscapes of the turn of the century,[7] so they produced an Anglo-Saxon ideal frozen into an Edwardian aristocratic landscape. In this there is a middle class idealisation of the pre-war years as a golden age when servants were cheap and one could live well on £500 per annum.[8] This Anglo-Saxonism was mirrored by a local desire to escape from the pressures of the modern world; Australia would be kept pure and wholesome by restricting any undesirable elements which threatened to enter the country. Richard White has correctly pointed to the cult of purity which developed during these years. Australians could not retreat into the shires; however they could 'get away from it all' in suburbia and in coastal holiday resorts. Patrick Morgan has emphasised the importance of this desire to escape from the world in Australia and clearly points to its major prophet as none other than R.G. Menzies.[9]

All of this is a long way from George Arnold Wood's vision of the 'spiritually active person'. The antithesis of Wood's ideal is, in fact, D.H. Lawrence's picture of Australians as shallow and lacking spiritual substance. Lawrence described freedom in Australia as freedom from responsibility and, in *Kangaroo*, Somers admits to almost being seduced by the desire to move to the fringes of civilisation in Australia and 'get away from it all'.[10]

Lawrence visited Australia in 1922; Elton Mayo left Australia in that year following the other great social theorist of the period, V. Gordon Childe, into exile. Others had already gone or soon followed, including Griffith Taylor, Clarence Northcott, Jack Lindsay and Persia Campbell. Peter Board, R.F. Irvine and Francis Anderson retired that year. The last expression of pre-war vitalism, *The New Outlook*, was published during 1922 and 1923.[11] A period of intellectual vitality had its last great flourish before it dissolved in the face of the great indifference of Australian life. And yet amongst the scattered remnants of the Cultural Liberals there was a flowering unequalled in Australian cultural history. Sitting on the fault line of Australian cultural development they applied the insights of their intellect and the fruits of their experience to produce an extraordinary set of writings. This section of the study will be devoted to those writings. All of the writers had been born before 1900 and all had completed university by the end of World War I. Their writings were a response to the crisis of the age, stimulated often by specific crises, including the end of the war, the Depression and the outbreak of World War II.

Consequently, the peculiar contribution of Australia to social and political thought occurred at that point of time when the practice underlying that thought had lost much of its impetus and had become discredited. Much of its vitality derived from a desire to investigate and understand the reasons for the failure of that practice and to respond to it. In the past there has been an inability to comprehend the collective importance of this group. The Australian roots of Mayo and Childe have tended to be ignored or played down. The others have been treated biographically, without adequate attention being paid to the intellectual heritage they shared and against which they reacted. Only Rowse has had some appreciation of the importance of the common liberal tradition, but his hostility and ideological preferences preclude him from a sympathetic understanding of that tradition.[12]

Idealism versus Realism

The placement of particular individuals in a tradition as elements of an ongoing conversation or argument promotes an increased understanding of their ideas. The whole illuminates the part just as each individual contribution takes the conversation into new and unfamiliar territory.

It should also be pointed out that after World War I, Cultural Liberals found it necessary to react to the different circumstances at two levels – first, in terms of understanding what had actually occurred in Australia and elsewhere during those years, and secondly, in terms of the adequacy of the tradition of thought which they had inherited as a means for understanding what had happened. Generally the writers to be considered can be placed in two groups:

1 The realists who sought to investigate the reasons for the failure of both the ideal as expressed by the tradition and the actual historical processes. They rejected Idealism (in the philosophical sense) in favour of a realist understanding of historical development, even if they continued to be haunted by their idealist roots. In this group can be placed Bernard Muscio, Clarence Northcott, W.K. Hancock and V.G. Childe.

2 Those who continued to state the case for the spiritual principle as the fundamental basis of social and cultural development. This group attempted to recover the sacred element in the hearts of men and use it as the foundation of social order and a just world. Often this meant

an investigation of psycho-analysis, building on a previous interest in the psychology of William James. Into this camp can be placed Ernest Burgmann, F.W. Eggleston, Elton Mayo and, with some reservations, the Barnard Eldershaw of *Tomorrow and Tomorrow and Tomorrow*.

One of the major transformations of the tradition of Cultural Liberalism which occurred in the wake of World War I was a shift from a mood of anticipation to one of criticism and analysis. The expectations of the early years of the century had been given form in the shape of Idealist philosophy as the Mind worked on the world and remade it in its own image. In the English-speaking world the major philosophical transition of the early twentieth century was from Idealism to Realism, from a philosophy founded on the pursuit of the ideal to one emphasising the need to analyse and carefully describe that which is.[13]

In Australia the advent of Realism is usually associated with the arrival of John Anderson in 1927 and with his subsequent attacks on all things sacred and patriotic.[14] Such a view is misleading because realism, both in its philosophical meaning and more generally as an outlook on the world, had been developing in Australia since World War I. The growing influence of Marxism indicated a growing realist mood and Marxist intellectuals such as Gordon Childe adopted a realist approach to history, largely rejecting the Idealism they had learnt at university. Similarly, the young Keith Hancock adopted a realist approach to the study of Australian development (a position he was later to reject), and the philosopher Bernard Muscio, who had pursued post-graduate studies at Cambridge, wrote a number of articles critical of Idealism from a Realist position. But while Childe and Hancock pursued careers in the Old World (Muscio having died young), Anderson was left as the great prophet of Realism in the Australian wilderness.

In considering the realist mood as it affected the tradition of Cultural Liberalism it is worthwhile separating two distinct, though often overlapping, elements of that mood. The first was a critique of Idealism considered as a philosophy or a way of understanding the world, and the second was a critique of the way in which Idealism had manifested itself in the world and of the effects and consequences which it had brought into being.

It is quite possible to develop an enthusiastic critique of the manifestations of Idealism without necessarily rejecting Idealism itself. Consequently, while Clarence Northcott was critical of the path Australian social development had taken he did not reject the ideals behind that development but rather sought ways of correcting its defects. Hancock was faced by a similar dilemma which he was to resolve ultimately by abandoning his realism.

Perhaps the point should be made that to be a realist in Australia after World War I was to run a risk. Just as the schools settled down to an Edwardian cosiness, so the universities did not look to break new ground. Philosophy was, by and large, dominated by a vague Christian Idealism, History remained pre-occupied with problems of Empire, and Walter Murdoch's cheery but banal essays set the standard of taste in *belles-lettres*.[15] Nevertheless there was a realist moment in the development of Cultural Liberalism, a precarious moment which emphasised the gulf between the values of the tradition and those which had come to dominance in Australia as a whole.

Muscio: A Philosophical Critique

Bernard Muscio died at a relatively young age without having had much opportunity to exert a great deal of influence on his own or the succeeding generation.[16] A student of the Idealist, Francis Anderson, he later succeeded him as Professor of Philosophy at the University of Sydney and was succeeded in turn by John Anderson. In his scattered writings he exemplified the outlook of the realist mood and its approach to the world. That is to say, he had modest expectations of philosophy whose task he saw as the 'reasoned study of such general problems about existence as cannot be solved experimentally'.[17] This 'reasoned study' involved, for Muscio, careful and reasoned analysis and precision in his use of language. He also adopted a rigorous, scientific approach in those areas which were amenable to experiment and empirical observation. In particular he was interested in industrial psychology.

Muscio's Realist philosophy necessarily involved him in a critique of Idealism and the evolutionary model of the growth of the mind which often accompanied it. In an early paper on the Hegelian Dialectic, he argued that the dialectic was essentially only an analysis of psychological phenomena. Similarly, the traditional distinction between Reason and Understanding could be reduced to that between two psychological theories with Understanding merely a name for exactness and Reason a name for a number of mystical and anthropomorphic tendencies. The dialectic simply did not exist 'and no theory of the Universe can be established by it'.[18]

Muscio continued this engagement with Idealism right up to his death in 1925. For example, he criticised the evolutionary position of J.S. Haldane and his claim that 'the universe itself is with us in our struggle'. Muscio pointed out that this picture of evolving nature always acting in our interest is contradictory – *either* we struggle *or* the universe is with us. Likewise, Muscio contended that an all-inclusive nature cannot possibly be seen as always good – the food which nourishes us one day may poison us the next.[19]

In the final piece written before he died, Muscio examined Keyserling's *Travel Diary of a Philosopher* in which Keyserling chronicled his attempt to realise ultimate reality by reducing his self to its essential nature as pure potentiality. Keyserling attempted to do this by taking on the values of the civilisations which he visited. Commenting on Keyserling's quest, Muscio rejected the ideal of the 'Protean' self seeking to realise some sort of universal experience; rather 'Profundity of experience is more likely to come from adopting a more limited ideal and following it to the end.'[20]

His major criticism of Idealism was of its vague aspirations which tended to find expression in philosophical ideals which did not hold up to rigorous scrutiny. 'Dialectic', 'Nature', 'the essential self' – all of these were terms in need of 'reasoned study'. In his discussion of religion, Muscio contrasted the mechanical and teleological approaches concluding that they did not necessarily conflict as they belonged to different realms. Moreover, he advocated 'a treatment of religious phenomena which shall connect them with psychical processes such as we know them'.[21]

Whereas Francis Anderson had seen philosophy as the ally of religion, Muscio saw the future of philosophy in connection with the sciences. Philosophy was to deal with those questions which were beyond the reach of science. 'For', as he argued, 'the Universe contains values and propositional forms as well as chemical reactions and mechanical forces'. Even as a student he had been an advocate of experimental psychology. In his lectures on industrial psychology he contended that 'science might be, and if possible ought to be, applied to every department of life'. On this basis he argued for industrial psychology as a means of making industry more efficient and able to supply goods to society in the most economical manner possible.[22]

Muscio's Realism was linked to a much more positivist, scientific outlook and manifested itself in a rigorous, analytical approach to philosophy. Nevertheless, it would be misleading to consider Muscio as a materialist philistine; for him philosophy was still concerned with questions of ultimate value. Idealism became a target of his criticism because of its intellectual inadequacies. It is now necessary to turn to those who considered the inadequacies of Idealism in practice.

Northcott: The Hopes of Efficiency

For Muscio, it was Idealism as a mode of apprehending the world which became the target of his critique and among his responses to it was a thorough-going positivism and the advocacy of a scientifically based industrial psychology to promote social efficiency. For Clarence Northcott, it was not so much the idealism which was at fault but the way in which it had come to manifest itself. It was in need of a corrective in the shape of a sweeping programme of efficiency. Like Muscio, however, Northcott rejected the faith in unlimited possibilities implicit in Idealism and came to recognise the need for limitations.

Northcott was yet another student of Francis Anderson whose interest in social questions was buttressed by his religious background.[23] His enthusiasm for national planning based on science, and a recognition of the limitations imposed by scarce resources on that planning, was also espoused by Griffith Taylor. Taylor's view that 'our national policy must be based very directly upon environment' did not endear him to those advocates of unlimited possibility, especially as Taylor held the unusual view that the Chinese were racially superior to Australians. Taylor's position 'that the days of great expansion . . . have gone never to return' made him many enemies.[24] Taylor's vigorous exposition of unpopular policies and his attempts to throw a wet blanket on the excessive exuberance of Australian idealism helped to create the image of science at war with the aspirations of the Australian people. Whereas the early advocates of culture had assumed that scientific rationality and the ideals of spiritual and political growth could be reconciled within an evolutionary, idealist framework, by the 1920s this could no longer be taken for granted. To adopt a realist, scientific approach meant to call the validity of 'Australian ideals' into question; rejection of those ideals was not the necessary outcome but the problem was how to solve the conflict. Taylor's geographical determinism was influential on a number of Cultural Liberals including W.K. Hancock and Marjorie Barnard.

Northcott's *Australian National Development* pre-dates Taylor's work but it is concerned very much with this relationship between orderly scientific planning and the ideals and aspirations of the Australian people. Northcott built up a picture of the Australian people as 'spirited and idealistic, even if their philosophy of life is a reckless optimism' and 'careless, unthrifty, reckless of misfortune, . . . incurably incautious concerning the future'. The Australian people, claimed Northcott, aim at the establishment of social democracy founded on a definite social principle or ideal: 'Into this ideal, they have read such terms as equality of opportunity, the realization of the welfare of the people as a whole, the development of the personality of the individual citizen and the establishment of social efficiency.'[25]

It is interesting that Northcott managed to conflate the 'ideals' of the Australian people with the values of educated liberals such as himself so that his ideals and those of the rest of the people appeared to be identical.

Northcott's study was essentially an investigation of the fate of that ideal in Australia, an analysis of the factors which had aided or impeded it. Central to this study was a rather distinctive racial theory: 'A homogeneous population will be more alike in character, more conscious of similar aims, and will react more surely and stably to the same impulses and ideals . . . Classes that are alike in race, speech and colour . . . will co-operate more readily and on more points than a heterogeneous people.' Later in the study Northcott commented favourably on the White Australia policy as a means of ensuring such homogeneity and he even included (unacknowledged) a sentence straight out of C.H. Pearson: 'They are guarding a land that offers the last opportunity for the development of the higher races and the higher civilization.'[26] Northcott's study had been carried out at Columbia University under the supervision of the notorious racist Franklin Giddings, a man who 'studiously avoided Jewish colleagues'.[27] Northcott's preference for a homogeneous population owes more than a little to the higher racism.

Despite Australia's relatively homogeneous population, Northcott traced the source of Australia's social divisions to the 'elements of the population' which comprise the following two groups: the non-assisted migrants who settled in the country and the assisted migrants who went to the cities. The non-assisted migrants settled on the land where they became rugged individualists. This individualism found its expression in a liberalism founded on competition, material advance, economic expansion and economics governed by immutable laws. The assisted migrants were employed in the cities and relied on the state for their advancement. They were supporters of the labour movement who viewed the individual as a member of a social unit which acted collectively such that individual interests were made subservient to the furtherance of a political and social ideal. Social progress came through restraining individualism and recognising the common humanity shared by individuals. The establishment of social democracy is very much the programme of this latter group. The 'sociological history of the last quarter of a century', claimed Northcott, '. . . is the history of the struggle of a social ideal to manifest itself'. In support of this ideal was labour and those social groups owing their origin to assisted migration. Opposed were the individualists – those dedicated to economic development. Support for the ideal of social democracy, claimed Northcott, derived from a 'deep-rooted sentiment latent in the country'.[28]

In essence, Northcott had taken the intellectual conflict of the late nineteenth century which had its roots in regional politics, and turned it into a class conflict based on a dubious social theory. As such, he robbed Free Trade of its inherent moral character and endowed some of the more dubious elements of Protection, such as its racism, with a moral gloss. Selfishness is transformed into idealism. Essentially this is because Northcott wanted to see an ideal at work and thus made the evidence fit into his pre-established categories. It is to Northcott, rather than to Hancock, that the 'party of progress' versus 'party of resistance' theory of Australian politics owes its origin. The Ideal must manifest itself through a particular social group and a particular political party if the Northcott argument is to work as sociology and history rather than as philosophy and theology.

What then were the characteristics of this social ideal? The major demands of the Australian people have been economic, born of the desire for every worker to receive such rewards for his labour as will enable him to live as a human being in a civilised community, but these demands have been 'enforced through a political program and by the political method'. Legislation has been used to put the programme into action, both as a means for the individual to realise 'his own personality in caring for his fellows' and as 'an instrument for the actualization of collective needs and purposes'. Northcott attached the term 'democracy' to this attempt to use legislation in the service of a social ideal.[29]

At the level of the particular, Northcott emphasised such things as the machinery for fixing wages, the development of health services as a way of maintaining 'a strong and healthy people with no racial poisons in their blood', and the advancement of education as a means of creating 'an educated democracy, the best brains of which have been selected and trained for its services, and in so doing to prevent, as far as possible, the congealing of the social strata, and the crystallization of class feeling'. In regard to education Northcott was basically endorsing the reforms of Peter Board in New South Wales.

Two goals are emphasised in this exposition of the development of the social ideal. The first is social efficiency. The second is the realisation of 'personality', a favourite liberal word which appears seemingly at every turn. Again, he wanted to make his description of Australian social development identical not only with the actual development but also with the motives of the democratic masses, despite the fact that such words as 'personality' and 'social efficiency' were abstract concepts found only in the vocabulary of liberals such as himself.

Northcott was clearly on the side of those advancing the 'social ideal'. When he came to explain the failures of this desire for social democracy he did place some emphasis on the class struggle emerging from the conflict of the two elements of the population and their competing ideals. Most of his critique, however, was directed against the deficiencies of the way in which the social democratic ideal had been applied. While he rejected the validity of the moral values of the individualists, his major criticism of the social democratic ideal was that it had lacked scientific good sense; in other words, the major problem was the 'national temperament, heedless of experience, unchecked by expert leaders, reckless of consequences'. Amongst its failures he included the failure to apply scientific methods to farming and to the development of natural resources, a tendency within the political system 'to prefer democratic equality to scientific efficiency' and an inability to appreciate and encourage the efficiency which comes from skill. Labour concentrated too much on remuneration and not enough on productive efficiency; wages had been divorced from any measure of productivity. Equally, in education there had been an inability to link the interests of the individual to productive tasks. Class consciousness had hindered social harmony and the political system had worked in such a way as to breed a distrust of leaders.

Northcott concluded that there had been 'not enough seriousness, not enough thoroughness . . . a loss of efficiency . . . the most pressing need of the country is a program of social efficiency'. This is curious considering that 'social efficiency' and 'personality' were supposedly the objective of the social democratic ideal. Northcott gave the game away when he mentioned that 'pleasures and amusements displace the opportunities for advanced individual efficiency and for civic service . . . there is too much preoccupation with the pleasures of the fleeting moment'. The closet Methodist finally shows his true colours! Clearly the Ideal had not lived up to his expectations of it; it may well have been the case that the legislation had delivered what the people themselves actually wanted.

So Northcott proposed a programme of social efficiency to correct the deficiencies of an ideal of social efficiency. Social efficiency, he claimed, 'is the idea of efficiency applied to the function of society'. For its realisation he believed that three factors were necessary: '(i) industrial competency, (ii) social harmony, (iii) the organization of society in conformity with a concept of social progress'. In a very real sense this is culture revisited – science, a civic awareness and some sort of higher moral ideal to bind it all together. In Australia only the last requirement had been fulfilled; clearly more emphasis must be placed on making the social order conform much more closely to scientific principles. By industrial competency Northcott meant the elimination of waste, the survey of resources and the formulation of plans, the 'scientifically planned development of what is available'. Out of this must come greater skill in industry and an industrial system geared to productivity. To achieve social harmony, class conflict must be overcome and a general agreement reached as to common social ideals. Only those social values which are 'consciously recognized and pursued, into which divergent purposes are transmuted . . . can produce social harmony'. Clearly it was the role of education to produce men and women capable of exercising that citizenship which is the foundation of social harmony. From where then are these values which guide the programme of social efficiency to come? 'The enunciation of these social values is the work of sociology.' Northcott also advocated the need for good leaders – men able 'to appreciate the changing social values' and use legislation as a means of implementing those values:[30]

Like Muscio, Northcott can be accused of scientism; his programme of social efficiency required scientists and social scientists to direct the programme as 'leaders' to define and mould its purposes. This is seen quite clearly in his programme of national efficiency for Australia. He advocated a much greater use of science, both as a way of developing resources and as a means of increasing production and minimising waste in industry. To overcome industrial strife he believed that a measure of democratic control in industry would foster co-operation. Likewise, he wanted to establish links between wages and productivity and to use education as a means of developing both vocational skills and the skills of citizenship. All of this was very much the 'American path to culture'.[31] But the key to the programme was the use of experts to assist in the drafting of legislation to make the ideals a reality. There must be a 'guiding minority [who will] use power in the interests of democracy'.[32] The programme of 'social efficiency' was meant to correct the deficiencies of the social democratic ideal by making it much more scientific. It was, however, a dirigiste vision of the future in which scientific experts would guide the mass of the population towards a more productive, healthy and efficient future. The role of the experts was central to the programme. Although Northcott attempted to graft this programme on to existing social democratic ideals, it is clear that he could do so only by a sleight of hand. In essence, an opposition exists within his work between science and idealism. The components of culture are in a very real danger of falling apart and into conflict; either you have scientific efficiency or democratic idealism. In this sense Northcott wanted both the idealism of the first decade of the century *and* the realism of the scientific critique of that idealism. He effectively closed off the other option which was an economically based Free Trade critique. The only option open to him was a rather confused restatement of culture as social efficiency and a dubious attempt to identify that vision of culture as the actual and ideal course of Australian social development.

The result was both confusing and unsatisfactory. Part of the problem was a consequence of the way in which he had set up his intellectual model. Northcott confused the idealism of the people with his Idealist interpretative scheme because only in this way could he make his scheme of social efficiency both the logical and historical outcome of the social democratic ideal. But, nevertheless, Northcott had been caught by the realist and revisionist mood growing up during the war; he was critical of the path of Australian social development and sought to extend the notion of culture to put it back on the correct path. The ambiguities in Northcott's arguments arose out of the difficulties he experienced in attempting to reconcile the moral imperative of the social democratic ideal with the scientific analysis of his social efficiency programme. These difficulties can be viewed as contradictions emerging in the conversation and argument of Cultural Liberalism, perhaps indicating its increasing inability to deal with the real world on its own terms. Northcott's solution perhaps, was to apply his knowledge of social psychology in England far from the problems of Australia.[33] With W.K. Hancock a similar difficulty emerged as he attempted to grapple with the conflict between Australian idealism and the realities of the wider world. The continuing popularity of his work *Australia* suggests that he managed to arrive at the centre of an important real problem, a problem which could be analysed but proved to be exceptionally difficult to solve.

Hancock: The Irony of Justice

Sir Keith Hancock began his career as a historian at the University of Melbourne before going to Oxford in the early 1920s where he subsequently became a Fellow of All Souls College. He came back to Australia in 1926 to take up the Chair of History at the University of Adelaide where he wrote *Australia*, but returned again to England to become Professor of History at the University of Birmingham in 1934.

His *Australia* remains a pivotal work for any understanding of Australian intellectual development because it is very much a guidebook to Australian modernity.[34] Subsequent generations plundered it for arguments about, and images of, Australian national character thereby transforming it into a quasi-mythological text torn out of its historical context.[35] This elevation of *Australia* from a participant in a conversation to a 'text' has meant that its descriptive and analytical qualities have been emphasised at the expense of the moral fabric in which they were embedded. Yet it is the problem of this moral fabric which lies at the very centre of the work. Hancock, having already tasted success in England, was attempting to come to terms with both his homeland and himself. Much of the power of the work derives from Hancock's frame of mind in which two distinct moral discourses jostled for control of his understanding.

In later life Hancock came to view *Australia* as somewhat of an embarrassment which he preferred not to re-read or discuss. In *Country and Calling* he proudly noted that it was his *Survey of Commonwealth Affairs* which was chosen as one of thirty books to represent twelve-hundred years of the work of British historians in the Festival of Britain Book Exhibition.[36] *Australia* remained in the field of vision of Hancock's

Australian contemporaries, yet for him it was only an episode in his moral and intellectual development. For the mature man it was the product of vigorous, immature youth; he had outlived its moral framework. Hancock tried and convicted *Australia* of being his *enfant terrible*. Having moved beyond its contradictions and uncertainties, he was in a position to dismiss his youthful folly. But much of the charm of *Australia* is a consequence of its *enfant terrible* quality – just as much of the power of Machiavelli results from his desire to shock. It is the tension in *Australia*, a tension caused by standing on a fault line of history, which permitted Hancock's insights in that work to be more than merely the observations of an *enfant terrible*.

At a psychological level this tension was bound up with conflicts of loyalty within Hancock himself, conflicts between ambition and loyalty to his homeland, between national and imperial loyalties. Intellectually the tension was created by bringing together two traditions of moral discourse which were fundamentally incompatible. These two traditions were the Tudor/Commonwealth tradition of social justice and the Machiavellian/realist tradition of analysis. As with Northcott, Hancock found himself torn between a desire to create a more just world and a recognition that the embodiment of that desire had not achieved many of its aims. During these years Hancock admitted to pursuing an interest in Machiavelli and said that he intended writing a book on the general problem of Machiavellianism and the modern state.[37] Through Machiavelli, Hancock was able to draw on the resources of the classical tradition of political thought dating back to Aristotle. A central argument of *Australia*, that the vices of the Australian people are the consequence of their virtues, has classical roots. In classical political theory any 'pure' political form, in this case democracy, will produce those excesses which will eventually overwhelm it.

The most curious element in Hancock's position is the way in which he conflated this classical realism with an economic realism. The constraints on human action are not so much the product of human nature or of the plans which human beings pursue, as of a fixed set of economic laws. Human beings follow the imperatives of social justice only to find themselves frustrated by economic realities. The laws of economics act as a limitation on the capacity of a community to achieve its moral aims. Morality and economics stand opposed to each other; this is a restatement of the old protectionist opposition between moral man and the amoral laws of nature. Whereas the classical tradition places the limitation in human beings themselves, the protectionist tradition places it 'out there'. The latter position had the unfortunate effect of convincing Australians that they were impotent victims of powerful forces outside of their control. Hancock's realism was composed of both classical and economic elements. The central feature of both elements was that of limitation; human actions do not contain boundless, unlimited possibilities. Similarly, expectations do not necessarily translate into desired outcomes; many outcomes are often ironic. Finally Hancock recognised that the charting of ideals through dangerous waters required a hard-headed intellectual approach and not just a vague faith in their ultimate success.

Did Hancock's realism rest on a recognition that Australian moral ideals were founded on sentiment and lacked a substantial intellectual basis? Hancock did not argue for the Tudor Commonwealth and its vision of moral excellence but he was clearly sentimentally attached to it. After having spent many years teaching Tudor history Hancock drew connections between the pre-capitalist values of sixteenth century England and those of the Australian idealists who created the Australian Commonwealth.[38] Australian ideals were pre-capitalist and therefore admirable; much of *Australia* is devoted to giving an unsentimental appraisal of the failings of these ideals. It is this appraisal which lies at the core of Hancock's analysis. As a middle-aged professor, Hancock came to choose sentiment over intellect and the tension found in his early work is missing. The loss of this tension can be traced in the essays he wrote immediately after leaving Australia in the early 1930s.[39] For the purposes of this study the works of Hancock after the early 1930s can, by and large, be passed over in silence.

Considered as an intellectual creation, *Australia* was doubly blessed as it was written at a time when both Hancock and Australia stood at the cross-roads. An ambitious young man, entranced by Oxford, Hancock wished to explore his heritage and to discover where his destiny lay. He could not, however, have written this work without the contributions of Edward Shann, Frederic Eggleston and Vance and Nettie Palmer.[40] From Shann, Hancock derived an economic history of Australia and a critique of Protection; from Eggleston, an analysis of the working of state enterprises in Australia; and from the Palmers, a picture of the failure of suburban Australia to generate a vital, living culture.

By the 1920s Australian civilisation was, as we have seen, in a state of profound crisis. The ideals which had nourished it in the pre-war years and had inspired such policies as arbitration were increasingly being called into question. Did they really deliver the goods? In his discussion of Hancock, Rowse characterises this crisis as New Liberalism's second thoughts and attempts to link it, crudely, to British imperial considerations.[41] No doubt these were a contributing factor but Rowse is incapable of recognising the simple fact, recognised by Hancock, that ideals, once put into practice, do have real consequences. As individuals act on the precepts provided by the ideals and in accordance with the rules established by the institutions to which these ideals have given rise, new states of affairs are created, some of which were desired and some of which were not. Clearly, by the 1920s the considerable number of undesirable consequences brought into being by courses of action set in motion during the early years of the century had became too obvious to ignore. It was this particular conjunction of circumstances which gives *Australia* its peculiar force and vitality. A young man, passing through a period of crisis on his own moral quest, writes a book about a country equally in crisis and is able to draw on the resources of the best minds in the country. The result – a remarkable work of synthesis bound together with a great deal of charm, wit and elegance.

Our major concern is with those critical elements of *Australia* which bind it to the tradition of Cultural Liberalism, both as an extension and as a critique of it. *Australia*, considered in the light of these concerns, is essentially a study in practical morality. Its central focus is the question of whether Australia has attained a state of justice – if not, why not? Hancock's own ethical position was developed through a critique of the flaws and weaknesses of Cultural Liberalism, or as he had encountered them in the teaching of Meredith Atkinson's 'sociology'. In the Atkinsonian dispensation, sociology was an unhappy mixture of sloppy analysis and moral uplift – in fact, everything the realists despised most about Idealism. Atkinson's major work, *The New Social Order*, described a Utopian vision of evolutionary spiritual development.[42] Hancock was not just interested in the actual course of Australian historical development, he was equally reacting to the moral framework created by liberals such as Atkinson to interpret that development. Put simply, in analysing the course of Australian development Hancock was obliged to develop a critique of Cultural Liberalism.

How was this to be done? Essentially, as we have already seen in Alasdair MacIntyre's discussion of tradition, there are only two ways: the internal method of judging the outcome of a tradition by its own standards, and the external method of bringing it into juxtaposition with other traditions so that they can be compared and contrasted. Hancock employed both approaches; he examined Australian idealism immanently and through the prism of realism. As we noted earlier, Hancock had the good fortune to be writing at a time when the Owl of Minerva had already flown, when the consequences of the policies inspired by Australian idealism had had time to manifest themselves fully. He also had the good fortune to be writing at a time when the intellectual inadequacies of that idealism were also becoming obvious.

Australia appears to be a purely secular account of Australian society and culture. Religion scarcely rates a mention and is ignored as a factor influencing Australian life. And yet in its pages can be discerned a theological battle as Hancock pitted Pelagian and Augustinian views, the one against the other. Cultural Liberals were essentially Pelagians who believed that an immanent spirit was progressively revealing itself in the world in the form of a more just and spiritual order. The movement of history indicated the possibility of an increasingly perfect and harmonious world permeated by goodness and spirituality. This political and social vision was underpinned by a Pelagian conception of human nature as capable of achieving goodness through its own efforts. Alasdair MacIntyre argues that one of Augustine's key criticisms of Pelagius was his ascription of self-sufficiency to human action.[43] Hancock criticised Australian democracy because it too believed that it could be self-sufficient and pursue its ideal of justice without considering the outside world. Through the adoption of the notion of limits on human action Hancock placed one foot in the Augustinian camp.

In *Today, Yesterday and Tomorrow*, Hancock acknowledged the importance of the Augustine/Pelagius division for an understanding of European civilisation. Machiavelli, he contended, was only apparently a secular Augustinian. He was a realist but, above all, he was a man who 'loved shocking people' through his accounts of human depravity.[44] Perhaps Hancock himself believed that he had not really been an Augustinian but, like Machiavelli, merely 'loved shocking people'. Realism thus became the device of an *enfant terrible* to be safely discarded once the shock had been registered. To accept this explanation is too simplistic; *Australia* works too well as analysis for Hancock not to have been sincerely attached to realism at the time, even if he remained a closet Pelagian. Hancock pitted the Commonwealth tradition with its pious hopes for justice, equality and co-operation against the realist tradition and its recognition that the springs of human action are various and often achieve other than what they intend. *Australia* is very much a realist critique of the Commonwealth tradition but however much Hancock wished to 'shock', he could not abandon Commonwealth values.

One reason for this is that he could not discern any moral qualities in realism because he associated it with the rule of impersonal necessity. Hancock was an heir to that tradition which associated ethics with the actions of a community seeking to escape the rule of necessity imposed by the laws of economics. Justice and commerce, justice and science are pitted against each other, the realm of freedom against the realm of necessity.

Hancock's realist critique of Australia perpetuates this dichotomy between the sentiment of justice and the reality of economics; and he was thereby caught in a trap of his own making. He could not choose both reality and ethics. As such, Hancock's critique was simultaneously an affirmation of an established tradition and a new departure from it. By confirming the validity of such existing categories as economics versus justice it was an affirmation. By taking the process of Australian development out of the realm of metaphysics and placing it in the realm of history it was a departure. One effect of Hancock's adoption of a realist/Augustinian position was to secularise development so that it was no longer an immanent movement of the spirit but the attempt, by real people, to put their ideas and beliefs into practice. Hancock's task had become an empirical investigation into the realities of Australian development, its peculiar form of nationalism, its achievements and failures.

Caught between idealism and realism at a time of rapidly deteriorating circumstances, Hancock found that only one rhetorical strategy was possible – irony. He could no more condemn the hope of justice than condone the realism which he was using to show its follies. Errors could be exposed, hopes expressed, but no solutions offered. The significance of Hancock's irony can be caught in the following sentence: 'Australians do not tolerate forms of thought or expression (such as irony) which are perplexing or offensive to the average man.' In other words, Australians could not appreciate the sort of enterprise in which Hancock was engaged. How could they possibly appreciate what he was telling them? A prime example of this irony is Hancock's discussion of 'parties of reform' and 'parties of resistance'. Whereas Northcott generally held to this view of Australian politics, a careful reading of Hancock indicates that he was consistently ironic about the 'resistance' of the non-Labor parties. Yet most people read him as an advocate of the 'parties of reform' versus 'parties of resistance' position. One must therefore tread very carefully when examining Hancock's discussion of any topic. Nevertheless, he did have a consistent picture of the average Australian as a simple soul, warm hearted, honest and true. This honesty expressed itself in a sentiment of justice and a desire for equality. He had a simple faith in the power of the state to achieve these goals.

Out of what does this faith arise? This is a central concern of Hancock's *Australia*: the sources and fundamental characteristics of Australian nationalism. 'Nations do not bring forth abundantly the flowers of civilisation until their roots have struck deep.' Hancock believed that Australian nationalism did not grow out of an established sense of community, a 'sending down of roots'; the roots which Australians had sent down had 'only here and there struck deep beneath the surface'. Discussing Australian literature, Hancock was led to comment that Australian writing was largely 'concerned with things of the surface'.[45]

As a young man Hancock had enjoyed a solid training in the classics which profoundly influenced his historical understanding. There is an interesting passage in Livy which provides a parallel to Hancock's discussion of Australia. Discussing the early republic Livy says that if the early populace of Rome had won their freedom too early they would have 'set sail on the stormy sea of democratic politics . . . before any real sense of community had had time to grow'. Livy goes on to say that true patriotism is 'founded upon respect for the family and love of the soil' and that whereas liberty is dangerous in an immature country a 'politically adult nation' can 'produce sound fruit from liberty'.[46]

Hancock was familiar with Machiavelli's *Discourses* (on Livy) and his concern with the importance of community and political maturity mirrors Livy's picture of Rome. The Australians, as Hancock described them, were very similar to the Romans before they became mature. Hancock also seems to have assimilated from classical authors two ideas: that the key to historical events is the character of the persons involved, and that actions are signs of character. The character in this case is a collective identity – the Australians – and Hancock set out to establish the fundamental qualities of Australians before examining the testing of their character in the crucible of action.

The model is essentially one of maturation. The Romans had begun as 'a rabble of vagrants, mostly runaways and refugees' but had managed to become a patriotic community.[47] Were the Australians also capable of maturing through experience and so developing their character? A key sentence in *Politics in Pitcairn* sums up Hancock's position:

> The most critical moment in the history of a man or a nation comes when the hard facts of present reality penetrate and tear the tenuous envelope which encircles that imagined world of perfect harmony and colour which a poetic vision creates and loves. What will the idealist do with himself and his ideal when the obdurate texture of biological and economic necessity, the real fabric of life in an actual historic situation, contradicts that flawless world of justice and beauty which lives in the individual soul?[48]

Australia is a study of Australians as they develop and express themselves through their actions until such time as they reach their critical moment and face the puncturing of their poetic vision. The Australians' character has been expressed in their political economy, their politics and their civilisation.

Such an approach initially seems puzzling to anyone used to European models of nationalism. What have politics and economics to do with national identity and the spiritual bonds of a people? Without roots in the soil, the Australians, like the Romans an emigrant people composed of many elements, were building a common life through their economics and politics. Their poetic vision was not to be found in their literature, art and philosophy but in their political and economic ideals. *Australia* is about an entity sharing a collective character called 'The Australians' who have attempted to build a nation and thereby revealed their character through their actions. Thus the book begins with foundations, or the establishment of the Australian character, then moves on to discuss Australia's political economy, its politics and finally its civilisation. In this way Hancock can confront the Commonwealth ideals of the Australian people with the 'hard facts' of economic reality and assess the degree of maturity they have attained.

Such a reading of Hancock's intentions is confirmed by the curious 'parable of the dog' with which he concludes his discussion on Australian civilisation: 'Yet we may believe that Australia, quietly and imperceptibly . . . is experimenting on the men as they experimented on the dogs. She will be satisfied at long last, and when she is satisfied an Australian nation will in truth exist.' The Australians are like the early Romans – only with time will they develop true patriotism. In this regard it is worth quoting Frederic Eggleston, writing after Hancock, who argued that the modern political unit is held together 'by a common pattern or system of ideas which is the property of all . . . and has been built up through long periods of common life in one area'.[49] Australians, according to Hancock, have been developing this common pattern but only with time will this pattern be consolidated and a genuine nation be brought into being.

In the short term, however, the Australians have emerged and have had their characters tested in the sense of bringing their ideals into contact with the cold, hard reality of the world. It is now possible to examine how Hancock handles the story of the Australians. They are indeed a unique group of people, a 'product of the blending of all the stocks and regional types which exist within the British Isles'; and it has been this sense of race which has been most important in cementing bonds between them. Like the Romans they were a 'scattered and shifting aggregate of uprooted units' which came to act collectively through the state. Australian nationalism, he described as the child of Australian democracy forged in the struggle of numbers against the interests of local landowners and the British.[50]

Thus, like Northcott, he identified Australian idealism with those who have sought to use the state to put their values into practice. The Australians were essentially a band of radical idealists seeking to put the collective power of the state at the service of individual rights. They were an homogeneous people with a common set of values and customs: 'The house-wife, whether her iron-roofed kitchen is situated on the "polar front" of Southern Victoria or in the steaming coastal plains of Queensland, observes the same hours of labour, cooks the same stews and puddings, and goes shopping in the same fashion of hat.' As a people sharing a common set of characteristics they also shared a common ideology, 'the sentiment of justice, the claim of right, the conception of equality, and the appeal to Government as the instrument of self-realisation'.[51] The Australians were thus a simple, good-natured, un-sophisticated people in search of justice and a better world. They were wrapped in the illusion of a 'flawless world of justice and beauty'.[52] This search for justice had manifested itself in three major areas: protection, state socialism and industrial arbitration. In all three cases the results had not been good. On the stormy sea of democratic politics the Australian ship of state had failed both the test of reality and that of its own principles of justice.

Consider first the case of Protection. Hancock argued that in order to conduct their social and political experiments the Australians had a need for a *cordon sanitaire* in the shape of immigration restriction and fiscal protection: 'The policy of White Australia is the indispensable condition of every other Australian policy.' Protection was the second fence put up around Australia in the attempt by Australians to make themselves self-sufficient. Protection was a 'faith and a dogma' amongst Australians as it enabled them to achieve their primary goal – a high standard of living for individuals. To achieve this goal the Australians had applied their notion of justice as expressed in the term 'fair and reasonable'. Workers were entitled to fair and reasonable wages while enterprises desired a fair and reasonable price for their goods. The primary determinant of wages was an ethical rather than an economically determined consideration. Again the late nineteenth century distinction between the moral community and the amoral laws of nature emerged, or as Hancock succinctly described it: 'What the economists call "Law" they [the Australians] call anarchy. The Law which they understand is the positive law of the State – the democratic State which seeks social justice by the path of individual rights.' Consequently, Australians regarded economic realities as something which 'their Government must struggle to soften . . . elude . . . or master'. Equally, the adoption of Protection was based as much on interests as on justice and became the tool of interests. If one industry had the right to a fair price then all industries did. Once set in motion Protection moved into every corner of the nation as one industry after another sought its assistance. But what does a fair price mean? 'Most of [Australia's] customers are poorer than she is; and they, too, have their idea of a fair price. If they can get what they want from other sellers, Australia, for all they care, may go out of business.'

The laws of economics ultimately cannot be avoided or eluded, although attempts can be made to do so. For example, Hancock commented that Australians 'have learned that it is more pleasant to dump than to be dumped upon'. The only conclusion was that self-sufficiency was an idle dream: 'There is no health in Australia unless she can maintain her competitive edge.' The quest for justice had reached a stage at which its consequences threatened those very conditions under which that quest was possible; 'the increasing costs of Protection are endangering the essential purpose of Protection'. And the cause of the problem? The Australians were 'easy-going, good-natured' but suffering from 'intellectual laziness . . . reluctant to refuse favours, to count the cost, to discipline the policies which they have launched'. The Australians had expressed their character through action and the consequences were hardly encouraging; their virtues had multiplied and turned into vices.

The same held true in the area of state socialism. Hancock asked if it were possible to reconcile popular control and efficiency. State control had the advantage that institutions could be used for the public good but there were real problems in defining the public good. The public good might mean supplying services at a 'fair price' or it might mean supplying those services in the cheapest, most efficient fashion. Hancock believed that the crucial factor was that Australia enjoyed neither socialism nor individualism but rather a form of state paternalism in which collective power was used to foster interests which were primarily individual. Groups and individuals claimed the mantle of justice to pursue their own sectional interests: 'Swarms of petty appetites attack the great common services for which the Government has made itself responsible'. As in the case of Protection, justice became a cloak behind which selfishness hid. Hancock also pointed to a lack of economic expertise amongst public administrators; Australians did not like economic laws and contrived to prevent them from being considered as significant.

But it was this lack of trained economic foresight and the attempt to override economic necessities in the name of justice which Hancock placed at the centre of his analysis. Writing of the failure of soldier settlement he said that 'it is, surely, facts of another class – the progress of agricultural knowledge, and invention, the growth of population, the demand of world markets – which will in the end determine the extent and character of country settlement'. He had already made a similar point early in the book: 'Science and invention and the resourcefulness of the practical farmer have succeeded where colonial parliaments failed.' And he made it again in his discussion of the 'Vast Open Spaces' – making use of Griffith Taylor's arguments.[53]

Idealism had come to grief on the rocks of economic and scientific necessity. But it was more complicated than that – the Australians had again demonstrated intellectual laziness and lack of resolution. They had confused the 'good life' with efficiency, not recognising that in attempting to achieve one they had sacrificed the other. But all that Hancock could finish with was irony; after having examined the foolishness of it all, he could offer no way out, no alternative. Implicitly, he was critical of the Australian notion of justice but appeared to be trapped into accepting it. He had locked himself up in an ethics versus science

prison because he was unable to be sufficiently critical of the ethics of
the Australians. The argument that Protection equalled selfishness,
expounded in the nineteenth century by people such as B.R. Wise,
would appear to have been beyond Hancock's moral universe.[54]

The same process of ironic development can be traced in Hancock's
discussion of wages policy in Australia. The Australian workers demanded
equality in the name of justice and, in that very name, had achieved a
system founded on the basic wage. The achievement was 'monstrous' as it
linked wages not to efficiency and productivity, but to justice. If a worker
was efficient and helped to reduce prices then, because his wage was
linked to the cost of living, he was rewarded by a scaling down of his wages.
With his wages regulated by public authorities, the Australian workman
did not worry about price rises – after all there were tariffs to protect his
job if he made the price too high. Australians 'do not count the cost
because it appears to be somebody else's cost', wrote Hancock. But some
were not so fortunate and Hancock pointed to the small wheat farmer
who must not only be efficient but also bear the costs of wage regulation.
Wage regulation and Protection created both equalities and inequalities:
'In modern Australia . . . the ideal of "fair and reasonable" expresses itself
only within a system of privilege.'

Again, however, Hancock's critique of 'fair and reasonable' remained
implicit and limited; he did not undertake a full-blooded realist critique
of its logical foundations. He could only point to the small population
of Australia and its overall prosperity concluding again with a clever
ironic statement: 'Australians have not grown rich because of their policies, but that, being already rich, they have been able to afford them.'

The final picture of the Australians is in the section on 'Civilisation'
in which Hancock summed up their development over the previous
thirty to forty years. Again Hancock praised the idealism of the
Australians and criticised their intelligence. He believed that their initial
successes were too easy and, like the Labor Party, they were lulled into
thinking that the triumph of justice was pre-destined. As a consequence,
once failure did set in a credulous idealism was replaced by an 'equally
credulous cynicism'. Hancock proceeded to describe Canberra as 'a
document of Australian immaturity'.[55] For there was the crux of the matter. The Australians, lacking true patriotism and roots in the soil, had
failed the test of reality. They had not mastered necessity but instead had
fallen victim to the storms of democracy.

A period of history had come to a close in Australia, a period comparable to the Tudor Age in England. Radicalism produced an ideal of
Commonwealth in both places, but that radicalism had exhausted itself
in Australia. The experiment had been made but the achievements were
'largely illusory'. The Australians had failed to assume responsibility and

deal with difficult problems preferring instead 'the line of least resistance'. They had succumbed to the temptations of 'politics' as the cure to all their ills because they lacked a fully developed character; their reliance on political tools was a symptom of immature development. The following passage sums it up:

> The exuberant, egotistical, idealistic nationalism of a generation ago was the sign, not that the Australians had already become a nation, but that they wished to become one. For nationality consists, not merely in political unity, but in spiritual achievement. Regarded from this point of view, the Australian people has not yet come of age.[56]

And of the future? Well, of course there was nature experimenting and the Australians would eventually become a nation just as the Romans did. Only time would enable the growing of roots and the adjustment to the realities and necessities of the world – then the immature, idealistic Australians would have a fully developed character. Perhaps they would even cease to be democrats. But for the moment there was only the irony of their attempts to create social justice to contemplate, perhaps as a warning to future generations. Hancock was a realist in that he pitted an idealistic community in search of justice against the realities and necessities of the wider world. But his realism did not eventuate in a thorough critique of the Australians' ideal of justice. This is because he was largely caught by the notion that ethics are rooted in human communities which then seek to impose themselves on a world lacking value and meaning. Like most of his contemporaries, Hancock owed something to pragmatism and its view that people imposed meaning on the world. Like Northcott, Hancock helped to open up the chasm between science and ethical ideals, between the objectivity of nature's laws and the subjectivity of human aspirations. But unlike Northcott, he did not seek to repair the breach. Instead, his work helped to confirm that the division was valid and to prevent other ways of examining the issue. By moving the focus on to the failings of immature but well-meaning Australians, he successfully evaded an examination of how 'well-meaning' they really were.

Childe: The Hopes of Progress

V. Gordon Childe, another former student of Francis Anderson, studied at Oxford, worked for the Labor Premier of New South Wales and pursued an extraordinary career as an archaeologist and historian. Indeed, he can be described as the founder of modern pre-historic archaeology.[57] He is the last of the thinkers in this study to be considered under the heading realism. For Muscio, Realism meant a rejection of Idealism and the adoption of a much more rigorous, scientific approach. Northcott can be considered a realist as he came to recognise the inadequacies of viewing the world as evolving towards a higher state, advocating instead a much greater role for scientists and experts. Hancock's depiction of Australia as a battleground between the sentiment of social justice and the realities of economics, places him in the realist camp.

The essence of realism possessed two major elements. The first was a reaction against philosophical Idealism and its fuzzy belief that the world was advancing onwards and upwards towards a more advanced spiritual and moral state. The second was an awareness of a need to be more tough-minded and analytically rigorous; in particular, this found expression in a desire to be more scientific. None of this generation was anti-scientific; if anything many of them could be accused of scientism. Even Mayo and Burgmann, who opposed abstract, scientific thinking, maintained a great respect for science. The same may be said of Marjorie Barnard and Flora Eldershaw; what they feared was the aridity of science without imagination. Childe, himself, admired the practical technologist rather than academic theoreticians.

This was a scientism born out of an idealist upbringing. Also, this was a generation on which the religious heritage continued to weigh heavily. Childe, like Hancock, was the son of a cleric. He was not taught by secularists but by men who maintained a strong moral sense as well as an Idealist view of the world. Like his contemporaries, Childe rejected Idealism but not idealism; Andrew Sherratt's claim that Childe stands halfway between nineteenth century speculator and twentieth century professional could be applied to many of his Australian contemporaries.[58]

This is the key to understanding Childe. He rejected Idealism but not other ideas inherited through his teachers from the nineteenth century, in particular ideas about history, evolution and progress. Discussing Malinowski, Ernest Gellner contends that there was a crisis in the human sciences (in particular, in the speculative history of humanity's origins) after World War I which was resolved by the development of functionalist anthropology.[59] Childe's response to this crisis, as to the crisis of evolutionary Idealism, was to restate the case for progress in essentially materialist and realist terms.

It is this realism which links Childe's pre-history and his foray into contemporary politics. He provided a realist account of the development of labour politics in *How Labour Governs*,[60] a hard-nosed analysis of the practice of the labour movement as opposed to the romantic idealism found in a pre-war work such as W.G. Spence's *Australia's Awakening*. As we saw in the case of Hancock, this realism did not necessarily imply a loss of faith in the ideals of justice – in any case, Childe had suffered far more from the 'Tories' than he had from his colleagues on the labour side of politics.[61]

In his pre-history Childe attempted to provide a realist and materialist account of how human societies have grown and developed. To
develop this materialist account, Childe looked back to nineteenth and
eighteenth century sources, not only to Marx but also to the Scottish
school of speculative history. Through Francis Anderson he had been
introduced to the nineteenth century school of philosophical history,
including Robertson Smith, Lewis Morgan and Engels.[62] More particularly, he desired to demonstrate that there was a natural course of
human development which, if followed, would create a dynamic, evolving civilisation and which, if ignored, would lead down the road to stagnation and totalitarianism. Childe's supposed Euro-centrism should be
considered in this light; for him Europe meant a dynamic evolving world
in contrast to the stagnation and static stability of the Middle East and
Asia. Again, this is a classic nineteenth century distinction, one which he
would have heard in Anderson's lectures.[63]

Despite his atheism, his materialism, his Marxism and his desire to
shock (which again may be compared with our use of the term *enfant
terrible* to describe Hancock's work), Childe can be placed in the tradition of Cultural Liberalism. He had many points of contact with other
participants in the tradition. First, as shall be demonstrated, he considered that evolution meant the extension of human powers through the
development of co-operation, the growth of knowledge and the movement of human nature towards a greater universality. Sherratt argues
that Childe's use of 'revolution', as in the 'Urban Revolution' was not
Marxist. Rather, his usage was closer to Anderson's use of the word in
Liberty, Equality and Fraternity, in which he provided an account of the rise
of humanity as the cumulative work of four revolutions.[64] Of course,
Childe was a materialist whereas Anderson was an Idealist, but there is a
similarity in the process even if not in the actual accounts.

Second, Childe placed a great emphasis on knowledge as practice
which was expressed through work. He was anti-theoretical in the sense
of seeing little value in mere abstract speculation. In this regard he was
quite close to Elton Mayo, who also regarded undisciplined theorising
with great suspicion and emphasised the importance of professional and
occupational traditions in the development of knowledge.[65] In fact, a
hostility to intellectualism, considered as abstract theorising, is a feature
of Cultural Liberalism. Science is a good thing but must not be allowed
to dominate other forms of human activity.

The third feature of Childe's thought which places him in the Cultural
Liberal camp is that, like his fellow compatriots, including Mayo,
Burgmann and Hancock, he used the word 'civilisation' when he wished
to discuss human activities and flourishings at a higher stage of development.[66] In the conflict between *kosmos* and *taxis* Childe, like Mayo, clearly

stands on the side of *kosmos*. But, like Mayo, Childe was not free of the influence of organic romanticism. *Kosmos*, the natural evolving order, stood not so much for competition as for an emerging co-operation. A comparison of Childe and Mayo with the Austrian school of such writers as Hayek, Popper and Jantsch, would prove illuminating (though outside the scope of this study) but it is clear that the ideas regarding spontaneous development and natural order, developed in Australia, would vary from those of thinkers such as Hayek. In particular, the emphasis on co-operation by these Australian thinkers would mark out their conception of *kosmos*.

It is now necessary to consider Childe's account of the rise of humanity and the philosophy on which it was founded.[67] There are a number of principles which underlie and inform that philosophy. The first of these is the conception of knowledge as a form of social practice which evolves as society develops and grows. Childe also opposed the idea that human nature was fixed and immutable. He believed that human beings change and develop as the society of which they are part progresses; they are the product of historical evolution. There is, therefore, a direct relationship between the growth of knowledge, the development of human nature and the evolution of society. They are complementary elements of a progress which is defined as the growth and extension of co-operative human enterprise.

Two consequences emerge from this conception of evolutionary growth. Firstly, it is inherently hostile to any ideal of an autonomous lifestyle, be it the quest for agrarian self-sufficiency by individuals, or the desire for economic autarchy by nations. As human nature is social it can only grow through contact with other people; to evade that contact is to replace principles which lead to co-operative social development with those which constrict the growth of knowledge and lead ultimately to social decay. Progress implies the division of labour and the intercourse of nations; for any society to progress it must participate in the life of the world as a whole.

Secondly, Childe's conception of evolution is voluntarist rather than mechanistic in that it does not view evolution as a mechanical programme following deterministic laws but as a continuing process in which human beings participate, in which, to take the title of one of his books, *Man Makes Himself*. His ideal of social development was affected by the vitalist philosophy of the early twentieth century which, in its Bergsonian form, stressed the free will of individuals and their capacity to make choices. For Childe, evolution implied the power of a society to choose and develop its knowledge and co-operative capacities – or alternately, to remain self-sufficient and to risk the slow death which such a static state of existence implies.

At the beginning of *Man Makes Himself* Childe stated that the purpose of his book was to establish the view that 'history may still justify a belief in progress in days of depression' and to 'vindicate the idea of progress against sentimentalists and mystics'. As an archaeologist and pre-historian dealing with the grand sweep of human history, Childe viewed the development of human society as growing naturally out of biological evolution. Evolution simply meant adaptation to the environment; progress could be considered as an extension of this process through the creation and development of culture. Social progress means successful adaptation, and Childe believed that cultural advances play the same role in history as mutations do in organic evolution.[68]

For Childe, the key to cultural advance lay in the accumulation of knowledge and the use of this knowledge to spur on technological development. Late in life Childe elaborated his theory of knowledge in a little book entitled *Society and Knowledge*. He viewed knowledge as being fundamentally social and practical in nature. By social, he meant that the categories through which knowledge is constructed and the world perceived have their foundations in the society's traditions and patterns of behaviour; in turn, these traditions are founded on co-operative human action. All knowledge which is merely personal and incapable of being expressed in symbols communicable to other members of society, or which lies outside of the common social categories is, according to Childe, meaningless. Knowledge is practical because its role is to aid adaptation to the environment, 'to provide rules for action'. A society is a co-operative entity; knowledge is 'an ideal reproduction of the external world serviceable for co-operative action thereon'.[69]

A number of consequences follow from this. Firstly, the test of 'truth' is whether something actually works and an ideology has power only in its capacity to foster action which is beneficial. There is no court of appeal beyond society, no timeless 'truth tables' by which propositions may be judged. In a sense then, all social ideologies are true in so far as they work in some shape or form and Childe conceded this, only to add that modern medicine can be established as being superior to magic 'if antiseptic and vaccines succeed better in preventing deaths, and so permitting social growth, than do incantations and witch-burnings'.[70]

Secondly, as knowledge is embodied in action it is also concrete and real. Tools, social arrangements, economic practices – all, for Childe, are the embodiment of ideas. The origin of European liberty, he believed, was to be found amongst the nomadic practices of the independent metal workers rather than in the abstract musings of Athenian philosophers. Knowledge is not merely practice but practice worked out in the form of social traditions by co-operative groups over perhaps hundreds of years. Childe cited the example of the invention of the steam engine and contrasted Watt's individual contribution with the 'social capital to which he contributed', a tradition of science and technology which stretched all the way back to the Iron Age. All knowledge is historical and social and is tested in the crucible of action; whatever works is best. In a sense, for Childe, the whole of human history has been like an extended science course during which knowledge, good solid practical knowledge, has accumulated, and of which modern man is the beneficiary. Childe conceived of history as being active and voluntarist; it does not have an essence but is in a constant state of becoming, 'making its path as it proceeds', and man plays an active and creative role in the historical process. Hegel's contribution to historical study was to establish that history was the 'rational and orderly but creative process of the emergence of new values'.[71] Most importantly, Childe did not believe that history had an end; the struggle and the creative process continued endlessly and no nation or society could opt out of the evolutionary contest and hope to survive. This dynamic conception of history owes as much to early twentieth century Vitalism as it does to the positivism of Marx and Darwin. Only in the twentieth century is such a combination of radical historicism and pragmatism conceivable and despite his self-proclaimed Marxism, Childe clearly also owed intellectual debts to William James and Bergson.

Despite its relativist tinge, Childe's idea of history was fundamentally that of progress, a progress founded on the growth of knowledge considered as technological practice. Societies can only survive and progress in so far as their relations of production 'favour the development of science, the march of invention and the expansion of productive forces'.[72] Successful adjustment to the environment means essentially the march of science. Morals, culture and the civilising process are of lesser importance and must be considered pragmatically as aspects of the social whole, as things which aid or hinder adaptation. How then did Childe explain the course of human progress and development? It is here that he introduced a second element into the dynamic of progress: diffusion. The progress of man and civilisation was to be understood as the interaction of the forces of evolution and diffusion.[73] Indeed it might be said that Childe's particular contribution to the study of the growth of civilisation was the way in which he employed the idea of diffusion to give the model of evolutionary social development an air of reality.

Childe's evolutionary scheme, found in *What Happened in History* and *Social Evolution*, is derived, via Engels, from the nineteenth century American writer Lewis Morgan.[74] It envisages three stages in human development, from savagery to barbarism to civilisation. Morgan had used it to explain the origins of the state, the family and private property, mixing up an analysis of Graeco–Roman civilisation with that of the Aztecs and with his own personal knowledge of the Iroquois Indians. As an archaeologist and scientist, Childe only made use of the technological aspect of Morgan's scheme, recognising that material objects could say nothing about kinship organisation or whether a society was matrilineal. Childe identified savagery with the hunting and gathering stage of human development: the Palaeolithic; barbarism with the development of agriculture and pastoralism – or what he termed the Neolithic revolution; and civilisation with urbanisation and writing. There is nothing new in this scheme, beyond Morgan it goes back to the speculative social philosophers of the Scottish Enlightenment although they would have identified civilisation with commerce. It is an intellectual construct, though one of great power and elegance.

But it is not a particularly dynamic model for explaining the central thesis of Childe's argument: progress as the growth of science and technology considered as social practice. In fact, Childe's account of social progress contains more than just the technological dimension; it is the movement of human understanding from the particular to the universal or the enlargement of man's vision through the enlargement of his society. Progress means the expansion of human capabilities as society moves away from the limited self-sufficient group towards a form of organisation founded on a complex division of labour and the constant interchange of ideas both between its members and with other societies. Obstacles to progress are anything which hinders this growth, be it family and kinship ties or the power of a despotic state.

Diffusion, or the intercourse of ideas, is the lubricant which Childe poured on savage, barbarian and civilised societies to get their social processes moving and to provide the necessary stimulus for the expansion of knowledge. Even Palaeolithic hunting communities had possessed a rudimentary web of intercourse in which 'ideas were exchanged and technical experience was pooled'. The Neolithic revolution, although it produced agricultural communities which were self-sufficient, accelerated this 'pooling of human experiences'. But it was the urban revolution and the unleashing of a dynamic commercial society which broke down the exclusiveness of traditional society. Trade, 'a means of intercourse, a channel by which ideas can be diffused on an international scale', promoted the diffusion of scientific knowledge and craftsmanship.[75]

Childe conceded that, traditionally, diffusionists and evolutionists belonged to different intellectual camps because while the diffusionists contended that civilisation had moved outwards from a single original source, the evolutionists argued that all societies passed through the same stages of development. While diffusion lacked a certain degree of rigour, evolutionary theory faced the problem that it was essentially abstract in character; it could not explain how human society had actually developed. In the early years of the twentieth century the major exponent of the diffusionist school had been Grafton Elliot Smith, who believed that civilisation had originated in Egypt. Smith, Australian-born and a graduate in medicine from the University of Sydney, had developed his theories while living in Cairo. Significantly, the other major Australian evolutionary theorist of this period, Griffith Taylor, was also a diffusionist who argued not only that 'progress in civilisation is essentially a question of contacts and culture, and only indirectly does it depend on race', but also that 'nationality is but a passing phase in the creation of a world civilization'.[76]

When any student of the nineteenth century society hears the word 'intercourse' the immediate reaction is to think of Free Trade. The belief that the intercourse of nations was the means through which science, liberty and commerce were diffused amongst the people of the earth was, as we saw earlier, a central plank in the platform of the Free Trade Liberals of colonial New South Wales. This emphasis on the exchange between societies of ideas and goods as the motor of the growth of civilisation represented a transference of the moral philosophy of the Scottish Enlightenment out of a framework in which it explained the growth of 'society' to one in which it could provide the principles most appropriate for understanding and justifying a new society created by imperial expansion. Whereas evolution made sense in the mother country, diffusionism and the need for constant intercourse with other peoples had obvious appeal in a colonial society, both as a scientific account of the dynamics of empire and as a moral doctrine showing the path to a better world. Colonial society had been created by diffusion and required continual commercial intercourse for its survival. To progress it needed to be in constant contact with developments occurring elsewhere in the world. In this way, the doctrines of diffusionism and the intercourse of nations were essentially strategies for improvement founded on the sound idea that contact with other peoples was a cure for provincial narrow-mindedness and thus a crucial element in the moral growth of any individual or society.

As New South Wales was the Australian home of Free Trade it is not surprising that Childe, Taylor and Smith were natives of that colony. Victoria, motherland of Protectionism, produced no comparable theorists. But even given its restricted appeal in Australia, diffusionism is largely a doctrine of the periphery. Its development in New South Wales is an example of how a European intellectual tradition could be reworked in an environment totally different from the one in which it originated. It is also worth reflecting that despite the victory of Protection at a national level, the intellectual tradition of Free Trade survived in New South Wales. Francis Anderson opposed Protection because it hindered the passage to universality. Childe was not alone among his students in adopting such universalism. Burgmann was critical of Protection, and G.V. Portus was also a supporter of Free Trade.[77] In both cases the essential link was between Free Trade and the growth of a universal outlook. Diffusionism was a natural extension of that desire for universalism as it provided a mechanism through which universalism could be attained.

Despite his self-proclaimed adherence to Marxism, and the occasional quotation from Stalin, Childe's account of human history seems to owe its greatest debt to Adam Smith and to the belief that the growth of knowledge is best served by ensuring that mankind is bound together by economic ties while being divided into a multiplicity of political units. The growth of civilisation is the tale of progress from Neolithic self-sufficiency to an interdependent world bound together by the division of labour and the interchange of knowledge and goods. It is the story of the rise of science and the pooling of human knowledge through increased intercourse. Also it is the movement of human society from particular to universal as, for example, in the replacement of customary law by universally valid codes of law. And finally, it is the cautionary tale of the failure of civilisations to develop political and social institutions appropriate to the forces of production which had allowed them to develop, and of the stagnation and decay which must occur when this happens. Childe cited the case of the Bronze Age when one of the effects of the growth of civilisation was the separation of craftsmanship and learning. This led to a stagnation in the area of applied science; trapped by the rigidity of their social structure and learning, these Bronze Age states were successfully challenged by new, more flexible societies which were able both to produce cheap iron and to democratise their agriculture, industry and warfare.[78]

It is impossible here to do justice to the richness of Childe's account of the rise of civilisation. Its theme can be characterised as that of constant expansion through migration, the diffusion of the 'arts of civilisation', and the constant growth of science and technology. Ideologically, it is the development of a more universal outlook such as occurred in the evolution of moral and religious ideas. 'The idea of humanity', claimed Childe, 'as a single society, all of whose members owe one another common moral obligations, is an ideological counterpart of an international economy based on the interchange of commodities between its parts'.[79]

Childe's heroes were the metal workers, the practical men ever in quest of technological innovation, whom he viewed as the ancestors of the modern scientist. He was rather contemptuous of the scholars and learned men who served as scribes and priests in the temples of the ancient Near East and were 'apt to turn to books in preference to nature'.[80] Equally, he had little time for the Greek philosophers and their ideology based on the *polis*. For him, Greek science was a failure because it had not found an expression in technical inventions, and the ideology of the *polis* was a disaster which had squandered the manpower of

Greece and dissipated its wealth. Most importantly it had proven incapable of providing an 'ideology compatible with an economic system based inexorably on international trade on at least a Mediterranean scale'.[81] In his final book, *The Pre-History of European Society*, Childe argued that the European tradition of liberty had its roots in the nature of prehistoric European society. In Mesopotamia, he argued, the urban revolution had been marred by the excessive power of the state and by the separation of the knowledge of the scribe and peasant. This brake on progress had not been applied in Europe because the European metal workers had not been tied to any one tribal society or patron. Competition between these craftsmen had provided an inducement to originality and rapid technical development; the consequence was increased efficiency. The key to European liberty, and to progress in general, was the establishment of an 'international commercial system linked by a turbulent multitude of tiny political units'.[82]

As he had scant respect for mere theorising, Childe did not consider classical Greece to be the climax of the ancient world. This honour was accorded by him to the Hellenistic world created by the conquests of Alexander the Great. The Hellenistic world saw the creation of a system of international trade and the unification of Greek philosophy with Babylonian and Egyptian science, resulting in the creation of a science which combined theory and practice. All the processes of civilisation – diffusion, commerce and technological advance – were intensified. And the result: 'The two centuries beginning in 330 BC brought forth a crop of mechanical inventions that cannot be paralleled in any comparable period till AD 1600.'

And yet this civilisation failed. Ultimately the contradictions in its economy meant that it could not exploit productively the inventions offered to it by science. The wealth created by economic prosperity had ended up in the treasuries of a few kings and in the pockets of a Greek ruling caste instead of in the hands of the productive section of society. Slavery proved to be a bar to technological advance. The dead hand of the state had dammed back the forces of civilisation and the consequence was a contraction of the economy and a growing impoverishment. Ultimately, in the later Roman Empire there was a relapse into self-sufficiency as large estates attempted to produce all of their own needs so as to avoid the need for intercourse. Finally the Roman Empire imposed a form of what Childe terms '*Nazional-Sozialismus*' to prop up an 'antiquated social system'.[83]

The moral is clear. The process of social adaptation is constant and never-ending and a society which fails to exploit inventions and technological advances because of its social structure will stagnate, contract and eventually go under. To survive, a society must be open to new and advanced ideas. Part of this process of adaptation is coming to terms with one's neighbours; the intercourse of ideas is a necessary condition for progress: 'progressive change is accelerated by intercourse with divergently adapted and differently organised societies'.[84] Attempted self-sufficiency is an indication of contradictions within a society, of social retrogression and of an inability to adapt to one's environment. Childe referred to Australia's chauvinistic demands for self-sufficiency in the context of the decline of the Roman Empire.[85] It is clear that he had no respect for the narrow Protectionism of his homeland.

Childe's picture of the development of human civilisation is an affirmation of a faith in progress and of a moral philosophy which preached the necessity for human beings and human society to grow and look outward. His writings are an implicit critique of the growing narrowness and chauvinism of twentieth century Anglo-Saxon society; much of it could be applied to England as well as Australia.

Childe may have been a realist and a materialist but in many ways he remained hopelessly idealistic. Unlike Hancock, for whom *Australia* assumed the status of an episode in his life, Childe continued to be an *enfant terrible* until the end of his days, attempting to shock his contemporaries out of their complacency. In many ways, Childe remained a perpetual 'jester' trying to tell the truth; equally realism remained a shock tactic in an age which had come to believe that its ideals were realities. And yet, as the case of John Anderson illustrates, a continued hard-line adherence to an uncompromising realism was not without its penalties. 'Andersonianism' ultimately adopted a sort of siege mentality in which the objective was to hold the line against a threatening wider world.

Such a position was in sharp opposition to the ideals of universalism and social sympathy held by Childe and his generation of Cultural Liberals. As with Hancock, Childe's realism was tempered by his faith in the ultimate creation of a universal co-operative world order. In this respect, Sherratt is correct;[86] Childe was restating the nineteenth century case for human evolution and development, a case he would initially have heard from Francis Anderson. It was a case for the development of human powers and capacities through the growth and diffusion of a vital, living civilisation devoted to expanding human knowledge. Like so many of his contemporaries, Childe was a vitalist who feared that Australia was settling down into a subservient and servile condition. Realism was one way to bring back some life; a new vision of progress was the other. Childe tried both ways and in so doing provided a new and powerful exposition of Cultural Liberalism. Perhaps it could be argued that, in his enunciation of a powerful vision of progress, he sought to repair the breach between science and ethics that realism had opened up, thereby restoring hope to those who despaired that the ideal would ever be attained.

CHAPTER 6

Liberalism and Its Critics: The Idealists

In the previous chapter, the 'realist moment' of Australian Cultural Liberalism was discussed. For Muscio, it was the philosophical inadequacies of Idealism which spurred on his Realist critique; for Hancock, it was the consequences of a naive idealism which incurred his criticism. But under the pressure of the developments of the age it was also possible to accept some of these criticisms and yet continue to adhere to a modified idealist version of Cultural Liberalism.

In the writings of Ernest Burgmann, Elton Mayo and Frederic Eggleston there can be discerned an attempt to discover new foundations for the idealist hopes of Cultural Liberalism in which scientific realism is reconciled with both the deeper needs of human nature and the need to create a civic community founded on democracy. Barnard Eldershaw's remarkable novel, *Tomorrow and Tomorrow and Tomorrow*, explores this issue further as it recognises the potential for scientific rationality to crush and repress the liberal spirit. For Barnard and Eldershaw it was not so much a matter of restoring a harmonious order as of ensuring that liberty could survive the onslaught of the constant threat of those forces seeking to overwhelm it.

Burgmann: Restating the Case for Personality

One of the great failings of secular historians writing on Australia has been their inability to understand and appreciate the religious sensibility. First there was George Nadel's characterisation of John Woolley as a secular thinker. In the case of Ernest Burgmann it is Tim Rowse's attempt to fit Burgmann into a liberal mould as a theologian with a humanistic bias and an interest in psychology.[1] Both Burgmann and Woolley were deeply religious, and Burgmann is the one Australian figure who has most in common with Woolley; a Platonic mysticism permeates the work of both men.

Burgmann inherited the tradition of Cultural Liberalism from Francis Anderson and he can be placed in that tradition as the heir not only of Anderson but also of Brennan, Badham and Woolley. After studying under Anderson at the University of Sydney before World War 1, Burgmann was ordained into the Anglican Church and became Warden of St John's College, Armidale. He transferred the college to Morpeth where he established the *Morpeth Review* and developed a reputation as a social activist. In 1934 he became Bishop of Goulburn.

If anything, Burgmann's writings are the most coherent and clear statement of the case for Cultural Liberalism in twentieth century Australia. He was not impressed by the critique developed by the realists, though he did assimilate much of the argument of Hancock's *Australia*.[2] Unlike Hancock, he did not revolt against the excesses of evolutionary Idealism – at times his writings seem as hopelessly Utopian as Meredith Atkinson's[3] – nor did he seek guidance from the likes of Machiavelli. Indeed, Burgmann was decidedly Greek in his Christianity and one searches in vain for even the ghost of Augustine in his writings. He never seems to have doubted the potential for human beings to move towards an increasingly integrated spiritual existence and to enter into the Divine. Unlike Muscio, he continued to believe that the passage to a more spiritual and moral life lay in following the path laid down by Nature, although he did recognise that Nature could be cruel and that death followed in the footsteps of life.[4]

Like Woolley, Burgmann combined a personal spiritual vision with a desire to improve the world and make it overflow with a genuine religious spirit – he was simultaneously a Platonist and an evolutionist. In a review of *The Platonic Tradition in English Religious Thought* he identified Platonism as the spiritual tradition of the Church existing alongside the Catholic and Protestant traditions.[5] That Burgmann practised this Christian Platonism can be ascertained from the following passage in which he plotted the route to Truth:

> The disciple of Christ will seek His mind in the stillness of meditative thought . . . But when all this has been done he will learn to muse on his knowledge in silent converse with the Spirit of the Great Galilean. To try to see how He views all these things will shut out our limited points of view and private interests, and enable us to escape from fears and prejudices. In the measure in which we can do this so far can we go in the direction of making the finding of truth possible.[6]

In this emphasis on stillness and disinterestedness Burgmann looks back not only to the Cambridge Platonists, but also to Meister Eckhart and the Alexandrian Fathers.[7] In like manner, in his advocacy of the unity of Truth, Beauty and Goodness, Burgmann betrayed his Platonic roots: 'The more perfectly truth, goodness, and beauty, in harmony and unified relation, are expressed in any person or event the more clearly is God present.' There is also an elective affinity between Burgmann's Platonism and Arnoldian culture with its emphasis on the disinterested self seeing things in their actuality as, for example, when Burgmann speaks of man discovering 'his own best self in thinking and working for unselfish ends'.[8]

Burgmann's Platonism was matched by his evolutionism, the belief that human beings, both individually and collectively, should develop naturally and harmoniously towards a more religious appreciation of the world. For Burgmann, the religious sense grows out of nature and man's natural development as human powers unfold and grow. Like Mayo, he had little time for conversion experiences and generally did not have much sympathy for Protestantism, viewing it as possessing a 'dry and sapless view of human life'.[9] In this he was following not only Francis Anderson but also William James's view of healthy-minded religion. Burgmann possessed a 'sacramental' view of nature of Wordsworthian intensity and this inclined him to consider the movement of human beings towards a greater spirituality as merely an element of the natural course of things.

Burgmann believed that the goal of development was the creation of a world in which every human being was recognised as a personal spiritual being able to realise his or her unity freely with the rest of humanity in a common brotherhood. From Francis Anderson he took over the belief that the central element of Christianity was its conception of Personality as that which enables the full flowering of human nature. In the Master of Arts thesis written for Anderson on 'Hebraic and Hellenic elements in Christianity', he wrote that Christianity both provides 'an inspiration to practical life' and 'gives man a Divine mission to be worked out by the exercise of his whole Personality'. Years later he was to write that 'The Christian conception of personality makes every individual potentially a person of infinite worth'.[10]

The central problem was to make religion an active spiritual force in the life of society and the world. Such activity was necessary because only individuals, traditions and nations possessing such spiritual vitality would continue to live and grow. Those who lose this vital force simply exhaust themselves and die. To grow, to expand, to move ever outwards in one's sympathies – these are nature's dictates. To disobey them is to die – sometimes spiritually, sometimes as a matter of fact. For as Burgmann put it: 'We are part of Nature and the God of Nature appoints death for those who cannot make the grade.'[11] There was a strong vitalist streak in

Burgmann inherited, like Personality, from Anderson and the milieu around the University of Sydney in the years leading up to World War I. This vitalism was matched by a fear of degeneration and decay, a fear that the Divine spark would be lost.

In Burgmann's writings the three key elements of Cultural Liberalism can be discerned. In the ideal of Personality there was combined a belief in human spiritual growth with an ideal of service to the community and citizenship. Burgmann was also an adherent of the ideals of rationality and science. The creator of the new world, he wrote, was the spirit of science which was God's latest revelation and clearest Word to modern man. The message of Christianity was that rationality as well as humanity was at the heart of the universe. Hence he could endorse 'rational living' and even eugenics and write of the need for the sciences to rescue Australia from the quackeries of popular leadership.[12]

The causes of science and religion were not in conflict. Rather, the task was to ensure that science was used properly for human ends in harmony with man's true needs as a spiritual and religious being. In all of Burgmann's writings the ideal of harmonious development is central, as is the need to reconcile pairs of conflicting elements. Just as science and religion can be unified, so can male and female, individual and collective, state and Church. This is not to say that he did not recognise the reality of conflict; he was fully aware that individuals in a civilised society were torn between their own personal impulses and the need to repress those instinctive urges.[13] Unlike Hancock, he did not despair of the possibility of reconciling harsh reality and ideal longings for justice by taking refuge in irony. Instead, Burgmann sought to restate the case for the traditional view that the resolution of conflict would ultimately occur as part of a harmonious evolutionary development. The whole could be attained and this theme of reconciliation is apparent even in his student days as he wrote his thesis on 'Hebraic and Hellenic elements in Christianity'. The interesting feature of Burgmann was that whereas his intellectual predecessors had moved their hopes for the fulfilment of harmony away from the Church and into the university, he reversed the process and again made the Church a certain element in any future harmonious world.

Central to Burgmann's hopes was the reconciliation of individual and collective. As a believer in natural, normal development Burgmann's central focus was on the development of the individual (education) and that of society (history). In both cases he was concerned that such development should take the form of a smooth, natural unfolding of human powers. His two major works written in the early 1940s each deal with one aspect of this development. *The Education of an Australian* is concerned primarily with individual development, while *The Regeneration of Civilization* deals with the problem of collective development.

Dealing with individual development Burgmann, like Mayo, was strongly attracted to psycho-analysis and he made a systematic study of psycho-analytical literature. He argued that psycho-analysis was useful in religion as a means of overcoming moral illness and senseless repression thereby allowing us as individuals to 'begin to win possession of our souls'. 'The need of the moment', claimed Burgmann, 'is the releasing of spiritual energy' and he believed that analysis carried out 'in the light of the Christian ideal' would bring light into the soul and lead to spiritual growth.[14]

This belief in education as proper spiritual growth informed both Burgmann's use of psycho-analysis and his observations on the growth and development of children. Burgmann was concerned that the child should grow and develop in the right emotional fashion.[15] To this end, he emphasised the importance of the mother as establishing the child's emotional development. Using his own childhood as an example he identified the mother as representing the immanence of God or God in Nature and the father with the transcendence of God and the moral personality. A proper upbringing should turn education into a 'continuous evolving scheme' without any sudden upheavals or convulsions. But, Burgmann claimed, there was too much emphasis on the growth of knowledge in the early years and not enough on physical and emotional growth. As a consequence almost all children, he asserted, were damaged in the first five years of their life.[16]

Education had to develop the whole person. Francis Anderson had spoken of the need to unify Willing, Feeling and Reason. His students, including P.R. Cole and Brennan, made use of this idea as did Burgmann.[17] He spoke of the ideal of the perfect man in which Love bound together:

Ego	which seeks Truth
Ego ideal (Super-ego)	which pursues Righteousness
Id	which rejoices in the Beautiful

Elsewhere he drew up the following table:

Emotion	Peter	Id
Will	Paul	Super-ego
Reason	John	Ego[18]

Peter stands for Jesus the Messiah, a human sacrament of the divine, Paul for Christ crucified or the power of God, and John for the incarnation of the eternal principle of wisdom.

The whole person must be developed because rational living 'depends upon the harmonious working of the whole personality'. Burgmann seems to have feared most the development of the ego in comparative isolation from the id and super-ego resulting in a 'barren form of intellectualism . . . divorced from any practical contact with the facts of life'. The fully developed person must have ego, id and super-ego working together harmoniously so that the human character can bring together and unify power, wisdom and knowledge.[19]

For Burgmann, there was a natural pattern of development which allowed this harmonious unfolding of powers to take place. As well as on the mother, he placed great emphasis on the family as the source of human roots and the guardian of freshness, variety and spontaneity. The family is the 'fundamental educational institution'. Nature itself is a great influence: 'Nature in its manifold moods exercised profound influences on man's inner being. She made him flexible and resilient to her moods.' To maximise this influence of Nature, Burgmann advocated sending all children at a certain age to boarding schools in the country. Such schools 'should be fitted into the landscape like an old-world village community'. In such a setting, Burgmann believed, Nature would exercise a maximum influence and children would become rooted in the natural environment. To this model of natural development Burgmann opposed the city school which was 'a factory for the making of wage earners' and the city milieu 'a dead-end for the human race'. He feared what he termed a 'mechanised environment' in which human beings made contact with Nature through some sort of machine and became denaturalised and deracinated. Through Nature one acquires roots and the harmonious development of one's personality. Out of this harmonious growth of its citizens a nation grows and evolves into a more mature and balanced condition. In a similar vein to Peter Board, Burgmann claimed that 'the growth of a nation, then, is fundamentally an educational process'.[20]

What sort of mature individual emerges out of this natural course of development? Obviously he or she is much more than just a physical or mechanical being. Man's abiding interests and permanent satisfactions are spiritual – it is the realm in which he finally comes into his own. The goal is man considered as a personality, a personal spiritual being 'whose destiny is to become fully and truly representative of the human race'. Burgmann believed that an individual was only truly alive when he or she was 'a fully personal being with rational purposes and spiritual interrelations with his fellows'. 'We die when we no longer feel our lives as purposive spiritual forces in a world of eternal values.'[21] A fully developed individual is rational, spiritual and dedicated to the service of his or her fellow human beings. Such a combination is only possible if the whole person is in harmony and the individual capable of unleashing their full spiritual powers.

Burgmann's discussion of the need for the growth of character and for spiritual roots recalls Hancock's comment that Australians had failed to put roots down in the Australian soil. Burgmann read Hancock carefully and responded to his analysis of Australian weaknesses: 'Australian life is weak on the traditional side and therefore easily disintegrated. We have not yet taken deep root in the Australian soil.' Burgmann believed in continuity and evolution; his radicalism, he claimed, was an extension of his conservatism and it would not be inappropriate to call him a Tory radical. The nation required 'hard continuous study' if it was to overcome its problems.[22] He listed the following as the chief needs of Australian civilisation: moral fibre, mental effort, technical achievements and political and social integrity.[23]

Above all, Australia needed to recapture its faith and to discover a vision which could provide the basis for this faith: 'We need to have a vision of greatness for Australia', he claimed in *The Education of an Australian*. The roots must be grown, the traditions of an energetic, active and intelligent people be established. But such growth did not imply Vance Palmer-style self-sufficiency; Burgmann considered that Protectionism 'meant death to the spirit of man'.[24] National growth, like individual growth, required active spiritual energy and ultimately would culminate in the evolution of a universal brotherhood.

For Burgmann there were two basic paths which humanity could follow: that of Nature which led to the integrated personality and harmonious social development, and that which ignored Nature, leading ultimately to degeneration and social disintegration. He saw around him many of the symptoms of this disintegration including betting, drinking and smoking. Just as Burgmann explained individual development in terms of growth and education, so he considered the collective development of humanity in terms of evolution from the primitive to the civilised. He left a variety of pictures of this evolutionary process scattered throughout his writings.

In his earlier writings, Burgmann contended that primitive man first moved in hordes under the leadership of a primal father. Within these earliest tribes there was coherence and unity as the individual submitted to the spirit of the group. Democracy emerged in its earliest form when the disinherited sons displaced the primal father. From this earliest revolution emerged the subsequent development of humanity – an oscillation between the two extremes of despotism and democracy. Equally, as tribes turned into nations two other key movements took place: nations turned into ever larger groupings, and a consciousness of individual rights emerged. These crucial developments can be viewed as two polarised pairs: despotism versus democracy, and collective versus individual. These two sets of forces could be seen clearly at work in

European history and Burgmann contrasted Britain and Russia. In Britain, the growth of parliamentary government had enabled power to devolve downwards towards the people and consequently fathers and sons had been able to co-exist. Russia, by contrast, had seen the fierce rebellion of the son against the father and the emergence of a radical version of democracy. England and Russia represented the two polarities of the modern world: capitalism and communism, individual and community. But both shared the same defect, they 'accept a materialist philosophy of life and set out to organise human beings as so much machinery'. There was a need to strike a balance between the interests of communism and capitalism, between the community and the individual. This could only occur if man was recognised as a 'personal spiritual being' and allowed to develop his Personality through serving the community. In other words, by discovering its religious nature as that which provides its abiding interests and permanent satisfactions, humanity will move back on to its true and natural path of development, and harmony and order will be restored to human affairs.[25]

Burgmann developed his view of the evolutionary development of humanity most fully in his 1942 work *The Regeneration of Civilization*. In this work Burgmann argued that every individual is composed of two selves: the group or social self which, through the conscience, exercises the conservative power of the group on him, and the individual self which exercises intelligence and develops reason. The social self values human customs and traditions and expresses itself in art and religion, while the individual self is attracted towards science as a means of exploring and controlling the world. Both are necessary for full human development: 'if there is harmony of purpose between the social and individual selves the mind is at peace'.

The co-operation of the two is also needed if humanity is to realise its universal obligations. The social self is small and local and requires the assistance of the rational, individual self if man is to realise his universal self; in this way local loyalties and universal obligations can be reconciled. As with Mayo, Burgmann saw the task as striking a balance between the need for local, personal relationships and the necessity of a universal bond which could unite all humanity. The task was the 'creation of a social self of universal proportions'. Equally, like Brennan, he saw the quest for knowledge as 'the activity of the whole man'. The quest for truth is best served by the co-operation of the social and the individual selves, by the co-operation of rationality and the intuitions provided by religion.

Human history, according to Burgmann, was the tale of ever greater scope and opportunity being given to the rational powers of humanity. It was this enlargement of rational thinking which had lifted man above the animal world. Pre-civilised man had been dominated by pre-rational thought in the shape of superstitions and magic. These had become part of the social self as a form of instinct and provided a sanction for social discipline. The birth of civilisation had been 'one of the greatest economic and political revolutions that the world has known'. In his account of this revolution Burgmann emphasised technological factors, in particular those inventions which had assured the food supply and an increase in population. The birth of civilisation resulted from the working of metals, specialisation of labour and the harnessing of non-human power for human needs. These developments led to new challenges and opportunities, to new processes of production, methods of social organisation and political government. In particular, these developments had given rise to war.

The effects of the rise of civilisation resolved themselves, for Burgmann, into the issue of the relation between rational and instinctive thinking and of the development of the two institutions, state and Church, which embodied these two modes of thought. Civilisation also transformed the nature of religion. The religion of the hunter/food gatherer had centred on sympathetic magic rites, myth and ritual; agricultural religion had emphasised the magical power of fertility, especially that of woman. Civilisation, however, was a 'man-made affair' which came into being when men took over farming from women. It expressed divinity in the 'clear and personal form' of the King, who initially had embodied both the secular functions of the state and the religious functions of the Church. But as civilisation developed these two functions went in separate directions as each became the preserve of a particular group of social functionaries.

The state developed as a paternal institution concerned with property and the legal, political and economic spheres of existence. The Church, as the 'God' element of the King, took on a maternal character and so its realm was that of art, education and welfare. As its roots were in the pre-civilised era when women were gardeners, Burgmann claimed that the 'Church is more deeply rooted in human culture than the State' and that it belonged 'to the permanent structure of man's civilised being'. Burgmann considered that the advent of civilisation had been a mixed blessing for humanity and that it harboured its own evils. Man the hunter had not been tamed and war was civilisation's constant companion. The only solution was the creation of a world order; but to achieve that a harmonious relationship between the various polarities created by civilisation, between instinctive and rational, social self and individual self, state and Church, needed to be achieved. A rational whole reconciling all of these elements alone could bring peace to humanity. It was the disruption of the harmonious balance existing amongst the various aspects of human nature, in particular the 'divorce between instinctive thinking and rational thinking', that lay at the root of the modern sickness of civilisation.

In the modern world, claimed Burgmann, it was impossible for man to be a rational soul or to attain harmony. Different institutions, of an incompatible nature, lay claim to the loyalty of the social self. In response, man set out to build up a kingdom of reason on his own and attempted to ignore the social self and to rely purely on rational knowledge as the foundation of society. This assertion of the individual self meant that a 'vast area of relevant and indestructible mental fact' was pushed to one side. The individual self forsakes the quest for wholeness and instead allies itself with one of the forms of the group self, such as a profession or the state. It escapes the moral force of the conscience which had previously expressed itself through the group self and comes to look upon education as merely the accumulation of information. Mechanistic explanations become the preferred means for explaining the world. The result is superficiality, the heightening of the pursuit of self-interest at the expense of a sense of responsibility, and the chaos of opinion.

More importantly, the social self has been left free to roam where it pleases, liberated from the influence of the rational self. The consequence has been the 'revenge of the social self'; hoary superstitions, including astrology and a belief in witches, have reappeared. 'The age of rationalism', asserted Burgmann, 'was chiefly noted for the most outlandish crop of nonsense the world has ever seen'. Society has become a 'chaotic, inhuman, planless affair'. This is the sickness of modern civilisation: 'the disruption of our personalities, in the divorce between conscience and knowledge, in the lack of an effective relation between true religion and sound learning'. Like Mayo, Burgmann considered that the crisis of modernity was the consequence of the breakdown of that harmony between the spiritual and the rational which should exist within the human personality. The restoration of that harmony, believed Burgmann, was the combined work of Church and state. Together they should work to form 'that social self that will give life a wholesome purpose' – the ultimate goal being the reunification of learning and religion. For Burgmann, the solution to the problem of modern disunity was a universal democracy which would harmonise the various parts of the group mind and define 'the place of each interest in relation to the whole'. It was a Utopian vision in which an enlightened citizenry would willingly seek to unify all of their activities and take on social responsibilities. 'To be a democrat', extolled Burgmann, 'is to be a whole person, trained to serve one's fellows and to find perfect freedom in that service'. Genuine democracy for Burgmann was a 'unity of harmonious activity' in which Church and state, instinct and reason, would all be reconciled, and the foundations laid for world unity. It was a unity which could not be achieved without a recognition of man's essential religious nature and its continuing role as an element of human existence.[26]

The regeneration of civilisation should result in the reconciliation of opposites as the basis of harmonious development. The most important reconciliation is that between individual and collective. There is, and will continue to be, a tension between the instinctive urges of the individual and the need to repress these urges in the name of civilisation. Hence, Protestantism represents individual impulses while Catholicism is founded on social repression; likewise, there is *laissez-faire* as opposed to communism. Both are necessary but only if a balance is maintained between them can harmonious social development proceed. In a similar way, Burgmann compared the role of the prophet and the priest. The priest stands for the conservatism of the corporate group and tradition; the prophet for vitality, individualism and radical renewal. Both are necessary if harmony is to be attained.[27]

In the modern world the key element is science and the challenge of creating a more rational world. Burgmann was an enthusiastic defender of government planning and supported a greater role for scientific and technical experts and a more rational approach to social problems. But he vehemently opposed scientism and materialism. There must be science but science considered in the light of religion and subordinated to a conception of humanity as both personal and spiritual. Thought in this new world 'to be adequate will ultimately take a religious form. In the final analysis the task for thought is a theological one.'[28]

Democracy is the way forward, but a democracy which has become imbued with a living myth capable of 'releasing the reservoirs of human nature' and 'an atmosphere which people breathe, a faith by which people live'. The vital living individual seeking to serve, like the prophet, is as essential as the order and stability provided by established traditions. In this regard, Burgmann's attitude to nationalism was contradictory. At certain stages he indicated that democracy was not possible without a well-established nationalism, at other times he complained that nationalism was cramping democracy and the liberal spirit and needed to be transcended.[29] It is clear, however, that Burgmann looked to a brotherhood of man, an international democratic and co-operative order. Again, his vision of democracy took on powerful Utopian elements; he seems to have desired an international order which reflected the spiritual and religious attainments of the mature individual.

This ideal international order was the ultimate product of the expanding circle of human sympathy and the increase in human rationality.[30] Considered in this light Burgmann's writings are perhaps the noblest, if most idealistic, statement of the tradition of Cultural Liberalism. In them are to be found all the central elements: a faith in scientific rationality, a belief in service as the expression of civic humanism, and a vision of humanity as vital and spiritual. For him, the path of Nature led to a society composed of personalities who could will harmony and enable continuous integrated social development. Social harmony was possible because the path of Nature was founded on an integrated human nature. The task was to restore that integrity. Ultimately all the polarities of the world could, and would, be reconciled.

Mayo: Restoring the Social Fabric

Elton Mayo is now primarily remembered for his 'human relations' approach to industrial psychology and for the Hawthorne experiments which he conducted while working at Harvard University. His approach to such problems grew out of the ideas he developed in Australia, particularly during his years at the University of Queensland during and after World War I.[31] The product of a well-known Adelaide medical family, Mayo had initially begun to train for a medical career but his interest turned to psychology and psycho-analysis. After a period spent lecturing in psychology and philosophy at the fledgling University of Queensland limited opportunities drove him to move to America in the early 1920s.

Like Burgmann, Mayo sought to bring harmony to individuals and to a social order torn apart by the divisions created by the coming of modernity. He also was interested in psycho-analysis and sought to preserve the integrity of the 'whole person' in opposition to the mechanistic and utilitarian tendencies of the modern world, tendencies which he believed were embodied in the modern state. Some commentators have seen his anti-statism as perhaps the most characteristic feature of his thought.[32] From an American or English perspective this might seem puzzling, but in the Australian context it is quite understandable. As we have seen, both Irvine and Francis Anderson had viewed favourably the role which the state had adopted in Australia and regarded it as aiding the cause of social progress. Nevertheless, both had been worried about the ability of the state to crush individual initiative and squeeze the life out of society. Irvine believed that there was a spontaneity and creativity which lay outside the state while Anderson argued that society was the place where free movement, manifold activities and spontaneous forms of self-organisation could occur.[33] As Vitalists, both placed the vital forces within individuals and society.

In his Lectures on the State, Irvine did discuss Belloc's idea of the Servile State and this concept became increasingly important amongst intellectuals in Australia.[34] Already, in 1892 C.H. Pearson had pointed to the growing power of the state and the consequent decline of independent activity both by individuals and free social institutions.[35] The capacity of the state to dominate and direct the life of society worried many intellectuals in Australia during the first half of the twentieth century, including Vance Palmer and John Anderson, as they sought ways to keep the vital spark alive in a sterile and deadening world.[36]

The problem of the Servile State arose for the Cultural Liberals because they believed that the rationality of the state should be the product of the wills of the individuals who compose it. It is those individuals who alone are vital; apart from them the state is inert and mechanical. While society is living and organic the state is lifeless and inactive; the proper relationship between society and state must accordingly give primacy to the living, growing society rather than to its artificial creation, the state.

Irvine and Francis Anderson could support state action on the basis that this action expressed the will of those individuals composing society. But Mayo believed that this relationship between society and the state was no longer working properly and that the mechanical principles of the state had become dominant, thereby preventing the natural organic growth of society. In other words, the prophecies of Pearson were coming to pass and the energy and vitality of society were running down as a prelude to degeneration.

Mayo's attraction to the organic view of society derived from his medical background.[37] A vision of society founded on organic and medical conceptions came naturally to him. The key elements in his position may be summarised as follows:

1 Society and its wider manifestation, civilisation, is best considered as a living and growing organism.
2 The state is a human product and fundamentally mechanical and inert.
3 Human beings, left to themselves, are naturally co-operative.
4 The key to healthy social growth lies in those co-operative groups which embody traditions of skill and profession. Considered collectively these traditions compose civilisation.

For Mayo, as for Burgmann, the growth of civilisation was a natural process which involved both a growing rationalisation and the expansion of the human capacity for vision and co-operation. The problem was to explain why this natural growth was not taking place and why society had instead moved on to an unnatural path dominated by mechanistic principles. Mayo began his explorations into this problem during World War I stimulated by the deep passions and irrationality which that war had brought to the surface. In particular, he was disturbed by the depth of class hostility and conflict and sought ways and means to restore harmony to society. With his desire to achieve a rational social order in which a balance existed between a wider vision and scientific rationality, Mayo was extending Cultural Liberalism into a domain which was fundamentally more secular than that envisaged by Anderson or Burgmann. His fundamental vision was formulated before he left Australia in 1922, and can be discerned in the two major pieces he published before departing. As we shall see, his American works were essentially an elaborate and more sophisticated reworking of these ideas.

In *Democracy and Freedom*, published in 1919, Mayo was concerned to discern those circumstances under which individual and social growth could occur in a positive and healthy fashion. In this regard, two issues took on a particular significance. Firstly, what is the role of knowledge within society and how is knowledge discovered, developed and transmitted? And secondly, what is, and should be, the role of the state in its relationship to society?

Mayo's model for the growth of society and civilisation had its roots in the Romantic tradition of slow, organic evolutionary growth. Usually this tradition is associated with the word 'culture' but Mayo used this word only once in this work, and then in a pejorative sense. Mayo associated 'culture' with the German *kultur* which he considered to be something imposed by the state. For Mayo the key words were 'civilisation' and 'society'. At first this may appear odd to anyone accustomed to the civilisation versus culture and society versus community distinctions. Mayo, however, was not working within that particular vocabulary. To a certain extent he meant by 'civilisation' and 'society' what other writers mean by community and culture, except that he did not link them to particular national cultures. Indeed, he was suspicious of the idea of 'self-determination' which, he said, when pushed to extremes becomes 'a modified form of Prussianism'. Both civilisation and society were, for Mayo, universal in nature and transcended national borders. Culture was national and invariably a tool of the state; rather than growing and evolving it was imposed so that citizens could be fitted into a pre-determined mould.

In contrast to this mechanical and coercive conception of *kultur*, Mayo presented a picture of civilisation as evolving through a slow process of self-development. As with individuals, societies slowly mature as they develop their abilities and capacities. Social growth should occur in a similar fashion; it is 'the accretion of slow centuries'. Civilisation, the expression of this social growth, is not an abstract set of relationships but 'concrete and actual in social traditions'.

For Mayo, this social growth was crucial in any discussion of the role of the state: human beings and the social traditions to which they belong must be allowed to unfold and develop. Through social growth men and women acquire new knowledge and new powers; they enlarge their spheres of activity. Put another way, civilisation is a collection of social traditions which evolve over the centuries, thereby enabling their members to increase their knowledge and enlarge their outlook. As Mayo put it, for individuals, society offers a sphere of activity in which ancestral tradition and present fellowship combine to aid and stimulate their powers of self-development.

Social development must preserve and encourage these social traditions. 'Man considered merely as an individual, alters little from age to age', claimed Mayo. 'It is in respect of knowledge and power to use, of social custom and tradition, and of capacity for depth of vision – it is in respect of these qualities that man changes; and it is these changes which make history.' As man 'advances to new powers and wider social relationships' the social order changes, and it is important that these changes be positive and take into account the historical social structure of civilisation. The basis of social organisation was, for Mayo, systematic co-operation, the will for its members to collaborate. If growth is to occur in an orderly and harmonious fashion then co-operation must be developed and extended. In addition, the growth of civilised society means a progressive rationalisation: 'Present-day humanity, in spite of party politics is far more widely capable of reasoned processes of thought than preceding generations.'

To describe the collective will of 'the complex and purposive activities which hold the traditions of civilisation and form its growing point', Mayo coined the term 'social will'. By this he meant the concrete expression of real people engaged in activities which are the product of traditions, as opposed to the abstract general will of that artificial construction 'the people'. 'The people' is simple and abstract; 'the social will' is the complex product of a collection of actual social traditions. Mayo, indeed, emphasised both the concreteness and the complexity of the social will. It finds expression: 'in moral institutions such as common law, equity, marriage and the law of contracts . . . in the various professions and trades, each of which conserves some special type of skill in the interest of the community'. The idea of the 'social will' was closely linked to Mayo's view of the way in which knowledge is constituted. Knowledge is the product of traditions transmitted from one generation to the next; 'the contribution of each successive generation to this common stock is relatively small'. It is the skill of individuals trained in these traditions which enables the written texts which they use to be interpreted. Only if the structural conditions are favourable can these traditions develop and be improved.

Mayo was anti-constructivist; knowledge was not something built up by individuals from the raw data presented to them by the world but was embedded in, and appropriated through, traditions. 'The social will' emerged out of the interaction of these traditions and the social order which it sought to express was not man-made. Despite his concern with the proper development of 'the social will', Mayo did not really explain how it could express itself as an identifiable entity. Nevertheless, it is the crucial element for an understanding of Mayo's conception of the relationship between society and the state. Industries were, for him, 'social functions' which is to say that he conceived of them as component parts of a greater whole, contributing to the maintenance and integrity of that whole. Hence he emphasised the fact that 'we are all creatures of an occupation'. Individuals are to be considered not as atomistic units but as members of specific traditions defined in occupational terms. It is curious that the only traditions recognised by Mayo were professional; he said nothing about family or religion or culture. This would seem to reflect the centrality of work and occupation in Australia at the expense of more traditional social institutions.

The social will is the collective and apparently harmonious expression of those social functions which compose a society. Party politics cannot express this unity because its starting point is the abstract individual. For Mayo, the central question was how to maintain the healthy growth of these 'social functions' and ensure their collaboration 'in the complex purposes of civilisation'. This can only be achieved if a proper relationship between state and society develops and if evolution is allowed to proceed in a natural and normal fashion. Mayo argued that the role of the state was to aid social development, and to 'conserve for the community its freedom of growth'. To that end the state cannot, and should not, initiate social change. Its role is to follow in the wake of social growth and to formalise those changes in law, to 'record and enforce moral relationships'. Human beings, the product of nature, will always precede their creation, the state. The assumption is that the unhindered and natural unfolding of human powers will lead to beneficial consequences. The state must not be permitted to interfere with this unfolding but must keep to its proper allotted function.[38]

Such a view only makes sense if it can be established that there exists a natural or normal process of social development. Mayo clearly believed that such a normal path of development did exist and his model was that of human individuals maturing and developing their powers in a harmonious and unified fashion. He abhorred both political revolution and religion founded on violent conversion experiences.[39]

Mayo did not concede that normal social development could therefore be taken for granted. Rather it had to be continuously worked for, 'constantly reachieved by the right use of reason'. There must be sane and rational public discussion and the continuous political education of the masses. But the most important factor making for social growth derived from Mayo's view of human beings as occupational creatures: 'It is the work we do for the community that determines the angle from which we see society and the world.' For a society to grow in an integrated fashion occupational groups must view themselves as fulfilling some useful function and the individuals composing those groups must feel that their work is socially necessary. More, however, is required. Mayo believed that it was essential for individuals not to be trapped by the outlook of their occupation but to look beyond it to the greater good of the social whole. Normal social growth can only occur if the various occupational groups actively co-operate. The common interest must not only prevail but must also be recognised as the common interest; civilisation depends for its survival on its 'capacity to achieve a social condition that will subsume castes under a community of interest and purpose'.

In Mayo's picture civilisation emerges as a complex organism composed of a number of 'industrial functions' which all contribute to its growth and stability. A healthy organism is one in which the various 'functions' all work together, just as the organs of the body work together to produce a healthy individual. Just as the individual matures into a more rational and integrated personality so society should take the same path. But, claimed Mayo, this was not occurring and modern social growth was neither healthy nor integrated nor rational. Modern democracies, Australia in particular, had failed to encourage sane rational debate of public matters. Instead, irrationalism was rampant; discussion about public matters was dominated by emotion and sentiment. Mayo claimed that the skilled politician appealed to the unconscious and emotional elements in human nature – he stimulated unreasoned fears. At election time he aroused and encouraged these fears. The deplorable but necessary consequence was 'the fear and nascent hatred which obtains between suburban drawing-rooms and Trade Halls in Australia'. Democracy, concluded Mayo, deliberately discourages reasoning and works against the growth of a healthy, rational social order whose members willingly co-operate with each other.

The root of this irrationality lay, for Mayo, in the disorderly growth of modern civilisation. Occupations had lost their sense of being a social function; only a few favoured professions, such as law and medicine, retained some vestiges of this sense. In place of this model of healthy organic growth there had emerged a conception of society as a scene of conflict between classes pursuing irreconcilable interests. It is as if the parts of the body had decided to compete against each other rather than working for the well-being of the whole body. Mayo traced this 'disease' back to the 'extreme industrial chaos' of the early nineteenth century and its division of society into two opposing groups: workers and employers. These divisions had hardened as each side developed a class outlook. Even worse, claimed Mayo, the divisions had become 'more complete in Australia than in other countries; industrial grievances have been generalised into a political party issue'.

The nineteenth century commercial system had deprived workers of their sense of social function and of all right to intelligent self-direction in their work. Individualism, competition and class hostility had come to replace co-operation, a sense of the common good and social function. Modern industrialism shattered social order, threatening the natural process of gradual evolution with the possibility of decay and chaos. Hence Mayo wrote: 'Class hostility means decadence, and methods of dealing with "industrial unrest" which admit and seek to perpetuate the fact of class-hostility are no more than steps downward on the easy path to destruction.'

There is a clear contrast: healthy growth, or the loss of vigour and energy leading to destruction. Conflict could only lead to decay. This conflict had given rise to two parties: the advocates of individualism and those of class war. Mayo conceded that both sides could create a logical case for their position once the premise of conflict was accepted. But he claimed that such arguments ultimately fail because they are developed out of 'over abstract and biased theories'. In so doing, Mayo was making a connection between the development of a particular type of society, one founded on competition, individualism and conflict, and a particular mode of knowledge, that is, abstract and sensationalist. The rise of the former had encouraged the latter. This contrasts with his ideal model of knowledge as the concrete product of specific traditions.

Democracy, founded on abstraction, had failed to come to terms with the social will. It had disregarded the actual historic structure of a civilised society and sought to put in its place an 'artificial organisation'. Mayo believed that with the extension of the franchise, individualism and sensationalist psychology had run riot. Modern democracy, like modern economics was founded on the abstract individual; abstract entities, such as the people, had come to replace realities such as 'the social will'.

As well as democracy, the growth of industrialism had led to the development of state control and regulation. This had also been a failure because state control rested on the unsound foundation of abstract knowledge. Ignoring the social will, state control could secure only 'an apparent unity' but could do nothing to 'promote real unanimity or mutual understanding'. It could not heal the rift between the two major conflicting groups of modern society: 'State control, in the form of industrial arbitration, tends to stereotype and make permanent the social fissure between employing classes and the employed.'

Political solutions to matters of social conflict cannot work because they rely on a mode of knowledge and a way of doing things which ignore social reality. Both socialism and *laissez-faire* make use of devices such as political organisation which are constructed out of abstract knowledge. Consequently, the state, via arbitration, 'is set the hopeless task of producing by regulation that which can only be spontaneous – growth'. Regulation is no substitute for the reality of people co-operating together to solve their problems. 'Human nature', contended Mayo, 'may be trusted to work out a gradual solution'. But it can do so only if it bases itself on the actual historic structure of civilised society. Democracy has failed to do this; instead it has 'been forced to substitute an artificial organisation for such structure. And this artificial substitute for human co-operation has brought all kinds of ills and abnormalities in its train.' All forms of mechanical regulation – be they that of state regulation or the 'system' of the practical businessman – are to be rejected on this ground.

Democracy, according to Mayo, has failed to recognise the social importance of knowledge and skill and placed too great a reliance on mechanical contrivances such as political organisation, legislation and 'systems'. But 'man can be saved by man alone'. The underlying principle of democracy, he continued, was a 'positive belief in social autonomy', the faith that men, considered as members of concrete traditions, should be free to order their own affairs. It placed 'sovereignty explicitly in the social will'. Considered in this way, democracy, according to Mayo, can provide the foundation for healthy social growth. State control is an unhealthy perversion; a reversion 'to the very condition of things which democracy was designed to destroy'. In Mayo's vision of civilisation composed of occupational groups considered as social functions, these functions can only collaborate if they are autonomous and self-regulating. The artificial 'political' structure of democracy cannot deal with these social functions as self-regulating entities, preferring instead to impose control on them. Founded on abstractions rather than realities it concentrates power in the state: unable to foster genuine co-operation it must rely on a fictitious political unity which the state then attempts to impose on society.

Mayo opposed both *laissez-faire* and state control in the name of social co-operation. Indeed, he considered state control to be the logical outcome of *laissez-faire*. Both are alike in being founded on abstract principles. For Mayo, organic social growth is necessarily co-operative and occurs spontaneously as the various social functions develop and extend their knowledge and understanding of the world. The future lay with democracy, but a democracy founded firmly on the social will and which allowed social life to grow and develop. For this to occur it was necessary to 'oppose . . . and, strongly, . . . all forms of governmental oppression'.

Mayo believed that state power originated in the necessities of defence but that it had no real place in a peaceful world. In particular, he opposed the linking of state power with *kultur*. Discussing the work of the Austrian–German socialist, Renner, he commented that 'Renner's gospel of "Kultur" and the means by which enlightenment shall be spread, does not notably differ from the doctrines of German militarism.' His ideal model was not national; his vision of the future was one in which 'the various societies of the world are really co-operating as one in the tasks of civilisation'. Properly developed, democratic civilisation contains within itself 'the social logic of peace'. In a very real sense, Mayo looked back to the mid-nineteenth century ideals of Free Trade which also had emphasised the peaceful co-operation of communities in the building up of civilisation. The way of nature was that of civilisation, peace and organic social organisation as opposed to that of state control, culture and war. If democracy recognises the supremacy of the social will as expressed in its professional and occupational traditions, then social health will pre-dominate and the 'social functions' will work together harmoniously.[40]

The concrete knowledge provided by particular traditions needs to be balanced by a universal ideal which links the traditions together and provides a vision of the common good. A universal civilisation requires a universal ideal as the basis of social cohesion so that humanity can be inspired towards a high purpose and liberated from the tyranny of the here and now. This is where Mayo saw a role for religion. Through religion, individuals acquire that universal outlook which enables them to look beyond the petty details of their day-to-day lives. The Church, argued Mayo in his pamphlet *Psychology and Religion*, is the 'proper guardian of past and future human values' because through it the individual could aspire to 'union with the universe', something which is of the highest value for social and personal morality. The problem, as Mayo saw it in 1922, was that the Church was losing its grip. It needed to reconsider its position, in particular, it needed to look at religion as a human fact answering to human needs and wants. 'Religion', he asserted, 'cannot build the life spiritual except upon a human foundation'. To retain its position as a spiritual guide to humanity the Church must take account of human psychology.

For example, Mayo argued that the Church must make use of the human life cycle in determining its religious practices; a youth of around fifteen or sixteen is particularly amenable to religious influences, whereas adults are more resistant; accordingly, maximum effort should be concentrated on those vital adolescent years. Like Anderson and Brennan, Mayo saw individual religious development as a slow evolutionary movement towards a more mature and universal appreciation of reality. Following William James, he distinguished between healthy-minded religion in which human 'powers unfold gradually . . . developing without disintegrating crises', and that of the twice-born which he considered to be the product of mental abnormality. Mayo believed that the pre-conversion experience of the twice-born was a form of hysteria resulting from an infantile life which had not prepared the individual for the world's wider social and intellectual interests. Calvinism, an excessive love of mechanistic theories of reality, the obsessiveness of socialist agitators – all of these were, for Mayo, indications of social pathology.

Just as the individual develops through the gradual unfolding and maturing of his powers, so civilisation has progressed through the sublimation of its primitive instincts. The primitive savage, Mayo contended, had possessed the mental condition of compulsion neurosis. The growth of civilisation was linked to a 'heightened capacity for self control'; as civilised man seeks to impose his purposes on the world, he finds that he must use his instinctive impulses to 'fund' energy for other activities. Developing his powers into 'an organic unity of purpose', man discovers that progress can only occur if inherited impulses are developed and controlled by personal ideals of intellectual and practical achievement. Civilised man must read the unity he finds in himself into the world and discover a means of merging his self into the universe. Just as poetry was Brennan's answer to this need, for Mayo it was the source of the religious experience.

Mayo's account of progress and the religious impulse has many points of contact with that of Brennan. Both adopted a pragmatic view of human development and emphasised the fusion of individual and universe in an organic totality. However, while Brennan opted for Gnosticism, Mayo regarded Christianity as the best way to achieve a measure of harmony. Unlike Hinduism, he argued, Christianity insists on the right relationship between two ways of thinking: meditation which widens our mental horizons and gives us vision, and concentration which gives us knowledge of lesser detail. We 'must live in the world', Mayo insisted, 'but we must look beyond it to the universe'.

A balance must be made between the world of everyday activities and the broader vision of religion. If too much attention is concentrated on the matters symbolised by modern economics, that is, on the avoidance of pain and the pursuit of pleasure, the result will be self-absorption and the possibility of social unrest and mental breakdown. Religion provides the necessary counter to this awful prospect:

> The civilisation that cannot number amongst its leaders men such as this [that is, men with vision] is surely doomed. Vision is the mental quality which inspires man to achieve knowledge and to construct a social order. And it is by reason of lack of vision in their leaders that the people of today are like to perish.[41]

When Mayo moved to America, to fame, glory and a professorship at Harvard, he carried with him the intellectual baggage he had developed in Australia. His two major works, *The Human Problems of an Industrial Civilization* and *The Social Problems of an Industrial Civilization*, essentially refined and elaborated on his established position.[42] New influences, such as Durkheim and Piaget, were assimilated into the framework he had worked out during his years in Brisbane. In *The Human Problems of an Industrial Civilization* the familiar dichotomy between social function, social integrity and co-operation on the one hand, and abstract individualism and the state on the other, formed the basis of his general discussion. He discussed the disorderly nature of modern society and attributed this to the breakdown of social control and the rise of political control 'as the sole organ in actuality of social organization' in the nineteenth century. The ultimate consequence of this destruction was that 'at the point of its highest culmination the social order is annihilated and a solitary organizing activity, the political State, is left facing "a disorganized dust of individuals"'.[43]

In *The Social Problems of an Industrial Civilization* Mayo reworked his ideas again in a more sophisticated fashion. Again, he emphasised that lack of co-operation was the central problem and that it could only be solved locally: 'it is always in the informal groups at the working bench and elsewhere that spontaneity of co-operation originates'. The major problems of modern industrial society are that groups are no longer prepared to co-operate with other groups and individuals have become prey to unhappy and obsessive personal pre-occupations. These are symptoms of major social disruption. The same villain – mechanical, abstract knowledge – also makes an appearance: 'a rapid, industrial, mechanical, physiochemical advance, so rapid that it has been destructive of all the historic, social and personal relationships'.[44]

On this basis, Mayo elaborated his ideas about the nature of knowledge, distinguishing between the direct experience of fact provided by knowledge of acquaintance, and the abstract reflective thinking involved in knowledge about. Equally, he distinguished between technical skill and what he termed social skill. Both needed to be developed and this took place in traditional societies. But in a modern industrial society technical, abstract knowledge had developed at the expense of social skills. Mayo cited the example of brilliant students with high intellectual achievement but little 'knowledge of acquaintance' of human situations. Such students might be extremely able but because of their excessive intellectualism were often unhappy and ineffective. They were devoid of social skills. To counter this, Mayo advocated that careful observation and an appreciation of the reality of human communication be used to temper the excesses of discursive human reasoning. Where nature had

failed, art must repair the damage, and Mayo contended that understanding must replace instinct. Social skills must be taught as the foundation of social insight.

Mayo also provided in this work a revised version of the breakdown of
the co-operative European civilisation and its replacement by the social
disorder of the modern world. In the Middle Ages, he argued, the
Christian Church made every man a participant in its common work and
man's chief duty was co-operation with every other person. Christian
Europe was a unified harmonious whole in which the 'doctrine of
human co-operation remained the guiding spirit of the developing civilization'. It was the decline of religious doctrine which had weakened
faith in human co-operation; the vision which the 'larger purpose of a
Christian civilization' had provided, disintegrated. As this Christian civilisation collapsed it was replaced by 'mere cultures' and co-operation
turned into conflict between groups and cultures. The collapse was exacerbated by the economic theories of the eighteenth and nineteenth century which he described as 'one of the major disasters the cause of
civilization has suffered'.[45]

Mayo believed that religion could no longer provide the vision
required to bind civilisation together as a co-operative enterprise. A substitute was needed for religious feeling and this could only be intelligent
human understanding. The will to co-operate had to be actively fostered.
Force and state coercion could not provide the answer, nor could political or economic measures. The problem was a human and not a technical one and required human solutions. Again, Mayo referred to social
skills and to what he termed the non-logical 'social code of behaviour'.[46]
It was this non-logical, though not irrational, code which formed the
basis of effective collaboration and it was this code which had broken
down in modern industrial society.

By this stage, Mayo had somewhat shifted his ground. The emphasis
on co-operation was still there as was the suspicion of the mechanistic
solutions of economics and the state. But with the loss of faith in the
power of religion to provide a vision for civilised co-operation, Mayo
began to look at social scientists and administrators to provide the solution. Properly trained, they would be able to reconstitute co-operative
groups able to work together for a common end. Admittedly, he did say
that a 'logic of understanding', an increased self-consciousness, must
now replace the unconscious awareness of the non-logical code.[47] But in
his earlier work there was an emphasis on autonomy and a belief that a
wider vision would come through natural processes. In this later work
there was the suspicion that administrators would make use of their
knowledge to manipulate people to ensure that the group was both
co-operative and functional. Somehow, as Mayo's work became more

professional and sophisticated, the vision constricted as he became more and more concerned with the functioning of organisations.

The analysis remained as acute but the solutions became increasingly unsatisfactory. Nevertheless, Mayo can be viewed legitimately as a participant in the tradition of Cultural Liberalism as he attempted to reconcile scientific rationality and the spiritual, non-rational side of human nature using an evolutionary conception of civilisation. Even if he opposed the mechanistic model of politics and the state, he still maintained a belief in the common good which is a mark of civic humanism. The essential continuity of his ideas can be seen in this quote from his last book *The Social Problems of an Industrial Civilization*: 'A society is a co-operative system: a civilized society is one in which the co-operation is based on understanding and the will to work rather than force.'[48]

But was the vision of a co-operative social order to remain no more than a pious hope? As well as the prospect of evolution there remained the possibility of degeneration – of the unravelling of the threads of civilisation. It was this fear of degeneration that dominated M. Barnard Eldershaw's extraordinary novel, *Tomorrow and Tomorrow and Tomorrow*.

Tomorrow and Tomorrow and Tomorrow: Cultural Liberalism Turned Upside Down

Tomorrow and Tomorrow and Tomorrow was written in collaboration by Marjorie Barnard and Flora Eldershaw under the name M. Barnard Eldershaw. Both women were graduates of the University of Sydney but had faced limited career opportunities in the Sydney of the 1920s and 1930s. Marjorie Barnard became a librarian and Flora Eldershaw a schoolmistress. They collaborated together on a number of novels and other works, the first being the prize-winning *A House is Built. Tomorrow and Tomorrow and Tomorrow*, their only political novel, was censored for political reasons during World War II before finally being published in 1947 as *Tomorrow and Tomorrow*. The entire, uncensored version was not published until 1983.

One of the key elements of Cultural Liberalism, as we have encountered it thus far, was its hope that ultimately evolution would lead to a better world. Cultural Liberals recognised that regression and degeneration were possibilities especially in the crisis-ridden twentieth century, but they maintained a Utopian hope that ultimately reconciliation could take place and the reign of harmony begin. Science, citizenship and spirituality could yet be combined and the realm of culture be established. The possibility of progress rested on the autonomous, 'spirituality active' individual capable of developing a vital power and bringing a rational order into existence through his or her will. Barnard and Eldershaw challenged this view.

Tomorrow and Tomorrow and Tomorrow has often been read with regard to its relationship with the Palmer circle.[49] It can also be read as a contribution to the conversation and argument of Cultural Liberalism. The Cultural Liberals·and the Palmers were concerned to establish some liberating force capable of saving Australia from servility. Marjorie Barnard and Flora Eldershaw had both been students of liberal historian George Arnold Wood. According to Barnard, 'George Arnold Wood ... had influenced me deeply. I was, and remain, a 19th century liberal' and it is no accident that 'liberty' lies at the core of the book.[50] The novel deals with many of the standard twentieth century liberal/progressivist concerns including the place of rationality and science, eugenics and degeneration. If anything, *Tomorrow and Tomorrow and Tomorrow* illustrates the enormity of the task facing Cultural Liberalism by World War II.

Barnard Eldershaw believed in liberty and the importance of the individual. But a black pessimism and a mood of despair pervades this novel such that it sometimes appears to invert the expectations of Cultural Liberalism. Instead of evolution it explores degeneration, and in place of the harmony of reason and spirituality it considers their conflict. Nevertheless, this novel clearly stands in the tradition of Cultural Liberalism especially in terms of the primacy it accords to the living spirit of culture.

'A sick world separates men, a living healthy world brings them together. The loneliness of the individual is the index of the system's decay.'[51] Here we have the traditional liberal model that in a living, organic community human nature will expand and reach out towards other human beings. Only Barnard Eldershaw plot this development in reverse; instead of evolving towards an organic harmonious state in which human nature realises its full potential, both of the societies portrayed in the novel – the capitalist world of the twentieth century and the technocratic socialist world of the twenty fourth century – are in a state of degeneration. Neither society embodies the harmony of culture.

The two societies can also be viewed as two possible pictures of twentieth century Australia. First, there is the commercial world ruled by competition, profit and the laws of economics, that realm of amoral necessity ruled by the iron law of cause and effect in which not even God will intervene to ease the burden of those who suffer at its hands.[52] Second, there is the rational world of co-operation and science dreamed of by the intelligentsia although lacking the important vital spark deemed so necessary by thinkers such as Irvine and Francis Anderson.[53] Although Barnard Eldershaw found the latter preferable to the former, both are subject to degeneration. Without some sort of spiritual principle, of which imagination and liberty are just different aspects, even a rationally ordered society will degenerate into servility. Both societies can thus be examined as instances of degeneration; then it will be possible to consider the relationship of liberty and the imagination to this degeneration.

Degeneration has always lurked in the shadow of progress, and fear of it stimulated the desire to work harder to ensure that evolution stayed on its true path. The degenerate present, the target of investigative mud-rakers, must not be allowed to ruin the glorious future. Fear of degen-eration had been present in Australia in the 1880s and 1890s; it had inspired Pearson's study of national character and stimulated Higgins to establish a 'new province for law and order'.[54] Both Gordon Childe and Frederic Eggleston recognised that evolution could regress and advanced social forms lapse into primitive ones. This was how they inter-preted National Socialism.[55] In *Tomorrow and Tomorrow and Tomorrow* these fears are unleashed and allowed full expression.

The question of rationality is central to Barnard Eldershaw's vision of the progress of twentieth century degeneration. The people of the twenty fourth century use the land rationally. So had the First People who had preceded the Australians;[56] they 'had lived scientifically follow-ing a rational, adjusted, permanent design'. The Australians had lived in an irrational manner, a 'very strange people, full of contradictions, adaptable and obstinate'. They lived 'in a perpetual high gale of un-reason', their 'whole life was stormy and perverse' while their cities were 'great vortices of energy that carried them nowhere'.[57]

This irrationality found its expression in their relationship with the earth. They 'begot a multiplicity of hybrid, unco-ordinated patterns and left upon the earth itself a half-meaningless scrabble. Their movements had been turbid and without rhythm.' Their whole style of life lacked an overall rational design; instead of a harmonious rhythm founded on bal-ance and order – a sort of modern Pythagorianism – 'they laid a different pattern on the earth, a free pattern, asymmetrical never completed'. They did not live in harmony with the earth, they did not follow nature and the rules that she had established for human existence. In this regard, Barnard Eldershaw were perhaps closer to the picture of nature painted by the Free Traders than they were to that of the Protectionists. They did not perceive nature as an amoral realm of necessity but rather as a pos-sible prototype on which to model human existence. The problem of the Australians was that they sought to impose an unnatural and destructive pattern of life on the world – and suffered the consequences. The source of this destructive force was competition and the search for profit: 'In competition men's efforts cancelled out . . . when competition merged into monopoly they were worse off, for as the forces became more power-ful they were more destructive. A terrible logic worked itself out.'

The laws of economics became positively malevolent. Unlike Northcott and Hancock, who viewed them as forces of necessity with which Australians had to deal if they were to have any possibility of realising their ideals, Barnard Eldershaw saw economic values as a positively evil force leading to the degradation of the character of individuals and of society as a whole. Twentieth century Australia is a sick world dominated by unnatural appetites and irrational patterns of life, 'all mad and strange and wanton'. Moreover, once in place, the irrational pattern of competition grinds on until the ultimate degradation is achieved. The logic of cause and effect works itself out with awesome consequences; hence Barnard Eldershaw chronicled the progress of an unnatural principle as it necessarily moves towards its goal.

Twentieth century Australia and the story of Harry Munster is intended to illustrate the process of degeneration under the guiding star of competition. This degeneration, however, is the mirror image of evolution. Evolution is meant to lead to the growth of social bonds through the extension of social sympathy, an increase in rationality and a strengthening of the spiritual principle in the world. In the world portrayed by Barnard Eldershaw, irrationality dominates, spirituality declines and social bonds break down. Moreover, this process of degeneration through competition occurs primarily in that most unnatural of settings – the city. That the city is the centre of twentieth century irrationality is apparent from the presentation of Sydney as it was in 1924: 'It was all without pattern or direction; no common purpose or thought held the crowd together, an infinite criss-cross of destinies, in the mass illegible and insignificant.'[58]

The pattern of life has nothing binding it together; and yet, for Cultural Liberals including both Mayo and Eggleston, it was precisely a well-developed rational pattern consciously willed by every member sharing in it which marked out a highly evolved civilised community.[59] But in Barnard Eldershaw's favourite word, all is 'phantasmagoria', an irrational 'whirl of activity' in which all is 'vastly, impressively unreasonable' and 'The people do little that is reasonable'.[60] All of this description makes sense if Barnard Eldershaw actually believed that there was a rational pattern of life, something along the lines of Northcott's national efficiency or Cole's personal efficiency, in which people were not deluded by advertising or seduced by gambling; nor did they eat greasy things out of paper bags.[61] This picture of the destructive effects of competition is repeated several times. For example:

Man building his life in repetitive images from bargain sale to war, from competitive bread winning to competitive nationalism . . . Gambling, astrology, necromancy, quacks, faith healers, fortune tellers . . . The city making men in its image, conditioning their characters as well as their daily lives . . . Increase reason and you strengthen magic, drive men into a mass, and everywhere the cracks of separation widen.[62]

As the book continues and depression turns into war, so the irrational elements intensify and the degeneration moves at a quickening pace. Once war is upon them the people are infected by the virus of war – 'There was at last no corner left in any man's mind where he could escape it' – and become ever sicker.

People could not hate the enemy without also hating one another, so that within society the cracks widened and competition hardened and increased, competitive living, competitive loving, competitive suffering and death. Out of their blind rage, irritation, discomfort, the people fashioned schisms.

This breakdown in social bonds was mirrored in other forms of individual behaviour. Gambling increased 'but it was savourless since nothing had value. Crimes of violence were frequent but meaningless, merely explosions of rage against society, the number of delinquent children was alarming because they had caught the contagion. Every sexual constraint was relaxed.'

As competition intensified and people became more degraded in their behaviour, so the process of degeneration moved inexorably on towards its goal – the consequence of the iron rule of cause and effect. Equally, all the individuals in twentieth century Australia degenerate and degrade themselves, without exception. The most obvious case is Harry Munster's wife, Ally, who becomes increasingly slovenly, eating greasy things out of paper bags, spending money on small luxuries and addicted to gambling. But other characters also decay: Gwen into a hard-faced drunkard, Chris and Arnie into selfish self-centred people. Even Paula deteriorates into an aimless, lonely existence while the central everyman figure, Harry Munster, withdraws into himself and fails to fulfil many of his social obligations.

There are thus two sides to the process of degeneration. Firstly, there is the growth of selfishness and self-interest as social bonds dissolve and individuals retreat into themselves. Social sympathy ceases to exist and the souls of men and women shrink and dry up. Secondly, this deterioration manifests itself in increasingly irrational behaviour: gambling, consumerism, the search for luxury, drunken and dissolute behaviour, even the use of make-up. This is all very Protestant and civic humanist – who else would refer to the old association between luxury and corruption?

The gathering apocalyptic mood of the novel becomes quite explicable. By the time Sydney is threatened with destruction there has been such a breakdown and an eruption of irrational sentiments that anything is possible. The city is the 'Golden Calf with its head in the sand'; therefore just as Moses had done once, so now another charismatic figure, Sid Warren, orders 'the overthrow of the golden calf'. Only in this way could the people be freed from 'the symbol of greed and profit . . . only by its utter overthrow could men free themselves' from the source of their degradation. 'The destruction of the city was . . . an act of repudiation . . . by destroying the accepted mould it forced man to create another.'

The destruction of twentieth century Sydney is portrayed so power-fully and imaginatively that the process of degeneration stands out force-fully. What is not readily apparent is that the section of the book about the twenty fourth century is also a study in degeneration. The world described in this section represents not so much a future state as a strand within twentieth century Australia – that of culture as expressed by the intellectuals of the social laboratory period of development. Consider the following statement: 'Man's first need is to eat. His second need is to be clothed and housed, and so on throughout all the items of the good life. The rational means of achieving these things is through the ordered functioning of the scientist and technologist.'[63]

These ideas would have been unexceptional in the mouth of James Barrett, or even H.B. Higgins and R.F. Irvine, except that the vitalist spark of culture is absent. They also describe the sort of world which C.H. Pearson believed state socialism was bringing into being. Twenty fourth century Australia embodies an order which is very much con-structed out of the ideals of the social laboratory. The big difference per-haps is that Barnard Eldershaw portray this world as the product of exhaustion and authoritarianism whereas an earlier writer, such as Catherine Helen Spence, could portray a future composed of co-operative communes which had come about as an evolutionary devel-opment in which the middle class had set the example.[64] Spence and Barnard Eldershaw were concerned with creating a rational lifestyle founded on co-operation; whereas the former looked forward to an increasingly vegetarian diet, the latter dreamed of the day when healthy natural food would replace the regime of the greasy paper bags.[65]

The world of the twenty fourth century is obviously more rational than that of the twentieth century. It embodies all the hopes of the scientific-ally minded intellectuals of early twentieth century Australia: scientific planning, a society founded on co-operation, a more 'natural' lifestyle. It makes use of eugenics, in that one has to be certified fit to marry, and of social psychology as individuals are tested and graded to fit them for their occupation. Under this 'rule of the best' everyone enjoys that material comfort which is considered to constitute the good life.

But it is clear that this order is becoming corrupt and degenerate. Although scientific principles are meant to pre-dominate, in fact influence now determines who will succeed and get the best jobs. The manipulation of individuals for social harmony has led to the practice of 'slow, cold, scientific violence' as a means of social control. The symbol of this new order is Sfax, the technical expert, 'specialised brains, no imagination, specialised stupidity'. The vital spirit of the people has been sapped and there is a lack of creativity, imagination and a desire for liberty. Few bother to display their creations in the community pavilion, and when the vote machine is finally operated the highest vote is recorded by those indifferent to the proposal. The triumph of power is corrupting the population, buying them off with comfort until finally the servile and despotic state triumphs.

Only liberty and imagination can rescue that society from servility. It is clear that liberty and imagination are closely associated in the minds of Barnard Eldershaw and are meant to represent a vital spiritual principle. In fact, liberty is never clearly defined at any stage of the book except to state that it is that which resists power. Liberty is that force which dilutes power; but it is also that thing which makes life worth living, it is the good life. It stands for fulfilment and activity as against comfort, but unlike the scientific order to which it stands opposed, it cannot be reduced to a definition capable of being manipulated.[66] Liberty was 'only a core to many cognate meanings':

> It has had a thousand manifestations. It is immortal, ever renewing itself. It was in the creative splendour of Greece, the toleration of Rome, the brotherhood of the Christian, England's justice, the ferment of the Renaissance, Revolutionary France, the Red Star of Communism . . . And every time it was defeated. Power has always devoured liberty.[67]

Liberty is a spiritual principle which brings meaning and purpose to life. In the novel, Ren stands for the principle of liberty; his father Knarf, for that of the imagination which is equally a spiritual principle. Similarly, the imagination cannot be defined; it is that which brings the world to life and makes it real and active. Hence Knarf had 'one of those moments when his mind made what seemed to him a direct contact with reality, dead knowledge came to life in him'. In using his imagination Knarf synthesises the book he is writing 'in a single flame, subjecting it once again to the melting fire of his imagination'.[68] The imagination brings life and reality, just as an excess of facts and technique are the kiss of death to anything vital. Both liberty and the imagination stand in opposition to the soul destroying tendencies of the existing order. For Irvine and Anderson there had been a unity of science and the spiritual principle, but Barnard Eldershaw effectively sundered that unity so that spirituality and the machine stand opposed to each other. Nor does any future reunion seem possible. The battle between power and liberty is constant and is an idea with its roots in seventeenth and eighteenth century Puritanism. Here the key influence would appear to be George Arnold Wood and his vision of the spiritually active individual.[69]

The vision of the spiritual principle battling against the Servile State and of the need for fulfilment as opposed to comfort is also reminiscent of John Anderson. This is not surprising; Anderson was also a secular Calvinist and like Vance Palmer had been profoundly influenced by Orage's *New Age*.[70] Both Anderson and Barnard Eldershaw shared a vitalist conception of culture in which liberty battled against the creeping disease of servility – indeed Janet Anderson identified her husband as one of Gilbert's 'little liberals'.[71]

Like Anderson, Barnard Eldershaw did not envisage an ultimate harmony, only the need for a continuous struggle in which, historically, liberty has always been the loser. Unlike Anderson, Barnard Eldershaw did not foresee an institutional focus for the defence of liberty; indeed, their image of the university is hardly flattering. Rather, those who battle for liberty and the imagination are outsiders and potentially disruptive of the established social order. Knarf's 'life did not mesh with the life of his community' and at one stage his friend Ord identified Knarf as a 'perversity . . . a man of imagination who would cut the thongs of life and bring in chaos again'. He is a man who finds his novel contains more reality than his wife. Illil, Ren's chief ally and the most stringent of the critics of the scientific elite, is physically sick and so excluded from the normal society of her world. She has been refused permission to marry.

Despite Barnard Eldershaw's hostility towards the twentieth century, they do seem to find elements of the imagination and liberty in it. The novel is identified as an antique form able to capture the flux of reality in a creative way. And the image of the brooding Anzac as a creative symbol is matched by the sympathy shown for the individualism of the pioneers who refused to buckle under and join the system preferring struggle and death to conformity. Barnard Eldershaw clearly distinguished between liberty and competition, and yet it is the competitive pioneers who come to symbolise liberty for Ren in his battle against the technocratic elite.[72]

In *Tomorrow and Tomorrow and Tomorrow* the themes of Cultural Liberalism are reworked and its fundamental elements reassembled. Competition is condemned as a source of degeneration and yet the suspicion remains that capitalist society is not entirely unfriendly to the creative spirit. The co-operative, scientific world of the future, however, has no place for liberty and the imagination. Science is not condemned, but the possibility of a harmonious world in which science, political activity and a living spiritual principle are reconciled is rejected. Rather, history is viewed as a constant struggle either between power and liberty or between a rigid social order and a living spiritual principle in which liberty fights a perpetual rearguard action. What has been discarded is the notion of evolutionary progress as a movement towards harmony and light.

It is a pessimistic vision, one suggesting the end of Cultural Liberalism. And yet at the close of the day came its final and perhaps most magisterial expression in the writings of Frederic Eggleston.

Eggleston: The Case for Liberalism

In the writings of Frederic Eggleston, politician, diplomat and social philosopher, is to be found the final restatement of liberalism after the disillusionment fostered by the realism of critics such as Hancock.[73] Having raised the spectre of the failure of the ideal in Australia, the realist critics had to face the problem of what would replace the liberal vision. John Anderson demonstrated one possible route as he retreated gradually into the university and cultural pessimism. As we shall see in the Epilogue, Manning Clark and James McAuley both believed that the day of liberalism had come to an end and that the future belonged to either Communism or Catholicism.

Eggleston belonged to an older generation and although he passed through a realist phase, he never ceased to hold on to his liberal faith. His *Reflections of an Australian Liberal* is the last great statement of Cultural Liberalism. In this work he described liberalism as upholding 'the sanctity of the human personality' and as a spur to the 'free creative activities of the citizen'. All of the traditional doctrines of liberalism were restated in this work, including 'Personality', voluntary co-operation, a high standard of citizenship and the ultimate importance of such values as toleration, decency, freedom and personal responsibility. Eggleston summed up the 'ultimate ideal' of the liberal as follows: 'that our communities should develop into brotherhoods in which the members behave towards each other in such a way as to produce the happiest social relations'.[74]

In coming to the final conclusion, Eggleston had travelled quite an intellectual journey from an optimistic vision of liberal improvement, through a more sanguine assessment of human possibilities, to a final acquiescence in the liberal faith. Eggleston's paper to the 1914 meeting of the British Association for the Advancement of Science, claimed that it was the use of the state to check 'the undesirable results' of the operation of 'pure economic and individualistic forces' which formed 'the keynote of Australian politics'. Although Eggleston recognised that state interference had not solved many social problems he would not apply the term the Servile State to the Australian situation. The state, he argued, had been 'a dynamic agent', encouraging individuals to work towards social reform. In other words, Eggleston believed that the individual and the state were working together harmoniously in the quest for a better world. He summed up his position in the following terms: 'social evils can only be remedied by a moral advance in the individual, in a better citizenship and higher activity; it is also true that this moral advance can be promoted rather than hindered by the action of the State'.[75]

In his unpublished piece, 'The mind of John Citizen', written in the 1920s, Eggleston contended that the Utopianism of the nineteenth century had been 'succeeded by an age of disillusion'. The faith in perfectibility 'died a glorious death with Mr Alfred Deakin' and it had been succeeded by an era in which the weaknesses of human nature were more fully appreciated. For Eggleston, it was W.M. Hughes who summed up the nature of this transition. Both 'The mind of John Citizen' and *State Socialism in Victoria* explored dimensions of this transition; the source of failure was not so much the state as the inability of individuals to live up to the ideals of liberalism and develop fully their 'Personalities'.

Planning, co-operative enterprise and the importance of the state were still emphasised. Most certainly Eggleston did not contemplate a return to *laissez-faire* and its mode of individualism as the solution to the 'age of disillusion'. He continued to condemn the mechanistic and dogmatic elements of utilitarianism and the Manchester school. and contended that there was much of value to be found in the philosophy of T.H. Green and Bosanquet. The fault did not lie with the philosophy, nor with the practices it encouraged – clearly it lay with the people who lagged behind the ideals required in a modern society. And in both of these works it is the inadequacies of 'John Citizen' and 'the self-contained man' which lie at the core of Eggleston's explanation of the failure of liberalism, conceived of as a doctrine of citizenship and Personality. The future of liberalism depended both on understanding John Citizen and on encouraging him to live up to the ideals required for life in the modern world.

The characteristic feature of the modern world, argued Eggleston, was the increased power of the average man. Therefore, a study of the 'mind' of John Citizen was imperative because progress required that individuals lift themselves 'out of the mire'. He held the key to the future. How did Eggleston view 'John Citizen'?

The primary problem, contended Eggleston, was that individuals did not think in moral terms but 'on purely economic lines'. In a similar fashion to R.F. Irvine, he condemned Australians for being too 'bourgeois', arguing that the dominant atmosphere in Australia was 'petty bourgeois'. By this he did not mean the vigorous individualism which distinguished entrepreneurs and capitalists on the grand scale. Rather, he meant to describe a frame of mind in which economic values were paramount but in a much more negative way. Instead of vitality and achievement, Australians were characterised by such virtues as thrift and diligence. They sought to restrain competition and fix prices much after the manner of the newsagent or the hotelier. The objective was economic security – the possession of a house and a reasonably sized bank account. Instead of seeking to develop new industries and enterprises, Australians preferred safe investments such as mortgages and real estate. Eggleston correctly summed up the consequences of this 'bourgeois' outlook: 'Such a state of affairs dwarfs ambition and the stimulus for improvement.'[76]

It would seem that Eggleston was somewhat misguided in describing this outlook as 'bourgeois'. Bourgeois invariably conjures up either images of great wealth or high levels of culture. He was essentially investigating the 'protectionist mentality' and its roots in the aspirations of the lower middle class. Equally, he correctly diagnosed the non-liberal (and consequently anti-modern) nature of this mentality. Liberalism had failed in Australia because its culture was not liberal.

In his conclusion to *State Socialism in Victoria*, Eggleston extended his analysis of John Citizen by adopting the term 'self-contained man' from Walter Lippmann to describe him. The 'self-contained man' possessed a mentality similar to that of the rentier; in contemporary parlance such a person would be termed a rent-seeker (that is, one who seeks to gain a living through state support rather than by developing a profitable enterprise). According to Eggleston, he was still 'imperfectly individualised' though already 'on the road to freedom'. A society of 'self-contained men' could form a loose and amorphous grouping capable of common action on occasions but was normally apathetic. It was difficult to move such men in a mass, or make them co-operate on behalf of an ideal.

Any progress required that the 'self-contained man' become a fully developed and responsible individual. Again, Eggleston did not find fault with science or planning as a means of organising modern society. Planning and co-ordination were necessary in the modern world. State socialism in Victoria was in difficulties because 'the people have not developed sufficient intelligence and disinterestedness and self-restraint to work it properly'. They had failed to develop a 'higher citizenship'.

Eggleston's solution to this situation was somewhat surprising considering his former views. He advocated a move towards *laissez-faire*. State interference, he contended, was obstructing the course of nature and preventing that tendency towards readjustment inherent in human affairs. To strengthen individual responsibility the state must withdraw and allow individuals to develop freely: 'The state can never replace individual responsibility.' In this way the 'self-contained man' will be encouraged to 'search his heart' and 'awaken' to 'higher responsibility'.[77] For Eggleston, only freedom could awaken that sense of individual responsibility required if modern co-operative enterprises were to function properly. By reducing state interference he hoped to break through the shell of 'John Citizen', 'the self-contained man' and encourage him to become an intelligent, disinterested and responsible citizen. He hoped that, in this way, a genuinely liberal world could be created.

This hope for a world composed of free, dispassionate and co-operative individuals formed the basis of Eggleston's major excursion into social philosophy – his 1941 work *Search for a Social Philosophy*. This work was dominated by two primary concerns. The first was to describe and explain the transition of humanity from a primitive to a self-conscious state. The second was to discover the principles of social cohesion and to understand how those principles changed as society developed and evolved. Eggleston's basic model, not surprisingly, was evolutionary. He believed that the cohesive factor in any community was provided by the operation of the mind. In his manuscript 'Mind and community', he commented that the idea of the evolution and creative development of mind formed the philosophical basis of *Search for a Social Philosophy*. Through the work of the mind the universe is being created. Reflecting the influence of Whitehead and process philosophy (and anticipating the recent work of Charles Birch), Eggleston conceded: 'The truth may be that God is immanent; the Kingdom of God is within us and we are carrying out His creative work by our lives as well as by our speculation'.[78]

The soul seeks out ever higher and more effective operational systems to fulfil its nature and achieve a more self-conscious, responsible, free and moral condition. This achievement was not individualistic but collective; Eggleston advocated Holism. Individuals achieve this higher moral condition through their voluntary co-operation with other individuals; they transcend the condition of the 'self-contained man'. This holistic transition towards a higher state was, for Eggleston, the movement of history: 'the whole of the historic process represents an effort of the human being to achieve freedom and to assert his individuality, an attempt never completely successful'. History proceeds as the 'active human mind' interacts with the environment; as the mind develops it creates experience, patterns of ideas and institutions which express the results of this interaction. On this foundation the quest for freedom and the common good proceeds. Eggleston's evolutionary model began with two basic elements. The first was the human mind, a 'small point of sensitivity', and the second was the universe, the environment within which human beings must live and which is at best 'insensible' and often 'hostile'.

Primitive man was a mind in an environment which he did not understand and of which he was afraid. He was a 'point of consciousness in a world that was hardly intelligible to him'. Desiring protection and security he was driven to use the human method of trial and error in an attempt to come to terms with his environment. Based on experience, logic and his power of reflection he developed working hypotheses and produced systems of practical ideas. But this was not enough. Primitive man also sought a generalised interpretation of life as a whole and, as a mind in a hostile environment, he was obliged to create it initially out of analogies based on his own life. Eggleston described this generalised interpretation as a 'pattern of ideas' which, he said, must form a 'connected whole'. By 'pattern of ideas', Eggleston meant a connected system of ideas, 'a system of working hypotheses' which related the mind of the individual to his environment. Such a pattern is Holistic – even to the extent of constituting an individual's personality. It establishes a pattern of reaction which enables an individual to deal with the environment without always returning to first principles. Evolution consists of the progressive development of this 'pattern of ideas'.

Eggleston thus seems to have argued in favour of a form of Idealist pragmatism: humanity began as a collective *tabula rasa* and advanced by adapting systems of ideas which gained acceptance if they were able to explain the environment. Moreover, Eggleston saw his 'patterns of ideas' as pertaining to discrete human units; every group had its own particular pattern which it had developed over time. As a good evolutionist however, Eggleston also contended that every group passed through the same stages of development and that different folk ways were 'alike in essence'.

The 'pattern of ideas' had provided all members of the group with their individual personalities. As human beings progressed from the primitive stage so the nature of the pattern had changed. The primitive mind, dominated by fear, was elementary, irrational and uniform. Rigidly holding to the established pattern it had, according to Eggleston, only reached the stage of consciousness. 'The primitive group', he claimed, 'has habits of common or joint thinking'. This rigidity reflects what Eggleston saw as the intensely knit, autarchic nature of the primitive group founded on status and the subordination of the individual to the group.

That was the starting point. But, contended Eggleston, there must be progress; it is essential for the 'healthy life' of the group. At first the pattern is rigid and closed but it is elastic and over time is transformed. Initially little more than an automatic conditioned reflex, the self slowly achieves consciousness and becomes aware of itself. The final stage is complete self-consciousness when the mind can direct and control its processes so as to secure the best possible results. The human mind possesses three processes which it uses to develop and refine the pattern moulding its personality: elaboration, rationalisation and 'energization'.

These processes weld together into a continuous gradual process of control. The movement is from relative passivity within the environment with ineffective, only half rational, attempts to secure a feeling in life, to increasing control with professional rationalisation and some simplification or elimination of the irrational element. The pattern is modified and changed by the mind 'interpreting biological and physical facts for use in common'; evolution is a slow and gradual social process involving the modification and restructuring of existing patterns. Hence, in discussing the discovery of iron Eggleston contended: 'the human mind perceived or imagined the significance of the discovery, and erected or developed the new forms in which society could use it. The history of iron as a social instrument is as long and tortuous as any other part of social evolution.'

The physical universe began with a mechanically organised cell. Subsequently organic cells developed and finally living things capable of organising their affairs by using their minds. The movement was always forward towards increasingly more highly organised units. So it was with people: 'in all things human the progress is towards increased consciousness, independence, freedom and self-control'. The pattern remained but became more flexible. As the human mind became freer it was able to harness the dynamic urges such as fear, sex and play to achieve goals which are moral and imaginative.

As this slow process of development proceeded, quite radical changes took place. From the rigid conformity of the primitive the pattern evolved towards a more rational, independent and elastic form. Social organisation moved from status through to contract until finally the highest stage, that of the ethical, was reached. As the group evolved and the pattern was transformed, consciousness turned into self-consciousness. Independent behaviour marked by individual self-control and social responsibility came to replace group control. The pattern remained but individuals came to accept it voluntarily; in other words, Eggleston was describing the 'emergence of Personality', the highest ideal of all good twentieth century liberals. Thus the ethical stage of evolution was reached, at which point the individual became a free agent imbued with a sense of ethical responsibility, 'doing his share towards keeping the social pattern healthy and harmonious'.[79] At this stage, individuals should co-operate spontaneously to achieve and maintain social cohesion. The result was the same as that envisaged by T.H. Green and Elton Mayo: will, not force, had become the basis of the state.[80]

Strangely, for a non-believer, Eggleston used the term 'Christian ethic' to describe this higher state in which individuals willingly sought to serve the common good and work for 'the welfare of our fellows and humanity'. The Christian ethic had made social co-operation possible and

Eggleston, the great Australian liberal, affirmed that 'a socialism which relies on goodwill as its main principle will succeed'. Evolution's goal was a community of responsible, co-operating individuals who recognised 'the claims of others and a desire to promote their interests'. This ethical activity, founded on personal responsibility and a disinterested desire to secure the common good was essential if the structure of civilised life was to be maintained. But Eggleston recognised that the civilised life was under threat in the twentieth century, primarily from the discoveries of modern science and the way in which political power had become powerfully organised. Totalitarianism and Nazism threatened a 'reversion to the primitive, intensely concentrated pattern or unit'. At a more mundane level, ethical evolution was being thwarted by the dominance of a somewhat narrow and sordid mental and social pattern. The inequalities of capitalism and the tendency to use force to solve social problems remained strong. The bourgeois outlook of 'John Citizen' still cast its shadow over the modern world.[81]

The faith of Eggleston in ethical progress and the Christian ethic did not falter. If modern society wanted to avoid decay and disintegration – after the fashion described by Barnard Eldershaw – then it must reform and improve itself. It must adopt the Christian ethic and follow the path of 'creative evolution' of 'God realizing Himself in the universe and in human life'. Liberalism and the triumph of personality remained the only solutions to the dangers of the age because they were the goals of evolution and progress. More than ever the world required these ideals: 'this particular moment of world history the dynamic strength of force reinforced by science, threatens us with grave possibilities of disaster unless Christian principles are at once applied'.

The Christian ethic 'puts on all the responsibility for disinterested social conduct'. It universalises human sympathy thus allowing for a spontaneous social order founded on duty, unselfishness and brotherly love. For Eggleston there was ultimately no alternative; only spiritual principles could build a better world. The whole future of humanity 'depends on enlightenment and intelligence'.[82]

Like Burgmann, Eggleston finally adopted a Utopian vision of a liberal democratic future. It was a noble vision, although it should be pointed out that his notion that social cohesion required a single, unified pattern shared by all members of society is potentially totalitarian. Again, like Burgmann, Eggleston restated the case for Cultural Liberalism – for the unity of science, culture and civic responsibility – only to have his argument dissolve into a vague Utopianism, and lose contact with social reality. In their depiction of the wasteland of technocratic socialism and their plea for the need to struggle constantly for liberty and the imagination, Barnard Eldershaw were much closer to the truth.

Just as Marjorie Barnard and Flora Eldershaw fell silent after the war, so Eggleston's *Search for a Social Philosophy*, along with Burgmann's *Regeneration of Civilization*, stand as the last great statements of Cultural Liberalism. Perhaps it had become a Utopian dream, but it is more likely that the Utopianism represented an exhaustion both of liberalism and the broad Church Anglicanism and Liberal Protestantism which had been its staunch allies. Cultural Liberalism had always survived by performing a delicate balancing act as it attempted to reconcile its various elements. Ultimately that balance could not be maintained. In the harsh divided world of the 1940s and 1950s the *via media* of Cultural Liberalism was succeeded by the mood of either/or created by the Cold War.

And yet, this period saw the flourishing of the two last great heirs of Cultural Liberalism: Manning Clark and James McAuley. Cultural Liberalism was in their blood even while they sought to transcend liberalism and abolish it as a viable road into the future. This study is incomplete without a consideration of these two men but they must form an epilogue to it; they came to bury liberalism not to praise it.

Epilogue and Conclusion:
Cultural Liberalism Spurned?

The Dynamics of Modernism

This study has considered Cultural Liberalism as an aspect of modernity. At the core of Cultural Liberalism was the ideal of the autonomous individual seeking to will a more moral and rational social order. The other key element of Cultural Liberalism was the conviction that harmony could be established so that scientific rationality, civic humanism and spiritual development could be reconciled. From World War I the tradition was in a state of crisis, but much of the criticism of it was made by its adherents and was designed to enable it to recover its essential ideals. There can be no doubt that Cultural Liberalism owed a considerable debt to its Protestant religious heritage as summed up in George Arnold Wood's ideal of the spiritually active individual. In its quest for harmony, in particular in its desire to reconcile individual and collective, it sought a *via media* between Manchester and Moscow where the spiritually active individual could create a just and rational world. But for how long could such a *via media* be kept open?

The importance of the Orage Circle in England and the *New Age* newspaper for Australian intellectuals has been noted in the previous chapter.[1] From this source Australian intellectuals, and not just liberals, drank the heady wine of Bergsonian vitalism and were warned of the dangers of the Servile State. Such ideas were conducive to individuals raised on a Protestant belief in individual responsibility and spiritual growth. Hence both Vance Palmer, the archetypal Melbourne intellectual, and John Anderson, his Sydney counterpart, owed a debt to the Orage Circle.

The *New Age* was also the site of the birth and development of English modernism with such writers as Ezra Pound and Wyndham Lewis. The key figure in this group was T.E. Hulme who published a number of essays in the *New Age* which appeared subsequently in his posthumous

176

collection *Speculations*.[2] Michael Levenson has argued in his important work, *A Genealogy of Modernism*,[3] that Hulme's ideas passed through a number of stages as follows:

1 a Bergsonian vitalist phase;
2 a pro-classicism phase following Hulme's interest in the French right-wing political movement, *Action Française*, and his reading of Pierre Lassere's book on French Romanticism;[4]
3 a final anti-humanist phase.

Levenson demonstrates that in a mere ten years Hulme moved from Vitalism to a rejection of Humanism and its belief that religion is an extension of the vital life spirit.[5] Hulme rejected the idea of spiritual evolution and its attendant ideals such as personality, in favour of a conception of religion founded on absolute and non-vital principles.[6] Hulme viewed human nature as limited and imperfect, in need of order and Absolute values, and had little time for any of the key ideals of Cultural Liberalism. His rejection of evolution, individualism and vitalism is significant because he had been an ardent Bergsonian; the logic of modernism seemed to imply a rejection of modernity. Was this rejection of modernity, liberalism and individualism from within the tradition of Cultural Liberalism also to be found in Australia?

To answer this question it is necessary to examine the ideas of James McAuley and Manning Clark, particularly as expressed in their two works of the 1950s: McAuley's *The End of Modernity* and Clark's *The History of Australia*, volume 1.[7] McAuley, poet, editor and convert to Catholicism, and Clark, historian, prophet and cultural icon, were perhaps the two most controversial figures ever in Australian intellectual life. Both men have been loved and reviled because they were not afraid to defend passionately those things of the spirit in which they believed. Both were heirs to the tradition of Cultural Liberalism and both came to repudiate it; the two men were friends and each recognised in the other a genuine spiritual affinity. McAuley repudiated the Sydney tradition of Gnosticism and vitalism which had tempted him as a young man, and converted to Catholicism. Clark, having rejected the two dominant traditions of Melbourne, the Protestant evangelical and the 'future of humanity', spent his life peering into the void and wishing that he might yet find safe harbour in Moscow or Rome.

In other words, both men rejected the variety of Protestantism which had taken root in their environment, be it evangelical Anglicanism or the atheistic vitalism which Calvinism had become at the hands of Norman Lindsay and John Anderson. For McAuley, the enemy was Gnostic nihilism as expressed both in Christopher Brennan and the counter-culture of the 1960s; for Clark, it was British philistinism which he instinctively associated with evangelical Anglicanism. Clark seems to have hated Evangelicalism with that passion reserved by those who have felt its intimate touch. And yet for all their repudiation, McAuley continued to harbour the Gnostic virus and Clark became one of the greatest of all evangelical historians.

The significance of their rejection of Gnosticism and Evangelicalism was that it meant that neither man could accept individualism or the middle road offered by Cultural Liberalism with its roots in broad Anglicanism and liberal Protestantism. That road was closed, and the choice became limited to Moscow and Rome; Communism or Catholicism.[8] Even so, much of their spurning of the *via media* had its roots in the ideals and values they sought to transcend.

Clark: An Evangelical Historian who hated Evangelicals

Manning Clark's hatred of Evangelicalism, and his life-long search for an alternative to it, derived ultimately from his family. He wrote of his brother once trying to shoot him in the course of an argument about religion, and of his father as a genuinely religious man hounded by the 'Moore College miserables and those respectability mongers in the Church of England'. But for the Clergy Provident Fund his father would have joined the Catholic Church, because it had 'kept alive the image of Christ'. The hurt felt by Clark was deep and, not surprisingly, was matched by an intense hatred which turned into a general antagonism towards his British heritage. This antipathy was heightened by the humiliation which he believed he had suffered during his time at Oxford.

Throughout his autobiographical *The Quest for Grace*, Protestantism and Evangelicalism were not treated kindly. He claimed that the Protestant churches 'have been captured by the Pharisees' and later described them as 'the guardians of a life-denying respectability cult'. This attack on Evangelicalism often spilt over into a diatribe against the middle classes in general and Clark admitted to enjoying the role of 'teasing the bourgeoisie'. The other side of the coin was disgust with the smugness of 'Christian cheerfulness, Church of England fashion'.[9]

This powerful reaction against Anglicanism and British institutions is the foundation on which Clark built his interpretation of the history of Australia. He seemed to want to throw away all things English and begin again without them. In his 1954 essay, 'Rewriting Australian history', Clark began by discussing the reasons why the study of seventeenth century British history had previously been so pervasive throughout the English-speaking world. It contained, he argued, what seemed to be the 'secrets of political liberty and material progress'.[10] These secrets were to be found in Protestantism and British political institutions and their roots lay in the seventeenth century upheavals.

But, claimed Clark, these ideals belong to the past; 'the era of bourgeois liberalism, of democracy, and belief in material progress is over'. The liberal ideal is 'bankrupt'. Farewell Protestantism, materialism progress and liberty. In their place there were two groups of true believers to be found in Australia: those who believed in the Communist Manifesto and those who believed in the last paragraph of the Apostles' Creed – Communism or Catholicism.[11]

In *The Quest for Grace*, Clark traced the origins of this dichotomy to a 1937 debate at the University of Melbourne on the Spanish Civil War. Neither side was satisfactory: Marxists needed 'to discover the image of Christ' and Catholics to see the need to destroy our 'corrupt society' but they provided the only two options.[12] The *via media* could be relegated to history. Clark later conceded that volume 1 of *A History of Australia* was 'lacking in all charity to Protestants'. At the same time he admitted to having formed a 'romantic picture of Catholic Christendom', no doubt as part of a reaction against his evangelical upbringing.[13]

So when Clark came to begin his history he believed that the day of British Protestant liberalism was over and that the future lay with either Catholicism or Communism (which he equated with the Enlightenment). The three protagonists in the coming of civilisation to Australia were Catholicism, the Enlightenment and Evangelical Protestantism – though, in effect, the core of the book focuses on the Evangelicals. Of course, it is the Evangelicals whom Clark understood best, especially when one of the two protagonists was Clark's ancestor, Samuel Marsden. This exploration of ancestral history was a subtle form of revenge on his family, especially when it is considered in the light of his view that the day of Protestantism was over.

Clark's preferences were expressed clearly in his depiction of Catholicism, the Enlightenment and Evangelical Protestantism. Catholicism is impregnated with the aura of sweetness and light, especially in his depiction of de Quiros's dream of Australia as a land dedicated to the Holy Spirit. This vision of Catholicism is confirmed later in the volume in Clark's picture of Therry as one of those 'sons of the Church' in which the 'image of Christ lived'. The Enlightenment did not receive a great deal of treatment except to be described as a 'message of hope for better things'. Sometimes Clark conflated the Enlightenment and Protestantism, but he saw its essential message of 'the dream of the brotherhood of man' as lying three generations in the future.[14]

No, it was the ascendancy, the temporary ascendancy of Protestantism which most exercised Clark's imagination. The picture most certainly was not charitable. Discussing the Dutch Calvinists in search of the South

Land he referred to their 'insatiable covetousness' and hope for an 'uncommonly large profit'. This connection between Protestantism and materialism can be seen clearly in Clark's depiction of Samuel Marsden. Marsden is portrayed as someone who is as much concerned with laying up his treasures in this world as seeking to teach his fellows about the next. Marsden was a good, successful farmer but Clark was less complimentary about his 'powers to wean his charges from vice'.

Moreover, Clark tended towards the view held by Mayo and Burgmann that adherence to Calvinism was the sign of an unbalanced personality. Catholicism brings the image of Christ, sweetness and light; Evangelical Protestants were unbalanced and obsessive. Two examples of the obsessive Protestant personality were John Hunter who was driven by his sense of his own righteousness, and Lachlan Macquarie possessed of the desire to vindicate his name. These were 'minds maddened by Protestantism'.

Not only were the Evangelicals materialistic and spiritually unbalanced, they were the agents of 'men whose one declared aim was material gain . . . men for piece-meal reforms, rather than men of vision'. They were the agents of British philistinism 'wedded to the existing political institutions; [their] leaders both lay and clerical . . . committed to the defence of the *status quo*'. But as Clark pointed out, the middle way of British philistinism was doomed:

> in succeeding generations its power melted like the snowdrift, possibly because it did not stand on entrenched ground, possibly because what it fondly believed to be its strength, its occupation of the space midway between the Catholic Church and the rationalists, proved its undoing in the coming encounter between belief and unbelief, but possibly also because of the disappearance of that social situation which it was designed to serve. In our period they were men of achievement: only the sorry force of their subsequent history drives the historian to search for their worm of failure.[15]

The *via media* was both loathsome and doomed and would be replaced by those who possessed 'entrenched ground'. The whole Protestant tradition was damned as evangelical and the 'sweetness and light' which an earlier generation sought in liberal Protestantism or Platonic Anglicanism was now to be found only in Catholicism. Clark closed the door on the British Protestant liberal tradition as hopelessly corrupt. In so doing he had to reject the Cultural Liberal tradition and transfer its hopes into another vehicle. This he did in his vision of a world caught between Communism and Catholicism – Communism had taken the hope of progress and the promise of science, Catholicism the spiritual image of humanity. He had replaced the harmony of the liberals with an either/or and the vain hope that somehow the two would be reconciled. He was left peering into the void.

Yet despite his dislike of Evangelicals, Clark's history is peculiarly evangelical; across the pages there is a parade of foolish, grasping and sometimes wicked men, squabbling and conducting fierce and often petty battles amongst themselves. Underneath this surface of petty grasping men seeking their own advantage, civilisation marches on, material advances occur and there is real 'progress'.

McAuley: The End of Modernity

James McAuley was equally explicit in his rejection of liberalism. In the preface to *The End of Modernity*, he discussed Lionel Trilling's *The Liberal Imagination* and pointed to the contradictions and limitations of the anti-metaphysical and non-religious modern mentality – both the liberal and the totalitarian variety. Liberalism cannot inspire great art and literature, he claimed, primarily because art and literature require 'the impressive ideas of traditional religion' if they are to aspire to greatness.

This rejection of what McAuley termed 'liberalist' ideas did not imply the rejection of liberal democracy and he did refer to 'developing another liberal outlook, authentic, coherent and realistic, based on perennial metaphysical and religious principles'.[16] By 'liberalist' McAuley appears to have meant that variety of liberalism founded on secular, positivist and materialist principles. In its place he hoped to create an order founded not only on religious and metaphysical principles but embodying what he considered to be the true nature of man. This vision of metaphysical reality McAuley found in Roman Catholicism to which he converted.

But McAuley was rejecting more than just secular liberalism. Just as Clark spent his life exorcising the ghost of Protestant Evangelicalism, so McAuley reacted against the dominant 'faith' of the Sydney intelligentsia – a mixture of Gnostic Progressivism and Vitalism. Shortly before his death McAuley returned to this theme as he opposed what he saw as the resurgence of Gnostic Romanticism in the counter-culture of the 1960s.[17] Clark denounced the Evangelicals in a most evangelical fashion; McAuley attempted to suppress his Romanticism but it obviously continued to haunt him. Ronald Conway, who proudly claims the title Gnostic, believes that this suppression (and what he believes was the unhealthy influence of B.A. Santamaria's political Catholicism) had an unfortunate effect on McAuley's work.[18]

McAuley's conversion to Catholicism came only after years of having saturated himself in the literature of spiritual progressivism, ranging from Blake to the German Romantics, as well as making a systematic study of Eastern religions. In a local context, he was following in the footsteps of Christopher Brennan whose poems he read in the 1930s.[19] Perhaps it was not an accident that McAuley was for a time organist at the Liberal Catholic Church (that is, the Theosophical Church) where Brennan had earlier been a frequent attendee.[20] It is certainly no coincidence that when McAuley attacked progressivism he attempted to encompass it under the term 'Gnosticism', by which he meant a particular spiritual orientation towards the world, although it must be said that he was also influenced by Eric Voegelin's use of the term.[21]

In the early 1940s McAuley had been an anarchist individualist, irreverent and somewhat wild.[22] He was clearly searching for something, which he found in Catholicism. McAuley's reasons for returning to the religious fold are revealing. He tells us that it had been a reading of James Frazer's *Golden Bough* which had finally killed his religious faith as a teenager and that it was 'in the midst of the actually primitive that it stirred and woke at last to a fuller and more assured life'. While visiting New Guinea, McAuley was moved to reconsider the whole question of modernity and the secular in the context of 'a world in which the facts of life and death were known; a world where the inexorable organic rhythms were insistent'.[23]

New Guinea helped to create McAuley's respect for the traditional, but his ultimate preference for tradition over the modern and the Gnostic was founded on intellectual grounds. Like Hulme, he found that modernity was intellectually dissatisfying. In McAuley's writings the issue of intellectuality is central. It appears that McAuley adopted the concept of intellectuality from the writings of Jacques Maritain although he had also been a student of that most intellectualist of philosophers, John Anderson. McAuley summed up his position on the role of the intellect in the preface to *The End of Modernity* in these terms: 'deep waters of feeling are stirred, and imagination induced to disclose its hidden treasures, only under the regnant star of intellectual ideas'.[24]

For McAuley, the triumph of modernity over the traditional order meant that emotional and sensational values had come to replace spiritual and intellectual values. Sentiment had triumphed over intellect. In *Australia*, as has been previously argued, Hancock commended Australians for their desire to create a more just world but recognised that the basis of their attachment to social justice was sentimental rather than intellectual. It was intellectual weakness which had prevented the triumph of their ideals. McAuley's contention that the rule of modernity equals the rule of sentiment was firmly rooted in reality.

Traditional order, that order which McAuley set up in opposition to the 'liberalist' position, was not only founded on firm intellectual principles. It was also constituted as a 'natural order . . . appropriate to man's natural constitution' because behind the diversity of cultural patterns exist 'certain anthropological constants'. One of these constants is the basic relationship between the sacred and the secular. The sacred must enjoy primacy over the secular because only then does culture become authentic 'giving form and meaning to men's experience, serving as a principle of coherence and order'. In such a normally constituted society there is social health and stability; a traditional hierarchy of values governs the members and the 'strands of spontaneous organic co-operation' remain strong and vibrant. There is social health not yet undermined by modern 'enlightenment' thinking. The term 'spontaneous organic co-operation' immediately conjures up the ghost of Elton Mayo whom McAuley did acknowledge having read, and his picture of 'traditional society' does allow him to be placed clearly in the Cultural Liberal tradition, especially in terms of its continuing opposition to the mechanical nature of modernity.

By 'intellectuality' McAuley meant an approach to the world founded on a concrete spiritual rationality. Positivists may believe that they possess the truly 'healthy' intellectual outlook but, as McAuley correctly argued, it is positivism which has helped to create much of the social disorder of modernity by turning the intellect into an instrument merely for dealing with abstract ideas. Most importantly, for McAuley the poet, the arts in a traditional social order marked by intellectuality exist under 'the presidency of the spiritual tradition and in symbiosis with other social needs and interests'. Art serves the natural needs of human beings standing in a normal relationship to the order of things.

For McAuley this traditional order came in two varieties: Gnosticism and Catholicism. Gnosticism, the temptation of Christopher Brennan, he came to reject because he believed it became overbearing, seeking to swallow up all reality in the name of the sacred. It was totalitarian as it, sought to identify completely a civilisation with a manifestation of the Universal Tradition, wanting to mould it according to the demands of a heavenly pattern. Christianity he commended for its modesty, noting that it was a tradition separate from any particular civilisation, containing no grand system, only a 'few bare principles of natural law and a meagre deposit of revealed teaching'. Whereas Gnosticism can have no place for the secular, Christianity allows the secular sphere a great deal of flexibility and freedom to develop. Christianity has the advantage of constituting a traditional order which not only unifies faith and reason but which also provides a firm set of intellectual principles establishing the proper relationship between sacred and secular. In many ways this is reminiscent of Burke and his belief that commerce and science should remain under the restraints imposed by traditional values.

Western modernity, in contrast to this traditional order, can be viewed as the consequence of secularisation understood firstly as the loss of intellectuality and metaphysical orientation, and secondly as the transformation of persistent Gnostic ideas from the sacred into the secular

realm. Following Erich Heller, McAuley contended that modern man
lives in the age of the 'Disinherited Mind' marked by the loss of a metaphysical orientation and rational principles of order. Faith had degenerated first into fideism, then into human rationalism and finally into an
exaltation of the sub-rational. For McAuley this loss of faith had three
major consequences:

1 humanism in which man became the measure of all things;
2 arbitrariness in which the human will came to deflect the intellect,
   and
3 individualism in which the human ego received the prerogatives of
   the Supreme Being.

Out of these three developments arose the modern mentality marked
by credulity at one pole and scepticism at the other. Man's capacities are
either over-exalted or excessively devalued; the true measure of man is
lost between sentimentality and brutality. Most importantly for McAuley,
the centrality of reason as an element of human personality had been
lost; he mourned the devaluing of the Graeco–Christian tradition which
had viewed man as 'capable of reason and choice' able to 'apprehend
objective values' and become 'a bearer of those values'.

Instead of a firm base rooted in faith and reason, modern man has
moved to the circumference of his being, to the world of sensation,
instinct, will and emotion. Emotional idiosyncrasy and individualism,
which both consider man as a sentimental being, have replaced the solid
conception of human rationality. Science, considered as the 'integral
body of human knowledge', has been replaced by particular sciences;
organic cohesion and spontaneity by the application of external and
mechanical forms of organisation. The world's goods have become
objects of an inordinate passion – the modern age is one of increased
conflict, an age of claptrap, revolution, mental illness and anxiety, an age
of nihilism breeding new ideologies.[25]

Much of this critique was not new; there are similar passages in Elton
Mayo and Bishop Burgmann.[26] What was new was McAuley's need to
move to Catholicism and the second element of his critique – the attack
on Gnosticism. McAuley described modernity as the secularisation of
anti-Christian illuminism or Gnosticism, viewing 'human perfection as
the end result of inevitable progress through rationalist enlightenment'.[27] To an extent McAuley confused neo-Platonism and Gnosticism.
The nineteenth century saw a secularisation of both neo-Platonism and
Gnosticism and it has often been pointed out that there are powerful
family resemblances between nineteenth century philosophies of
progress – especially of the German variety – and the neo-Platonic

philosophies of Plotinus and Proclus.[28] Modernity owes something to both neo-Platonism and Gnosticism. McAuley himself pointed out that it was in poetry that modern Gnosticism developed in reaction to the completely secularised and anti-metaphysical outlook of the Enlightenment.

Secular progressivism, McAuley contended, had both discredited traditional Christianity and caused poetry to wither at its roots. In response to this situation poets from the French Revolution onwards made the 'Journey into Egypt' seeking 'to become Magi',[29] attempting to rescue poetry by recourse to the ancient traditions of Occultism and Gnosticism. In the process they sought to raise poetry to the status of a religion by making the poetic word into the 'Logos of a new dispensation, the informing spirit of a new age'. This is the Magian heresy to which Christopher Brennan had succumbed and by which the young James McAuley was tempted. But, as McAuley continued, the road to Egypt is really a journey into subjectivity: 'Meaning to conquer the Absolute, they instead opened up new regions of subjectivity.' In other words, such great poetry as the Magian heresy helped to create, it created only by encouraging the poet to explore the inner regions of his soul. Ultimately it was a fraud leading nowhere – the end of modernity meant that poetry had to go beyond this Romantic deviation into the occult.[30]

Here is to be found the logic behind McAuley's rejection of Gnosticism in favour of the rational faith of Catholicism. For McAuley, Gnosticism contained within it a belief in the unbounded imagination, an emphasis on feeling and subjectivity and a faith in progressivism. Like the secret doctrines on which poets like Mallarmé had built their castles in the air, Gnosticism led nowhere except to the alienated condition of the modern age. McAuley, like Flaubert, was a Romantic; he knew the dangers of its excesses. In choosing Catholicism he sought to overcome what he feared most in himself. As opposed to the subjectivity and danger of the unlimited imagination lurking behind the apparent rationality of modern thought, he found in the 'irrational' religious attitude of Catholicism a balance between reason and experience embedded in a set of revealed truths received by faith but made to suit human nature.

McAuley was both an heir of Cultural Liberalism and one of its harshest critics. By becoming a Roman Catholic and embracing the neo-Thomism of Maritain, he indicated that he was both seeking the harmony which was the promise of Cultural Liberalism and denying that it could be found in that tradition. Like Brennan he was seeking spiritual illumination, and like Mayo an ordered and stable world in which human capacities could develop and unfold. But McAuley denied that such an order could be constructed out of the materials of modernity. In so doing he rejected both the scientism of the preceding generation and their hope that humanity was evolving towards some sort of higher state. The 'End of Modernity', for McAuley, meant the end of that individualism on which Cultural Liberals had hoped to build their new order. In Catholicism, McAuley, the heir of Cultural Liberalism, discovered that which Cultural Liberalism had promised but had failed to provide.

A similar point could perhaps be made about Clark. Both men had been stimulated by the liberal tradition itself to deny the *via media* of liberalism. They had attempted to break with the conversation of Cultural Liberalism only to have their rejection of the tradition couched in terms which the tradition had provided for them. With Clark and McAuley, rather than with Barnard Eldershaw, Cultural Liberalism appeared to have come to the end of the road because they sought not to defend liberty in the face of despair but to condemn it as the very source of that despair.

Conclusion

There is a certain irony in the fact that Cultural Liberalism should have suffered harsh criticism at the hands of two of its most gifted participants. The end of modernity as discussed by James McAuley, really did mean both the end of modern Australia and the collapse of its most significant intellectual and cultural tradition. In the depths of the coldest intellectual winter of the Cold War it did seem that liberalism did not have a future.

From the perspective of the 1990s this seems surprising. Communism no longer exists as a serious body of doctrine and has collapsed under the weight of its own contradictions. Since Vatican II, Catholicism has changed its character significantly and has sought to liberalise itself. We stand in the middle of an extraordinary renaissance of liberalism which has become the dominant ideology of the 1990s. The discipline of historical study should be sufficient warning against any belief that this reversal of fortune is any sense permanent. In a decade or two there may be scholars laughing at the foolishness of the pundits of the early 1990s. Nevertheless, this revival of liberalism must affect our vision of the past and of the traditions which constituted it.

The key question must be: where does Cultural Liberalism stand in relation to the resurgence of liberalism in the 1980s and 1990s? This is a complex issue but it most certainly can be argued that contemporary liberalism owes very few intellectual debts to Cultural Liberalism. Viewed from the wider perspective of the English-speaking world, contemporary political philosophy has been dominated by the debate between the liberals and the communitarians. Liberals have been concerned primarily with the individual as the building block of the political order, while communitarians have emphasised that individuals cannot be considered apart from the associations and communities in which they are embedded.

Communitarians such as Charles Taylor and Alasdair MacIntyre have an appreciation of the religious dimension of human nature.[31] Moreover, like Cultural Liberals, their understanding of liberty is closer to civic humanism or republicanism than to the liberal idea of 'negative liberty'.[32] There are similarities between Cultural Liberals and communitarians, and indeed republicans, that would seem to place Cultural Liberalism on the opposite side of the fence from contemporary liberalism. Such a view, I believe, is to create divisions where none need exist. Hugh Emy has described liberalism as a house of many mansions although he also bemoans the fact that liberalism in Australia has been captured by 'one particular school, the economic liberals'.[33] Cultural Liberalism in Australia has been, and remains, a genuine form of liberalism even if it has been often marginal to the mainstream of Australian politics. Its significance lies in the spiritual nourishment that it brings to liberalism, and its capacity to redeem liberalism from that philistinism to which a purely secular outlook all too easily leads.

Cultural Liberalism has survived in Australia but, as one would expect, not as a mainline body of political theory. One finds a variety of it expressed, for example, in such works as the biologist Charles Birch's *On Purpose,* and in the writings of psychologist and social critic Ronald Conway.[34] Both of these men adjudge human beings as rational, spiritual creatures capable of striking a balance amongst the disparate elements of their nature and bringing them into harmony. Conway is open to the influences of Gnosticism while remaining firm in his refusal to be lured by its excesses. The current situation of Cultural Liberalism, nevertheless, is not a strong one. To understand its present circumstances and future prospects there are three key areas that need to be examined: the current state of the universities, contemporary liberalism and republicanism.

In the nineteenth century the Australian universities asserted their claim to be 'religious' institutions in a society divided by the dogmas of the Protestant and Catholic churches. In many ways this was no more than an expression of the traditional idea that the Church was that estate of human society devoted to intellectual and spiritual matters. The university was to be that estate in the Australian colonies. Of course, it never attained that role and by the early twentieth century the dominant idea of the role and place of the university emphasised its position as a servant of the state. Nevertheless, the older idea of the university survived primarily in those bastions of tradition, the Arts faculties.

The so-called 'Dawkins revolution' of the late 1980s, which has transformed the nature of higher education in Australia, once again emphasised the subordination of the university to the state. Moreover, the accompanying increase in state interference was matched by a campaign within the humanities to discredit the traditional humanist ideal of the university and to replace it with a functionalist, anti-humanist and bureaucratic one. The university environment of the 1990s has not been conducive to the flourishing of Cultural Liberalism because Cultural Liberalism stands opposed to the narrow, utilitarian vision of humanity that is at the centre of the post-Dawkins university. This is in stark contrast to the past when the universities were the natural home of Cultural Liberalism.

Contemporary liberalism does not owe a great deal to the tradition of Cultural Liberalism as it has been discussed in this study. Its roots lie predominantly in economic rationalism and in the revival of free market economics dating from the mid-1960s.[35] Intellectually, the influence of the Austrian philosopher and economist, Frederick Hayek, has been paramount and although Hayek was an evolutionist, he lacked any real conception of human spirituality or of society as essentially a co-operative entity. Contemporary liberalism's model of human nature is not all that far removed from the one that animates the post-Dawkins university. Both support radical reform to make Australia more efficient and able to take its place in the harsh world of international competition. In contrast, although Cultural Liberals had often advocated Free Trade and a wider international outlook, they had done so in the hope that this would lead to an era of peaceful co-operation when the nations of the earth recognised their common humanity.

As for republicanism, there is little in mainline Australian republicanism that suggests that it is very much more than a variety of bunyip nationalism. For Mr Keating and his fellow republicans, the republic is essentially the completion of the Australian nation. As such, it too would seem to have as its aim a more efficient and competitive Australia, the so-called 'Asian republic'. But regarding the sorts of people who will inhabit this republic and the values they will profess and seek to put into practice, the republican movement has been silent. Instead, there has been a tendency amongst republicans to accept the past of the deconstructionists and to seek to build a 'New Australia' freed from the burdens of that past.

Perhaps what is most significant about the proponents of all of these developments in the Australia of recent times is their shared view of human nature and their emphasis on discovering the means for turning Australia into an efficient nation state. From their perspective, Cultural Liberalism would appear to be old-fashioned and antiquated, a survival from the days when Australia could still afford the luxury of an ideal of humanity that did not have efficiency as its central focus. Cultural Liberalism has also been the victim of the rise of the 'new individualism' in Australia, a mode of individualism that has downplayed duty and obligation in favour of self-expression and self-fulfilment.

The crucial factor about Cultural Liberalism was its recognition that human beings possess a spiritual dimension. Even as its adherents enthusiastically advocated the cause of science and efficiency, they did so in a framework that had as its goal a humanity able to fulfil its intellectual and spiritual potential. As against the somewhat shallow and harsh philosophy of contemporary liberalism, Cultural Liberalism appreciated the richness of the human condition. From this point of view, there is much to be said in favour of the recovery of Cultural Liberalism as a tradition of liberalism capable of tempering the potential excesses of a post-modern Australia that in its quest for economic efficiency has forgotten the importance of other dimensions of human existence. By re-establishing a bridge to the past in the form of tradition there would be the hope of securing a more sound foundation for the Australia of the twenty-first century than that offered by liberals or republicans, both of whom would happily (and selectively) discard the past.

Cultural Liberalism may have been a minority tradition in Australia and its participants were often pushed to the periphery of power and influence. Nevertheless, it retained its critical intellectual power which can still be recovered and analysed through the writings of those who developed it. Moreover, by considering this body of writings as a tradition rather than as the products of a disconnected collection of individuals, the ideas gain a new coherence and order.

A tradition considers cultural and intellectual development as the product of the unfolding of an argument or conversation by a particular group of people. It does not claim universality but merely says that arguments and ideas can be made intelligible by being considered as elements of a tradition. In a way, this tradition becomes its own hermeneutic; as its ideas are explored they can be explained and understood through the conversation and arguments which the tradition has already established. Such a hermeneutic was created by combining a number of Australian thinkers under the heading of Cultural Liberalism. The tradition did become self-explanatory. Instead of a disconnected set of individual thinkers it was possible to portray a continuing conversation and argument.

The use of tradition as an explanatory tool made possible both the exploration of a number of ideas over an extended period of time and an understanding of their significance. It was also possible to establish similarities in the intellectual approach of thinkers who would not normally be thought of as belonging together. For such figures as Gordon Childe, Christopher Brennan, Marjorie Barnard, Clarence Northcott, Elton Mayo and Frederic Eggleston who would not normally be considered as a group, the idea of a tradition provided a means of demonstrating connections. One can see these connections in such themes as the desire for a coherent set of rational principles to bind society and the world together, a conception of knowledge which acknowledged the importance of science but resisted the encroachments and excessive intellectualism of scientism, and a view of human nature which emphasised its spiritual dimension.

In this way, the idea of a tradition has overcome the fundamental problems of previous approaches to Australian cultural history: the inflexibility of the all-inclusive evolutionary nationalist model and the chaos of the deconstructionist approach. As well, it permits the portrayal of some of the richness of Australian political, social and cultural ideas during the first half of this century. From Charles Badham to Francis Anderson to V. Gordon Childe to Elton Mayo to James McAuley, there was a remarkable intellectual vitality which found expression in a distinctive body of specifically Australian ideas. That distinctiveness emerged not from some essential 'Australianness' but from the interaction of the ideas of Cultural Liberalism with the peculiar nature of modernity in Australia.

And yet Cultural Liberalism ultimately came to grief under the weight of the vision it carried within itself. The key to understanding this failure lies in its pretensions to universality. The burden of balancing so many elements in the end became too great and the hopes of harmony and unity dissolved into a Utopian dream. This faith in universality was the great illusion of modern Australia. It is by no means the case that the jettisoning of that illusion must imply that what remains of the tradition has lost its significance. Rather it remains as part of the intellectual property of the nation, capable of being taken up and refashioned to meet contemporary demands. Contemporary liberalism and republicanism in Australia are impoverished because they seek to deny, elude or alter the past. Consequently they succumb to what might be called the 'tyranny of the present'. Through the recovery of a tradition rich in its appreciation of the human condition, we may not only combat that tyranny but also place some flesh on the dry bones of what passes for political and cultural debate in contemporary Australia.

Notes

1 Introduction: Culture, Tradition and Modernity

1 On post-modernity and its relationship to ideas of culture see A. Milner, *Contemporary Cultural Theory* (Sydney, 1991). On post-humanism see J. Carroll, 'The post-humanist university: three theses', *Salisbury Review*, 7, 2 (1988), pp. 20–5.

2 R. Rorty, *Contingency, Irony, and Solidarity* (Cambridge, 1989).

3 See J. Frow, 'The social production of knowledge and the discipline of English', *Meanjin*, 49, 2 (1990), pp. 353–67.

4 For a discussion of this matter see my review of three key works: J. Rickard, *Australia: A Cultural History*, S.L. Goldberg and F.B. Smith (eds), *Australian Cultural History*, and B. Head and J. Walter (eds), *Intellectual Movements and Australian Society*, in *Australian Journal of Politics and History*, 35, 2 (1989), pp. 294–7.

5 G. Sorel, *Reflections on Violence*, T.E. Hulme (tr.), (London, 1915), pp. 134 ff.

6 See D. Walker, *Dream and Disillusion: A Search for Australian Cultural Identity* (Canberra, 1976), pp. 44–50.

7 V. Palmer, *The Legend of the Nineties* (Melbourne, 1954), p. 9.

8 *Ibid.*, p. 167.

9 This is a view also expressed by Marjorie Barnard. See M. Barnard, *A History of Australia* (North Ryde, 1978), p. 13.

10 Palmer, *Legend*, pp. 48–9.

11 E.B. Tylor, *Primitive Culture*, Boston, 2 vols (1874).

12 Palmer, *Legend*, p. 52.

13 *Ibid.*, p. 50.

14 *Ibid.*, p. 70.

15 On the idea of the remnant, see B. Knights, *The Idea of the Clerisy in the Nineteenth Century* (Cambridge, 1978), ch. 4, and on the Australian context, see P.R. Stephensen, *The Foundations of Culture in Australia* (Sydney, 1935), p. 88.

16 See especially, V. Burgmann and J. Lee (eds), *A People's History of Australia*, vols 1–4 (Fitzroy, 1988).

17 See in particular, G. Turner, *National Fictions* (Sydney, 1986); V. Burgmann and J. Lee, (eds) *Constructing a Culture* (Fitzroy, 1988); and R. White, *Inventing Australia* (Sydney, 1981).

18 See J. Anderson, 'The servile state', in his *Studies in Empirical Philosophy* (Sydney, 1962), pp. 331–9.

19 On the importance of Althusser, see Milner, *Cultural Theory*, pp. 59–60, and for Gramsci, see L.J. Hume, 'Another look at the cultural cringe', *Political Theory Newsletter*, 3, 1 (1991), p. 33.

20 D. Horne, *Ideas for a Nation* (Sydney, 1989).

21 J. Docker, *Australian Cultural Elites* (Sydney, 1974), pp. 156 ff.

22 T. Rowse, *Australian Liberalism and National Character* (Melbourne, 1978), pp. 15–33.

23 For the development of contemporary cultural theory, see Milner, *Cultural Theory*.

24 R. White, *Inventing Australia: Images and Identity 1788–1980* (Sydney, 1981), pp. viii–ix.

25 H. Butterfield, *The Origins of Modern Science* (London, 1957), p. 87.

26 E. Gellner, *Plough, Sword and Book: The Structure of Human History* (London, 1988), p. 13.

27 The phrase, 'the presence of the past' comes from Rupert Sheldrake's *The Presence of the Past* (London, 1988). Although Sheldrake's position in biology is controversial, the application of his ideas to human cultures is worthy of consideration, see especially pp. 239–53.

28 A. Finkielkraut, *The Undoing of Thought*, D. O'Keeffe (tr.), (London, 1988), p. 7.

29 A. MacIntyre, *Whose Justice? Which Rationality?* (London, 1988), p. 301.

30 Rorty, *Contingency*, pp. 16 ff.

31 Carroll, 'The post-humanist university', p. 25.

32 J. Gray, 'The politics of cultural diversity', in *Salisbury Review*, 7, 1 (1988), p. 41.

33 D. Hume, 'The natural history of religion', in R. Wollheim (ed.), *Hume on Religion* (London, 1963), p. 62.

34 P. Brown, *The Cult of the Saints* (London, 1981), pp. 13–16.

35 H. Stretton, *Political Essays* (Melbourne, 1987), pp. 202 ff.

36 M. Blondel, *L'Action* [1892], (Paris, 1973), p. viii.

37 See for example, Montesquieu, *De L'Esprit des Lois*, Tome 1 [1748] (Paris, 1974), pp. 14 ff.

38 J. Gray, *Liberalisms* (London, 1989), p. 257.

39 A. MacIntyre, *Whose Justice?*, p. 13.

40 T. Fuller (ed.), *The Voice of Liberal Learning: Michael Oakeshott on Education* (Yale, 1989), p. 39.

41 Horne, *Ideas*, pp. 251–5.

42 Fuller, *Voice of Liberal Learning*, pp. 53–4.

43 E. Gellner, *Nations and Nationalism* (Oxford, 1983), pp. 35 ff.

44 J. Rickard, *Australia: A Cultural History* (Melbourne, 1988), p. x.

45 F.B. Smith and S. Goldberg (eds), *Australian Cultural History* (Cambridge, 1988), pp. 3–4.

46 N. Meaney (ed.), *Under New Heavens* (Sydney, 1989), pp. 8–17.

47 See, for example, S. Castles, M. Kalantzis, B. Cope, M. Morrisey, *Mistaken Identity: Multiculturalism and the Demise of Nationalism in Australia* (Sydney, 1988), ch. 8.

48 W. Osmond, *Frederic Eggleston: An Intellectual in Australian Politics* (Sydney, 1985), p. 50.
49 Civic Humanism may be understood as that form of humanism, deriving from the Renaissance, which comes into being when humanists choose the active political life over the contemplative life. This means that the individual cultivates his virtue through political activity. By the late nineteenth century civic humanism had also become associated with ideas of service to the common good and the state, as expressed in both Arnold's conception of culture and the new liberalism of T.H. Green. On the earlier development of civic humanism, see especially J.G.A. Pocock, *The Machiavellian Moment* (Princeton, 1975).
50 J. Gray, *Liberalism* (Milton Keynes, 1986), p. 82.
51 J. Anderson, 'Classicism', in D.Z. Phillips (ed.), *Education and Inquiry* (Oxford, 1980). The problem with the term 'modernity' was also drawn to my attention by the comments of Barry Hindess at the V. Gordon Childe Conference (Brisbane, 1990). My conception of modernity has been shaped in particular by the writings of the Gellner school: Ernest Gellner, Michael Mann and John Hall.
52 S. Schama, *Citizens: A Chronicle of the French Revolution* (Harmondsworth, 1989), pp. 183 ff.
53 See in particular, Peter Gay's discussion of Enlightenment in his *The Enlightenment: An Interpretation, Volume 1, The Rise of Modern Paganism* (London, 1973), especially chapter 2.
54 Gellner, *Plough, Sword and Book*, pp. 87, 158.
55 Gellner, *Nations and Nationalism*, pp. 35–8.
56 Gellner, *Plough, Sword and Book*, pp. 118–22.
57 See Gellner's comments on the future of cognition, *ibid.*, p. 265 ff.
58 On 1900 as the beginning of a period of crisis in European civilisation, see N. Stone, *Europe Transformed* (Glasgow, 1983), pp. 389–412. On the European analogues see G. Hawthorn, *Enlightenment and Despair: A History of Social Theory*, 2nd ed. (Cambridge, 1987). See also on England, R. Williams, *Culture and Society* (Harmondsworth, 1971) and F. Inglis, *Radical Earnestness: English Social Theory 1880–1980* (Oxford, 1982). On New Liberalism, see A. Vincent and R. Plant, *Philosophy, Politics and Citizenship: The Life and Thought of the British Idealists* (Oxford, 1984) and M. Freeden, *The New Liberalism: An Ideology of Social Reform* (Oxford, 1978).
59 Rowse, *Liberalism*, S. Macintyre, *A Colonial Liberalism* (Melbourne, 1991) and M. Roe, *Nine Australian Progressives: Vitalism in Bourgeois Social Thought* (St Lucia, 1984).
60 Rowse, *Liberalism*, pp. 11, 15.
61 Gray, *Liberalism*, p. x.
62 Rowse, *Liberalism*, pp. 37 ff.
63 Macintyre, *Colonial Liberalism*, p. 5.
64 Compare for example, J.D. Bollen, *Protestantism and Social Reform in New South Wales 1890–1910* (Melbourne, 1972).
65 A. Gouldner, *The Future of Intellectuals and the Rise of the New Class* (New York, 1979), p. 48.
66 Gellner, *Nations and Nationalism*, pp. 8 ff.
67 J. Hall, *Powers and Liberties: The Causes and Consequences of the Rise of the West* (Penguin, 1986), p. 20; M. Mann, *The Sources of Social Power*, vol. 1 (Cambridge, 1986), pp. 301 ff.

68 Gouldner, *The Future of Intellectuals*, p. 21.
69 See for example, B.B. Biggs, *A New Class?* (New York, 1981), and D. Stabile, *Prophets of Order* (Boston, 1984).
70 E. Etzioni-Halevy, *The Knowledge Elite and the Failure of Prophecy* (London, 1985), pp. 9–15.
71 Gouldner, *The Future of Intellectuals*, p. 48.
72 For an interesting attempt to relate ideas and ideology to specific social locations, see D. Kelley, *The Beginning of Ideology* (Cambridge, 1981).
73 In the former category can be included Childe, Hancock and Manning Clark, in the latter Burgmann, G.V. Portus and A.P. Elkin.
74 Gouldner, *The Future of Intellectuals*, p. 29.

2 Traditions of Modernity in Australia

1 D. Horne, *Ideas for a Nation* (Sydney, 1989), p. 69.
2 M. Roe, *Nine Australian Progressives: Vitalism in Bourgeois Social Thought* (St Lucia, 1984), pp. 315 ff.
3 See especially my 'Keeping the shutters firmly closed: the social laboratory, liberal intellectuals and the growth of the "protectionist mentality"' in G. Melleuish (ed.), *Australia as a Social and Cultural Laboratory?* (University of Queensland, 1990), pp. 12–20.
4 On the economic development of nineteenth century Australia, see N.G. Butlin, *Investment in Australian Economic Development 1861–1900* (Cambridge, 1964). On the distribution of wealth, see W.D. Rubinstein, 'Elites in Australian history' in R. Manne (ed.), *The New Conservatism in Australia* (Melbourne, 1982), pp. 67–87, and 'Men of wealth' in S.L. Goldberg and F.B. Smith (eds), *Australian Cultural History* (Cambridge, 1988), pp. 109–122. On class structure, see R. Connell and T. Irving, *Class Structure in Australian History* (Melbourne, 1980) and on the early Labour movement see W.G. Spence, *Australia's Awakening* (Sydney, 1909), and Bede Nairn, *Civilising Capitalism: The Labour Movement in New South Wales 1870–1900* (Canberra, 1970). For a general picture of the early Commonwealth, see S. Macintyre, *Oxford History of Australia, Volume 4, The Succeeding Age, 1901–1942* (Melbourne, 1986), chs 1–4.
5 On this, see my 'The Sydney intellectual milieu *c.* 1850–1865' (unpublished MA (Honours) thesis, University of Sydney, 1980).
6 *University of Sydney Calendars*, 1912, 1913, 1914.
7 L. Hartz, *The Founding of New Societies* (New York, 1964).
8 See for example, P. O'Farrell, *Vanished Kingdoms: Irish in Australia and New Zealand: A Personal Excursion* (Sydney, 1990), and my 'Australian individualism and Australian liberty', in L. Dobrez (ed.), *Identifying Australia in Postmodern Times* (Canberra, 1994).
9 Rubinstein, 'Elites', p. 70; J. Hirst, *The Strange Birth of Colonial Democracy* (Sydney, 1988), pp. 243 ff. and pp. 263–4; C.H. Pearson, *National Life and Character* (London, 1894).
10 R.W. Leach, 'A need for radical history', *Australian Studies*, 11 (1989), p. 5.
11 For a more detailed treatment of Free Trade ideology, see my 'Beneficent providence and the quest for harmony: the cultural setting for colonial science in Sydney 1850–1890', *Journal and Proceedings, Royal Society of New South Wales*, 118 (1985), pp. 167–80.
12 P. Higonnet, *Class Ideology and the Rights of Nobles during the French Revolution* (Oxford, 1981), ch. 1.

13 See in particular Hirst, *Strange Birth*, pp. 266–73, and my 'Daniel Deniehy, Bede Dalley and the ideal of the natural aristocrat in colonial New South Wales' in *Australian Journal of Politics and History*, 33, 1 (1987), pp. 45–59.

14 *Sydney Morning Herald*, 5 July 1860; J. West, 'Friendly intercourse of nations: a lecture', *Sydney Morning Herald*, 8 July 1858.

15 Antony, Earl of Shaftesbury, *Characteristics of Men, Manners, Opinions, Times*, J. Robertson (ed.), (Indianapolis, 1964); F. Hutcheson, *An Inquiry into the Original of our Ideas of Beauty and Virtue* [1726], (New York, 1971).

16 On Wise, see the entry on him by J.A. Ryan in J. Ritchie (ed.), *Australian Dictionary of Biography, Vol. 12* (Melbourne, 1990), pp. 546–9.

17 B.R. Wise, 'The revival of commercial restrictions' in *Australian Economist*, 1, 18 (1889), p. 142, and 'Cash nexus debate', *ibid.*, 1, 2 (1888), p. 10; B.R. Wise, *Industrial Freedom: A Study in Politics* (London, 1892), p. 18.

18 Wise, *Industrial Freedom*, pp. 116, 122–3.

19 *Ibid.*, p. 331.

20 *Ibid.*, pp. 331, 333.

21 *Ibid.*, pp. 123, 119; B.R. Wise, *The Commonwealth of Australia* (London, 1909), p. 334.

22 W. Scott, 'The cash nexus' in *Australian Economist*, 1, 1 (1888), pp. 2–6, B.R. Wise, pp. 10–11, J.T. Walker, p. 11, J. Plummer, p. 12, S.A. Byrne, p. 13.

23 For example, M. Simmat, 'Unproductive consumption', *Australian Economist*, 1, 9 (1888), pp. 66–9, and A. Duckworth, 'The territorial environments of man', *Australian Economist*, 1, 19 (1889), p. 147.

24 Quoted in A. Pratt, *David Syme* (London, 1908), p. xli.

25 P. Miller, *The New England Mind: The Seventeenth Century* (Cambridge, Mass., 1954), pp. 407–31.

26 See S. Kern, *The Culture of Time and Space 1880–1918* (London, 1983), p. 104.

27 On the other hand, Stuart Macintyre in a personal letter to me has emphasised Syme's radicalism. He points out that Syme followed, rather than led, the move towards Protection in Victoria. See also Macintyre's book, *A Colonial Liberalism* (Melbourne, 1991), pp. 103–4.

28 *Age*, 9 October 1880, 1 August 1888.

29 J. Hall, *Powers and Liberties: The Causes and Consequences of the Rise of the West* (Harmondsworth, 1986), pp. 156–7 and pp. 163 ff.; N. Stone, *Europe Transformed 1878–1919* (Glasgow, 1983), p. 11.

30 H.S. Hughes, *Consciousness and Society: The Reorientation of European Social Thought 1870–1930* (Frogmore, 1974), pp. 105 ff.; K.D. Bracher, *The Age of Ideologies: A History of Political Thought in the Twentieth Century* (London, 1984), pp. 17–25.

31 F.L. Baumer, *Modern European Thought* (New York, 1977), pp. 368–9.

32 F.A. Hayek, *Law, Legislation and Liberty, Vol. 1, Rules and Order* (London, 1982), pp. 35 ff.

33 Stone, *Europe Transformed*, pp. 74 ff., pp. 96–106, pp. 129–42. See also, G.R. Searle, *The Quest for National Efficiency* (Oxford, 1971) and Roe, *Nine Australian Progressives*, ch. 1.

34 'What will the coming man in Australia be like', *Athenaeum*, 2, 28 (1876), p. 18.

35 J. Roe, *Beyond Belief* (Sydney, 1986), pp. 38 ff.

36 On Pearson, see J. Tregenza, *Professor of Democracy: the Life of Charles Henry Pearson* (Melbourne, 1968).

37 Pearson, *National Life*, pp. 18, 19, 13.

38 *Ibid.*, pp. 101; pp. 102, 237, 294, 276; pp. 191, 146, 303; pp. 168, 322; p. 343; p. 363.

39 *Bulletin*, 20 January 1894.

40 *Bulletin*, 18 May 1888.

41 S. Griffith, 'A plea for the study of the unconscious vital processes in the life of the communities', *AAAS: Report of the Sixth Meeting* (Sydney, 1895), pp. 659–67.

42 P. Kelly, *The End of Certainty* (Sydney, 1992), pp. 1–12.

43 E. Shann, *An Economic History of Australia* (Cambridge, 1930), p. 341. See also, X. Pons, *A Sheltered Land* (Sydney, 1994), pp. 116–28.

44 See *Parliamentary Debates, Commonwealth of Australia*, Vol. 4, 1901–1902, pp. 4631–4812.

45 S. Griffith, 'Speech', *Record of the Jubilee Celebrations of the University of Sydney* (Sydney, 1902), p. 28.

46 W.J. Brown, *The New Democracy* (London, 1899), pp. 136–7, 172–3; G.C. Henderson, 'Democracy the theory and practice' (August 1899) and 'Democracy: theoretical and practical' (1919), Henderson Papers, Archives Department, Public Library of South Australia.

47 *Inaugural Ceremony of the University of Queensland* (Brisbane, 1911), pp. 28–9; J. Barrett, *The Twin Ideals: An Educated Commonwealth*, Vol. 1 (London, 1918), p. 8.

48 T.W. Edgeworth David, 'The aims and ideals of Australasian science', *AAAS: Report of the Tenth Meeting*, G.M. Thomson (ed.), (Dunedin, 1904), p. 9; *Final Report of the Royal Commission on the Government, Administration, Teaching and Finances of the University of Melbourne*, (Melbourne, 1904), p. 9.

49 W.H. Bragg, 'Address', *AAAS: Report of the Twelfth Meeting*, J. Shirley (ed.), (Brisbane, 1910), p. 30.

50 T.W. Edgeworth David, *Inauguration of the University of Queensland* (Brisbane, 1909), pp. 18, 2.

51 Edgeworth David, 'The aims and ideals of Australasian science', p. 43.

52 Barrett, *The Twin Ideals*, p. 288.

53 C.E.W. Bean, *In Your Hands Australians* (London, 1918), pp. 82–3; A.G. Stephens, 'Australian education' in L. Cantrell (ed.), *A.G. Stephens: Selected Writings* (Sydney, 1977), p. 429.

54 W.G. Spence, *Australia's Awakening* (Sydney, 1909), pp. 377, 280; quoted in W.K. Hancock, *Australia* (London, 1930), p. 212; Spence, *Australia's Awakening*, p. 281; *Adelaide Advertiser*, 20 July 1914.

55 W.M. Hughes, 'The limits of state interference', *AAAS: Report of the Eleventh Meeting*, W. Hawkin (ed.), (Adelaide, 1908), pp. 624–5, 631.

56 H.B. Higgins, *Shakespeare's Aims and Ideals* (Melbourne, 1907), p. 5. On Higgins generally, see especially J. Rickard, *H.B. Higgins: The Rebel as Judge* (Sydney, 1984) and P.S. Callaghan, 'Idealism and arbitration in H.B. Higgins' *New Province for Law and Order*', in *Journal of Australian Studies*, 13 (1983), pp. 56–66.

57 H.B. Higgins, *Robert Browning: His Mind and Art* (Melbourne, 1906). See also, Rickard, *H.B. Higgins*, on Higgins as Prometheus, pp. 231 ff.

58 H.B. Higgins, *A New Province for Law and Order* (Sydney, 1922), pp. 150, 61, 38.

59 See W. James, *The Varieties of Religious Experience* (Glasgow, 1960), Lectures IV, V, VI and VII.

60 R. Conway, 'The end of the great Australian stupor?', *Interchange*, 32 (1983), p. 10; on the traumatic effects of World War I on Australian culture, see B. Smith, *The Death of the Artist as Hero* (Oxford, 1988), p. 227.

61 P. Morgan, 'A world of one's own: traditions and divisions in Australian life' in R. Manne (ed.), *The New Conservatism in Australia* (Melbourne, 1982), p. 99.

62 On this question of cultural contacts, see my 'Justifying commerce: the Scottish Enlightenment tradition in colonial NSW', *Journal of the Royal Historical Society*, 76, 2 (1989), pp. 122–31.

63 See J. Moses, 'Australia's academic garrison 1914–1918', *Australian Journal of Politics and History*, 36, 3 (1990), pp. 361–76; R. White, *Inventing Australia* (Sydney 1981), p. 143; G. Davie, 'John Anderson in Scotland', *Quadrant*, xxi, 7 (1977), pp. 55–7.

64 Morgan, 'A World of One's Own' , pp. 102–3.

65 M. Wiener, *English Culture and the Decline of the Industrial Spirit, 1850–1980* (Cambridge, 1981). See also Geoffrey Sherington's comments on the public school in Australia after World War I in his 'Education and enlightenment', in N. Meaney (ed.), *Under New Heavens* (Sydney, 1989), pp. 227–8.

66 C.M.H. Clark, *The Quest for Grace* (Ringwood, 1990), and W.K. Hancock, *Country and Calling* (London, 1954).

67 On Stephensen, see C. Munro, *Wild Man of Letters: The Story of P.R. Stephensen*, (Melbourne, 1984).

68 L. Ross, *William Lane and the Australian Labour Movement* (Sydney, 1935), ch. 1.

69 D.H. Lawrence, *Kangaroo* [1923], (Harmondsworth, 1987), p. 72; p. 146; p. 379.

70 See V.G. Childe to R.P. Dutt, 4 April 1931, reprinted in *Hummer*, 29 (1990); R. Conway, *The End of Stupor?* (Melbourne, 1983), pp. 6–7, and *The Great Australian Stupor* (Melbourne, 1970), pp. 241 ff.

71 Smith, *Death of the Artist*, pp. 226–9; G.V. Portus, 'The Australian Labour Movement and the Pacific', *Pacific Affairs*, III, 3 (1930), p. 924.

72 J. Herf, *Reactionary Modernism* (Cambridge, 1984).

3 Ethos and Myth: The Dynamics of Cultural Liberalism

1 J. Carroll, 'The post-humanist university: three theses', *Salisbury Review*, 7, 2 (1988), p. 20.

2 A. MacIntyre, *Whose Justice? Which Rationality?* (London, 1988), p. 13.

3 See my 'From certainty to alienation: the development of Romanticism in colonial New South Wales', *Melbourne Historical Journal*, 15 (1983), pp. 108–18; J. Docker, *Australian Cultural Elites* (Sydney, 1974).

4 W. Osmond, *Frederic Eggleston: An Intellectual in Australian Politics* (Sydney, 1985), pp. 45 ff.

5 Plato, *Republic*, viii, 514A–521B.

6 H. Jonas, *The Gnostic Religion* (Boston, 1963), pp. 320–40.

7 On this, see D. Morse, *Romanticism: A Structural Analysis* (London, 1982), pp. 191 ff.

8 B. Croce, *Philosophy, Poetry, History: An Anthology of Essays*, Cecil Sprigge (ed. and tr.), (Oxford, 1966), pp. 1103–4.

9 M. Butler, *Romantics, Rebels and Reactionaries* (Oxford, 1981), p. 182; L. Goldmann, *Le Dieu Caché* (Paris, 1959), p. 51, note 2.

10 M. Peckham, *Beyond the Tragic Vision* (New York, 1962).

11 G. Thurley, *The Romantic Predicament* (London, 1983), pp. 1–23.

12 D. Morse, *Perspectives on Romanticism* (London, 1981), p. 101.

13 Melleuish, 'From certainty to alienation', pp. 108–18.
14 On this, see B. Knights, *The Idea of the Clerisy in the Nineteenth Century* (Cambridge, 1978), pp. 178–213. See also C. Harvie, *The Lights of Liberalism* (London, 1976), pp. 31 ff.
15 See D.S. Luft, *Robert Musil and the Crisis of European Culture 1880–1942* (Berkeley, 1980), pp. 178 ff.
16 Porphyry, 'The life of Plotinus' in A.H. Armstrong (ed.), Plotinus *Enneads 1 1–9* (Cambridge Mass., 1966), p. 71.
17 D.H. Lawrence, *Kangaroo* [1923] (Harmondsworth, 1986), p. 27.
18 R.W. Church, *The Oxford Movement* (London, 1892), p. 79.
19 S. Prickett, *Romanticism and Religion* (Cambridge, 1976), p. 97; D. Newsome, *Two Classes of Men* (London, 1974), p. 63.
20 S. Griffith, 'Speech' in *Record of the Jubilee Celebrations of the University of Sydney* (Sydney, 1902), p. 26.
21 J.J. Rousseau, *The Social Contract*, and *Discourses*, G.D.H. Cole (tr.), (London, 1973), pp. 268–77; H. McLeod, *Religion and the People of Western Europe 1789–1970* (Oxford, 1981), pp. 3–4.
22 R. Nisbet, *The Sociological Tradition* (New York, 1966), pp. 221–63; see also, J. Burrow, *Evolution and Society* (Cambridge, 1966).
23 S.T. Coleridge, 'On the constitution of Church and State' in John Colmer (ed.), *Collected Works*, vol. 10, (Princeton, 1976), pp. 55, 44, 48.
24 M. Arnold, *Culture and Anarchy* (Cambridge, 1971), pp. 11–90.
25 T.H. Green, *Lectures on the Principles of Political Obligation* (London, 1941), p. 124.
26 A. de Tocqueville, *Democracy in America*, Vol. 2, J.P. May and M. Lerner (eds), (New York, 1968), pp. 549–644.
27 Lawrence, *Kangaroo*, p. 146; S. Weil, *The Need for Roots* (London, 1978), pp. 13–19.
28 Sir Charles Nicholson, 'Inaugural address' in H.E. Barff, *A Short Historical Account of the University of Sydney* (Sydney, 1902), p. 27.
29 J. Woolley, *Lectures Delivered in Australia* (London, 1862), pp. 76, 10, 17, 22.
30 Griffith, *Record of the Jubilee Celebrations*, p. 28; 'Tennyson's "In Memoriam"', *Sydney University Magazine* (January 1855), p. 64; J. Roe, *Beyond Belief* (Sydney, 1986), pp. 39 ff.
31 G. Melleuish, 'The theology and philosophy of John Woolley', *Journal of Religious History*, 19, 2 (1983), pp. 418–32.
32 C. Badham, *Speeches and Lectures* (Sydney, 1890), p. 1.
33 *Ibid.*, pp. 105–7; p. 31; p. 58.
34 *Ibid.*, p. 130.
35 *Ibid.*, pp. 44–5.
36 On the notion of the 'saint', see E. Gellner, *Muslim Society* (Cambridge, 1981), chs 1 and 6; W.J. Gardner, *Colonial Cap and Gown* (Christchurch, 1979), pp. 43 ff.
37 A.B. Piddington, *Worshipful Masters* (Sydney, 1929), pp. 1–6, 101–20; R.R. Garran, *Prosper the Commonwealth* (Sydney, 1959), p. 76; Judge Backhouse, 'Recollections of the university – with some thoughts of the future', *Union Book of 1902* (Sydney, 1902), pp. 246–51; A.G. Stephens, *Chris Brennan* (Sydney, 1930), p. 30; C.J. Brennan, 'Charles Badham' in T. Sturm (ed.), *Christopher Brennan* (St Lucia, 1984), p. 372.
38 H.A. Strong, *Address to the Students Attending the Classical Lectures* (Melbourne, 1879), p. 13.

39 T.G. Tucker, *The Place of Classics in Education* (Melbourne, 1886), pp. 29, 15, and see also T.G. Tucker, *Things Worth Thinking About* (Melbourne, 1909); G. Dutton, *Snow on the Saltbush* (Ringwood, 1984), pp. 150–2, and D. Green, 'Training our leaders: the university and society', *Age Monthly Review*, December–January 1987/88, pp. 22–3.

40 T. Huxley, *Science and Education* (New York, 1897), pp. 137–51, 205–13.

41 W. Scott, *What is Classical Study?* (Sydney, 1885), pp. 35–6; W. Scott, 'The cash nexus' in *Australian Economist*, 1, 1 (1888), pp. 2–6; W. Scott, 'On fixing a minimum wage' in *AAAS: Report of the Sixth Meeting* (Sydney, 1895), pp. 149–65.

42 J.T. Wilson, 'Presidential address' in *Union Book of 1902*, p. 87.

43 F. Adams, *The Australians: A Social Sketch* (London, 1893), pp. 56–7.

44 W. Mitchell, *The Two Functions of the University and their Cost* (Adelaide, 1917); J. Barrett, *The Twin Ideals: An Educated Commonwealth*, Vol. 1 (London, 1918), p. 124; R.F. Irvine, *The Place of the Social Sciences in a Modern University* (Sydney, 1914), pp. 30–6.

45 S. Ratnapala, *Welfare State or Constitutional State?* (Sydney, 1990), p. 32.

46 On the 'New Education' and Herbart and Froebel, see R.J.W. Selleck, *The New Education* (London, 1968), especially pp. 190–204 and 227–71.

47 P.R. Cole, *Herbart and Froebel: An Attempt at a Synthesis* (Teachers' College, Columbia, New York, 1907).

48 T.W. Edgeworth David, *Record of the Jubilee Celebrations*, p. 95; T.W. Edgeworth David, *The Inauguration of the University of Queensland* (Brisbane, 1909), p. 18.

49 T. Anderson Stuart, *Record of the Jubilee Celebrations*, p. 77; O. Masson, *The Scope and Aims of Chemical Science and its Place in the University* (Melbourne, 1887), pp. 12–18; *Report of the Commissioners on Agricultural, Commercial, Industrial and Other Forms of Technical Education* (Sydney, 1905), p. 254.

50 Barrett, *Twin Ideals*, pp. 54, 81, 24.

51 Western Australian Parliament, *Report of the Royal Commission on the Establishment of a University* (1910), Appendix 1: Examination of MacCallum, pp. 21, 23; Appendix 2: Examination of Naylor, p. 27.

52 *Final Report of the Royal Commission on the Government, Administration, Teaching and Finances of the University of Melbourne* (1904), p. 9.

53 W.H. Bragg, 'Address', *AAAS: Report of the Twelfth Meeting, 1909*, J. Shirley (ed.), (Brisbane, 1910), p. 29.

54 Sir George Knibbs, 'Science and its service to man', *AAAS: Report of the Sixteenth Meeting 1923*, W.R.B. Oliver (ed.), (Wellington, 1924), p. 45.

55 On Taylor, see his autobiography *Journeyman Taylor* (London, 1958).

56 T.G. Taylor, 'Letter to his father', 1 October 1908, Griffith Taylor Papers, Ms 1003/1/83, National Library of Australia; T.G. Taylor, 'National research', *Argus* (5 January 1916), Griffith Taylor Papers, Ms 1002/9/1134, National Library of Australia; on the problems, see for example, T.G. Taylor, 'Geography and Australian national problems', *AAAS: Report of the Sixteenth Meeting 1923*, pp. 433–87; letter from Robertson, Director of Education, Western Australia to T.G. Taylor, 9 September 1921, Griffith Taylor Papers, Ms 1003/9/685, National Library of Australia.

57 T.G. Taylor, Education, 18 October 1928 (had been discussed in newspapers June 1928), Griffith Taylor Papers, Ms 1003/9/941, National Library of Australia.

58 Series of Letters, F.A. Todd to T.G. Taylor, 29 June, 2 July and 3 July 1928; T.G. Taylor to F.A. Todd, 29 June, 2 July and 3 July 1928, Griffith Taylor

Papers, Ms 1003/9/939, National Library of Australia; letter, Edgeworth David to Taylor, 13 March 1929, Griffith Taylor Papers, Ms 1003/9/1035, National Library of Australia.

59 G.V. Portus, *The University in Australia*, Fisher Library (University of Sydney, n.d.), pp. 177–8.

60 Barrett, *Twin Ideals*, p. 288.

61 On sociology in Australia during these years, see H. Bourke, 'Sociology and the social sciences in Australia 1912–1928', *Australian and New Zealand Journal of Sociology*, 17, 1 (1981), pp. 26–35.

62 His father was an emigrant brought to Australia by J.D. Lang. On Board, see A.R. Crane and W.G. Walker, *Peter Board: His Contribution to the Development of Education in New South Wales* (Melbourne, 1957).

63 P. Board, *Report Following Upon Observations of American Education*, (Sydney, 1909), p. 39.

64 P. Board, 'Economic and social values in education', *AAAS: Report of the Eighteenth Meeting* (Perth, 1928), p. 694.

65 P. Board, 'Mental science and education', *AAAS: Report of the Twelfth Meeting* (Brisbane, 1910), pp. 702 and 704.

66 *Ibid.*, p. 705.

67 Board, *Report*, p. 41; P. Board, 'Mental science', p. 711; P. Board, 'Australian citizenship', *Journal and Proceedings of the Royal Australian Historical Society*, 5, 4 (1919), p. 196.

68 *Ibid.*, pp. 197–8.

69 P. Board, 'History and Australian history', *Journal and Proceedings of the Royal Australian Historical Society*, 3, 6 (1916), pp. 292–3.

70 Board, 'Economic and social values in education', pp. 700–1.

71 *Ibid.*, p. 703.

72 Cole had been a student of Francis Anderson before he did post-graduate studies at Columbia University. He eventually became vice-principal of Sydney Teachers' College and was the author of many books on the history and theory of education. For further information on him, see C. Turney, 'Scholar and Writer – P.R. Cole' in C. Turney (ed.), *Pioneers of Australian Education*, Vol. 3 (Sydney, 1983), pp. 296–330.

73 Cole, *Herbart and Froebel*, pp. 95, 107.

74 P.R. Cole, *A History of Educational Thought* (London, 1931), pp. 293, 296, 297, 302, 301.

75 P.R. Cole, 'The development of an Australian social type', *Journal and Proceedings of the Royal Australian Historical Society*, xviii, ii (1932), pp. 51–7; p. 59; p. 62.

76 P.R. Cole, *Personal Efficiency* (Melbourne, 1936), pp. 44–7, 42–3.

77 P.R. Cole, *A History of Educational Thought*, p. 268.

78 On Irvine, see M. Roe, *Nine Australian Progressives: Vitalism in Bourgeois Social Thought* (St Lucia, 1984), ch. 9.

79 R.F. Irvine, 'The new humanism', Irvine Papers, Ms 6278, Folder 1, National Library of Australia.

80 R.F. Irvine, 'What's wrong with the world?', Irvine Papers, Folder 1, National Library of Australia, pp. 8–11. This is another version of the New Humanism.

81 R.F. Irvine, 'A university for the people', Irvine Papers, Folder 1, National Library of Australia.

82 R.F. Irvine, 'Commerce and the university', Irvine Papers, Folder 4, National Library of Australia, pp. 4–5; R.F. Irvine, 'Municipal administration', Irvine Papers, Folder 2, National Library of Australia, p. 13; R.F. Irvine, *National Organisation and National Efficiency* (Melbourne, 1915), p. 6.

83 R.F. Irvine, 'Progress and public spirit', Irvine Papers, Folder 1, National Library of Australia, p. 13; R.F. Irvine, 'Town planning: is it a necessity?', *Building*, 12 April 1917, pp. 86, 90.

84 R.F. Irvine, 'Patriotism and·nationalism', Irvine Papers, Folder 1, National Library of Australia, pp. 1–30.

85 R.F. Irvine, 'Lectures on the state', Irvine Papers, Folder 5, National Library of Australia.

86 R.F. Irvine, '*Laissez-faire* or the limits of individual freedom', Irvine Papers, Folder 1, National Library of Australia.

4 Ethos and Myth: The Humanities Strike Back

1 See M. Roe, *Nine Australian Progressives: Vitalism in Bourgeois Social Thought* (St Lucia, 1984), ch. 9.

2 On Piddington, see Roe, ch. 8.

3 B. Aspinwall, 'The Scottish religious identity in the Atlantic world 1880–1914' in S. Mews (ed.), *Religion and National Identity* (Oxford, 1982), p. 511. On Chalmers, see S.J. Brown, *Thomas Chalmers and the Godly Commonwealth* (Oxford, 1982).

4 L. Foster, *High Hopes* (Melbourne, 1986), pp. 25–6.

5 C.M.H. Clark, *A History of Australia*, Vol. 5 (Melbourne, 1981), p. 209.

6 M. MacCallum, *Tennyson's Idylls of the King and the Arthurian Story from the XVIth century* (Glasgow, 1894), pp. 323–4, 327–9.

7 *Ibid.*, pp. 335–6.

8 *Ibid.*, pp. 342, 347–8, 351, 349.

9 *Ibid.*, p. 354.

10 M. MacCallum in *Record of the Jubilee Celebrations of the University of Sydney* (Sydney, 1902), pp. 54–5.

11 Hermes, XVI, 6 (1910), p. 119.

12 On Wood, see R.M. Crawford, *A Bit of a Rebel* (Sydney, 1975).

13 G.A. Wood, 'The Miltonian ideal', in T.F. Tout and J. Tait (eds), *Historical Essays by Members of the Owens College Manchester* (London, 1902), p. 365.

14 *Ibid.*, p. 369.

15 G.A. Wood, *St Francis of Assisi* (Sydney, 1908), p. 21.

16 G.A. Wood, 'Savonarola and his times', George Arnold Wood Papers, University of Sydney Archives, p. 26.

17 G.A. Wood, 'Tennyson', George Arnold Wood Papers, University of Sydney Archives, pp. 15–16.

18 *Ibid.*, p. 32.

19 G.A. Wood, 'The Bible as history', George Arnold Wood Papers, University of Sydney Archives, p. 39.

20 G.A. Wood, 'Reign of Queen Victoria', George Arnold Wood Papers, University of Sydney Archives, p. 39.

21 *Ibid.*, p. 43.

22 On Anderson, see the entry in the *Australian Dictionary of Biography, Vol. 7, 1891–1939*, B. Nairn and G. Serle (eds), (Melbourne, 1979), pp. 53–5.

23 These lecture notes were taken by Miss D. Burns BA, and are to be found in the Burgmann Papers, National Library of Australia, Box 32.

24 F. Anderson, 'A modern philosopher – Green of Balliol', *Union Book of 1902*, p. 180.

25 F. Anderson, *The Religion of a Christian Student* (Sydney, 1930), p. 17.

26 F. Anderson, *On Teaching To Think* (Sydney, 1903), pp. 18, 23.

27 F. Anderson, 'Sidelights', *AJPP*, IX, 1 (1931), pp. 1–4.

28 Anderson, 'A modern philosopher', p. 197.

29 F. Anderson, *Christian Liberty and Ecclesiastical Union* (Sydney, 1923), p. 6.

30 Anderson, 'A modern philosopher', p. 177.

31 F. Anderson, *Liberty, Equality and Fraternity* (Sydney, 1922), p. 22.

32 F. Anderson, 'Liberalism and socialism', Presidential Address to Section G, *AAAS: Report of the Eleventh Meeting* (Adelaide, 1908), pp. 222–3.

33 F. Anderson, 'The poetry of Matthew Arnold', *Centennial Magazine*, 1, 2 (1888), pp. 114–17.

34 F. Anderson, 'Psychology and education', *Australian Journal of Education*, 2, 1 (1904), pp. 7–9.

35 Notes to Francis Anderson, 'Introduction to Philosophy', Burgmann Papers, National Library of Australia, Box 32, p. 30.

36 Anderson, *Christian Liberty*, pp. 39, 16–17.

37 Anderson, 'A modern philosopher', p. 190.

38 F. Anderson, 'Religious faith and modern thought', Francis Anderson Papers, University of Sydney Archives, V, p. 26.

39 Anderson, *Liberty, Equality and Fraternity*, p. 4.

40 *Ibid.*, pp. 4–5, 12, 8–9.

41 *Ibid.*, pp. 7, 17–20.

42 *Ibid.*, pp. 22, 21, 23.

43 Miss Burns's notes based on Anderson's lectures, Burgmann Papers, National Library of Australia, Box 32.

44 V.G. Childe, *The Dawn of European Civilization* (London, 1925), p. xiv.

45 See Eggleston's account of primitive man in chapter 6 of this study.

46 Miss Burns's notes on History of Philosophy, Burgmann Papers, National Library of Australia, Box 32.

47 The following discussion is based on Miss Burns's notes taken from Anderson's, Lectures on Ethics 1911, Burgmann Papers, National Library of Australia, Box 32. There are no page numbers in the notes.

48 Miss Burns's notes record the name 'Inglis' but Anderson was clearly referring to Frederick Engels.

49 F. Eggleston, *Search for a Social Philosophy* (Melbourne, 1941), p. 104.

50 F. Anderson, 'The state and the professions', Francis Anderson Papers, University of Sydney Archives, p. 6.

51 Miss Burns's notes based on Francis Anderson, Lectures on Ethics, Burgmann Papers, National Library of Australia, Box 32.

52 *Ibid.*

53 F. Anderson, 'The present religious situation', *AJPP*, 1, 3 (1922), pp. 216–22.

54 *Hermes*, X, 2 (1904), p. 46.

55 *Hermes*, XI, 3 (1905), p. 43.

56 'Philosophy and modern life', *Hermes*, XIV, 4 (1908), p. 77.

57 'Have we a university?', *Hermes*, XVIII, 3 (1912), pp. 94–6; 'University and state', XVIII, 2 (1912), pp. 47–8; 'Public life', XIV, 1 (1908), pp. 25–7.

58 'D.P.', 'Eternal Beauty', *Hermes*, XVIII, 2 (1912), p. 57.

59 L.H. Allen, *Gods 'and Wood-Things* (Sydney, 1913).
60 L.H. Allen, 'Possibilities of art in Australia', *The Conservatorium Magazine* (October 1917), p. 4.
61 John Le Gay Brereton to H. Duncan Hall, 26 June 1926 in Letters, John Le Gay Brereton to Duncan Hall, Ms 7229, National Library of Australia.
62 For Brennan's life, see A. Clark, *Christopher Brennan* (Melbourne, 1980).
63 C.J. Brennan, 'Curriculum vitae', in T. Sturm (ed.), *Christopher Brennan* (St Lucia, 1984), p. 178.
64 C.J. Brennan, *Prose*, A.R. Chisholm and J.J. Quinn (eds), (Sydney, 1965), pp. 5–11.
65 *Ibid.*, pp. 46, 84; pp. 73, 74, 46, 78; pp. 82, 161; pp. 163–4.
66 C.J. Brennan, *Poems* [1913], (Sydney, 1972), final two pages.
67 See, for example, A.G. Stephens, *Chris Brennan* (Sydney, 1930); R. Hughes, *C.J. Brennan: An Essay in Values* (Sydney, 1934); H.M. Green, *Christopher Brennan* (Sydney, 1939).
68 C.J. Brennan, 'Charles Badham', in Sturm (ed.) *Christopher Brennan*, p. 372.
69 Stephens, *Chris Brennan*, p. 30.
70 T. Molnar, *The Twin Powers: Politics and the Sacred* (Grand Rapids, 1988), pp. 85 ff.
71 J.H. Newman, *Oxford University Sermons* (London, 1887).

5 Liberalism and Its Critics: The Realists

1 M. Roe, *Nine Australian Progressives: Vitalism in Bourgeois Social Thought* (St Lucia, 1984); D. Walker, *Dream and Disillusion: A Search for Australian Cultural Identity* (Canberra, 1976), pp. 119 ff.; for an analysis of the social effects of the war, see R. Evans, *Loyalty and Disloyalty* (Sydney, 1987).
2 On the discrediting of *kultur*, see G.V. Portus, *The Cult of Kultur* (Newcastle, 1915); and E. Mayo, *Democracy and Freedom*, (Melbourne, 1919), pp. 70–1.
3 See Evans, *Loyalty*, pp. 63–4.
4 Many of Australia's leading historians, from Hancock and Clark to Stretton and Bolton, went to Balliol.
5 See R.G.S. Trahair, *The Humanist Temper* (New Brunswick, 1984), pp. 221–3, 271–2, 349–53.
6 G. Sherington, 'Education and enlightenment', in N. Meaney (ed.), *Under New Heavens* (Sydney, 1989), pp. 227–8; R.G. Menzies, *The Place of a University in the Modern Community* (Melbourne, 1939). On art, see R. Haese, *Rebels and Precursors: The Revolutionary Years in Australian Art* (Ringwood, 1988), pp. 39–40.
7 Haese, *Rebels and Precursors*, pp. 8–12.
8 E.H. Collis, *Lost Years: A Backward Glance at Australian Life and Manners* (Sydney, 1948), p. 114.
9 R. White, *Inventing Australia: Images and Identity 1788–1980* (Sydney, 1981), pp. 140 ff.; P. Morgan, 'A world of one's own: traditions and divisions in Australian life' in R. Manne (ed.), *The New Conservatism in Australia* (Melbourne, 1982), p. 100.
10 G.A. Wood, 'The Miltonic ideal' in T.F. Tout and J. Tait (eds), *Historical Essays by Members of the Owens College, Manchester* (London, 1902), p. 363; D.H. Lawrence, *Kangaroo* [1923] (Harmondsworth, 1987), p. 381. On the sterility of middle-class life between the wars in Australia, see S. Hazzard, *Coming of Age in Australia* (Sydney, 1985), pp. 9–20.

11 On expatriation, see H. Bourke, 'Intellectuals for export: Australia in the 1920s' in F.B. Smith and S.L. Goldberg (eds), *Australian Cultural History* (Cambridge, 1988), pp. 95–108; M. Roe, 'The new outlook' in P. Gathercole, T.H. Irving and G. Melleuish, *Childe and Australia* (St Lucia, 1995).

12 T. Rowse, *Australian Liberalism and National Character* (Melbourne, 1978).

13 On the development of twentieth century philosophy, see J. Passmore, *A Hundred Years of Philosophy* (Harmondsworth, 1968), chs 11, 12; on the shift within literature, see M. Levenson, *A Genealogy of Modernism* (Cambridge, 1984).

14 On Anderson, see A.J. Baker, *Anderson's Social Philosophy* (Sydney, 1979).

15 On what he calls 'the dominance of idealism', see S.A. Grave, *A History of Philosophy in Australia* (St Lucia, 1984), pp. 24–46; on Murdoch, see G. Dutton, *Snow on the Saltbush* (Ringwood, 1984), pp. 133–8.

16 On Muscio, see the obituary in *AJPP*, IV, 3 (1926), pp. 157–9 and also the entry on him by W.M. O'Niel in B. Nairn and G. Serle (eds), *Australian Dictionary of Biography, Vol. 10, 1891–1939* (Melbourne, 1986), pp. 650–1.

17 B. Muscio, 'The meaning of philosophy (1)', *AJPP*, I, 4 (1923), p. 238.

18 B. Muscio, 'The Hegelian dialectic', *Mind* (October 1914), n s xxiii, 92, pp. 540–1.

19 B. Muscio, 'Dr Haldane's religion', *AJPP*, III, 2 (1925), p. 133.

20 B. Muscio, 'A philosopher in search of his soul', in *AJPP*, IV, 2 (1926), p. 110.

21 B. Muscio, 'The mechanical explanation of religion', *Monist*, xxviii, 1 (1918), p. 130.

22 B. Muscio, 'Our philosophical heritage', in *AJPP*, II, 3 (1924), p. 161; B. Muscio, 'Experimental psychology as an educative subject', *Hermes*, XVIII, 3 (1912), pp. 106–7; B. Muscio, *Lectures on Industrial Psychology* (Sydney, 1917), pp. 6, 25–6.

23 Northcott eventually moved to England where he worked as Labour manager for Rowntrees and later as Director of the Institute of Personnel Management. For further biographical details, see J.D. Bollen, *Protestantism and Social Reform in New South Wales 1890–1910* (Melbourne, 1972), p. 125.

24 G. Taylor, 'Geography and Australian national problems', *AAAS: Report of the Sixteenth Meeting 1923* (Wellington, 1924), pp. 489, 485.

25 C. Northcott, *Australian National Development* (Columbia, 1918), pp. 9, 19 and 29.

26 *Ibid.*, pp. 31 and 158.

27 G. Hawthorn, *Enlightenment and Despair: A History of Social Theory*, 2nd edn (Cambridge, 1987), p. 208.

28 Northcott, *Australian National Development*, pp. 49–50 and 85–6.

29 *Ibid.*, pp. 58 and 89.

30 *Ibid.*, pp. 170, 185; pp. 169–70; pp. 87, 210, 209, 220, 246, 242–3; pp. 247, 255; pp. 256, 260, 261, 272, 274.

31 For Northcott's programme, see *ibid.*, pp. 277 ff. and for the 'American path to culture', see P.R. Cole, *A History of Educational Thought* (London, 1931), pp. 293 ff.

32 Northcott, *Australian National Development*, p. 294.

33 See, for example, C.H. Northcott (ed.), *Factory Organization* (London, 1928), chs I and IV.

34 See R. Conway, *The End of Stupor?* (Melbourne, 1983), pp. 1–3.

35 See R.W. Connell, 'Images of Australia', *Quadrant*, XII, 2 (1968), pp. 9–19.

36 W.K. Hancock, *Country and Calling* (London, 1954), p. 166.

37 *Ibid.*, pp. 112–14.
38 See in particular W.K. Hancock, 'A veray and true Comyn Wele' in his *Politics in Pitcairn and Other Essays* (London, 1947), pp. 94–109.
39 See Hancock, 'England and Australia' and 'A veray and true Comyn Wele', in *Politics in Pitcairn*.
40 Hancock, *Country and Calling*, pp. 96–7; W.K. Hancock, *Australia* (London, 1930), pp. vii–viii.
41 T. Rowse, *Australian Liberalism and National Character* (Melbourne, 1978), pp. 81 ff.
42 Hancock, *Australia*, p. 285 and *Country and Calling*, p. 70; M. Atkinson, *The New Social Order: A Study of Post-war Reconstruction* (Sydney, 1919).
43 A. MacIntyre, *Whose Justice? Which Rationality?* (London, 1988), p. 155.
44 W.K. Hancock, *Today, Yesterday and Tomorrow* (Sydney, 1973), p. 46.
45 Hancock, *Australia*, p. 292; ch. XI; p. 75 and pp. 271, 58.
46 Livy, *The Early History of Rome*, A. de Selincourt (tr.), (Harmondsworth, 1971), p. 105.
47 *Ibid.*
48 Hancock, *Politics in Pitcairn*, p. 103.
49 Hancock, *Australia*, p. 289; F. Eggleston, *Search for a Social Philosophy* (Melbourne, 1941), p. 147.
50 Hancock, *Australia*, pp. 53, 70, 63.
51 *Ibid.*, p. 75.
52 Hancock, *Politics in Pitcairn*, p. 103.
53 Hancock, *Australia*, pp. 77, 89, 85, 86, 99–100; pp. 97, 100, 128; pp. 140, 143; pp. 139, 25, 168–9.
54 See chapter 2 of this study.
55 Hancock, *Australia*, pp. 185, 190, 191–2; p. 193; pp. 277, 282.
56 *Ibid.*, p. 284.
57 On Childe's life, see S. Green, *Prehistorian: A Biography of V.G. Childe* (Bradford on Avon, 1981) and for an account of his thought, see B.G. Trigger, *Gordon Childe: Revolutions in Archaeology* (London, 1980).
58 A. Sherratt, 'V Gordon Childe: archaeology and intellectual history', *Past and Present*, 125 (1989), p. 184.
59 E. Gellner, *Culture, Identity and Politics* (Cambridge, 1987), pp. 47–74.
60 V.G. Childe, *How Labour Governs* in F.B. Smith (ed.), (1923), (Melbourne, 1964). For a recent discussion of this work, see T.H. Irving, 'New light on *How Labour Governs*: rediscovered political writings by V. Gordon Childe', *Politics*, 23, 1 (1988), pp. 70–7. See also the papers by Irving, Beilharz, Hindess and Maddock in Gathercole, Irving and Melleuish, *Childe and Australia*.
61 See especially R. Evans's paper on Childe in Queensland in Gathercole, Irving and Melleuish, *Childe and Australia*.
62 See chapter 4 of this study.
63 See, for example, *The Dawn of European Civilisation* (London, 1925), p. xiv.
64 A. Sherratt, 'V. Gordon Childe', p. 179; F. Anderson, *Liberty, Fraternity, Equality* (Sydney, 1922), p. 4.
65 For a discussion of Mayo and Childe, see my 'The Place of V. Gordon Childe in Australian intellectual history' in Gathercole, Irving and Melleuish, *Childe and Australia*.
66 See my 'The case for civilisation: an Australian perspective' in *Thesis Eleven*, 34 (1993), pp. 156–64.

67 This analysis will be founded on Childe's popular and general works rather than on his more technical archaeological works, as the central focus of this study is Childe considered as a Cultural Liberal rather than Childe as the father of modern archaeology.

68 V.G. Childe, *Man Makes Himself* (London, 1966), pp. 2, 14, 36.

69 V.G. Childe, *Society and Knowledge* (London, 1956), pp. 68, 54.

70 V.G. Childe, *What Happened in History* (Penguin, Harmondsworth, 1982), p. 23.

71 V.G. Childe, *History* (London, 1947), pp. 12, 68, 67.

72 *Ibid.*, p. 83.

73 V.G. Childe, *Social Evolution* (London, 1954), p. 13 ff.

74 L. Morgan, *Ancient Society* (New York, 1907), pp. 3–18.

75 Childe, *What Happened in History*, pp. 38, 69; Childe, *Man Makes Himself*, pp. 150, 140.

76 G.E. Smith, *Human History* (London, 1930), pp. 271 ff.; T.G. Taylor, *Our Evolving Civilisation* (Toronto, 1946), pp. 105, 6.

77 For Burgmann, see chapter 6 of this study. Cf. Portus's comment that if New South Wales had remained Free Trade 'her manufacturers [would have] eclipsed those of her southern neighbour' in 'If Australia had not Federated', Portus Papers, Archives Department, Public Library of South Australia.

78 Childe, *History*, p. 72; and *What Happened in History*, pp. 184–91.

79 Childe, *What Happened in History*, p. 221.

80 Childe, *Man Makes Himself*, p. 183.

81 Childe, *What Happened in History*, p. 239.

82 V.G. Childe, *The Pre-History of European Society* (London, 1962), p. 172.

83 Childe, *What Happened in History*, pp. 260 and 288.

84 Childe, *Social Evolution*, p. 173.

85 Childe, *What Happened in History*, p. 284.

86 Sherratt, 'V. Gordon Childe', p. 182.

6 Liberalism and Its Critics: The Idealists

1 T. Rowse, *Liberalism and Australian National Character* (Melbourne, 1978), pp. 157–9. For a discussion of Burgmann, see P. Hempenstall, 'The bush legend and the red bishop: the autobiography of E.H. Burgmann', *Historical Studies*, 77 (1981).

2 E. Burgmann, 'The existing order and disorder within the nation', Burgmann Papers, National Library of Australia, Box 30.

3 See M. Atkinson, *The New Social Order: A Study of Post-War Reconstruction* (Melbourne, 1919).

4 E.H. Burgmann, *The Education of an Australian* (Sydney, 1944), pp. 48–9.

5 E.H. Burgmann, 'Review: the Platonic tradition in English religious thought', *Morpeth Review*, 1 (1927), p. 22.

6 E.H. Burgmann, 'The Christian attitude to Russian Communism', *Morpeth Review*, 2, 20 (1932), p. 6.

7 See for example, J. Smith, 'Of the true way or method of attaining to Divine Knowledge' in his *Select Discourses* [1660], New York, (1979), pp. 1–2 and M. Eckhart, 'About disinterest', *Meister Eckhart: A Modern Translation*, R.B. Blakney (tr.), (New York, 1941).

8 E.H. Burgmann, 'The necessity of religion', *Morpeth Review*, 1, 11 (1930), p. 9; E.H. Burgmann, *Religion in the Life of the Nation* (Morpeth, 1930), p. 34;

9 E.H. Burgmann, 'The churches and the New Age', *Morpeth Review*, 3, 26 (1934), p. 9.

10 E.H. Burgmann, 'Hebraic and Hellenic elements in Christianity', Burgmann Papers, National Library of Australia, Box 31, p. 91; Burgmann, *Religion in the Life of the Nation*, p. 23.

11 Burgmann, *The Education of an Australian*, p. 51.

12 Burgmann, 'The churches and the New Age', p. 10; E.H. Burgmann, 'Geneva, Moscow, and Jerusalem', *Morpeth Review*, 3, 27 (1934), p. 13; E.H. Burgmann, 'Rational living', Burgmann Papers, Box 37, pp. 15–20; 'Today in history', Burgmann Papers, National Library of Australia, Box 21, pp. 27–8.

13 E.H. Burgmann, 'Our present discontents', *Morpeth Review*, 2, 15 (1931), pp. 6–7.

14 E.H. Burgmann, 'The place of psychology in religion', Burgmann Papers, National Library of Australia, Box 37, pp. 8–9.

15 Cf. for example, E.H. Burgmann, 'The first five years of life', lectures delivered March–August 1930, Burgmann Papers, National Library of Australia, Box 33.

16 Burgmann, *The Education of an Australian*, p. 20; Burgmann, 'The first five years of life', p. 87.

17 F. Anderson, 'Psychology and education', *Australian Journal of Education*, 2, 1 (1904), p. 8; C. Brennan, *Prose*, A.R. Chisholm and J.J. Quinn (eds), (Sydney, 1965), p. 78; P.R. Cole, *Personal Efficiency* (Melbourne, 1936), p. 38.

18 Burgmann, 'The first five years of life', p. 88; E.H. Burgmann, 'The insurgence of democracy', Burgmann Papers, National Library of Australia, Box 30, p. 69. See also his 'The analysis of the soul', Burgmann Papers, National Library of Australia, Box 37.

19 Burgmann, 'The analysis of the soul'.

20 Burgmann, *The Education of an Australian*, pp. 31, 42, 27, 55, 77.

21 E.H. Burgmann, 'What is man?', *Morpeth Review*, 1, 12 (1930), p. 9; E.H. Burgmann, 'Life or death', *Morpeth Review*, 2, 16 (1931), p. 4.

22 *Ibid.*, pp. 6 and 7

23 E.H. Burgmann, 'What are the chief needs of Australian civilization?', Burgmann Papers, National Library of Australia, Box 21.

24 Burgmann, *The Education of an Australian*, p. 89; E.H. Burgmann, 'The existing order and disorder within the nation', Burgmann Papers, National Library of Australia, Box 30, p. 27.

25 Burgmann, *Religion in the Life of the Nation*, pp. 20, 21, 22, 29.

26 E.H. Burgmann, *The Regeneration of Civilization* (Melbourne, 1942), p. 18; pp. 32, 36; pp. 41, 46, 48; pp. 49–55, 59; pp. 70, 59, 78; pp. 78–80; pp. 82–5, 88, 89, 99, 106, 100.

27 See for example, E.H. Burgmann, 'Religion as an article of faith or a guide to action' (1938), Burgmann Papers, National Library of Australia, Box 37 and 'The insurgence of democracy', p. 67.

28 Burgmann, *The Regeneration of Civilization*, pp. 102–3, 106–7; Burgmann, 'The churches and the New Age', p. 11.

29 Burgmann, 'Geneva, Moscow, and Jerusalem', p. 9, and 'Notes and essays [on] politics', Burgmann Papers, National Library of Australia, Box 30; Burgmann, 'Notes and essays [on] politics', and 'The existing order and disorder within the nation', p. 27.

30 Burgmann, *The Regeneration of Civilization*, p. 120.

31 On Mayo's life, see R.G.S. Trahair, *The Humanist Temper* (New Brunswick, 1984).

32 J.H. Smith, 'Foreword', *The Social Problems of an Industrial Civilization* [1949], (London, 1975), pp. xi, xxxii.

33 See chapter 4 of this study.

34 R.F. Irvine, 'Lectures on the state', Irvine Papers, National Library of Australia, Folder 5.

35 See chapter 2 of this study.

36 On Palmer, see D. Walker, *Dream and Disillusion* (Canberra, 1976), pp. 44–50; and for Anderson, see his 'The Servile State', in J. Anderson, *Studies in Empirical Philosophy* (Sydney, 1962), pp. 328–39.

37 See H. Bourke, 'Industrial unrest as social pathology: the Australian writings of Elton Mayo', *Historical Studies*, 20, 79 (1982), p. 225.

38 E. Mayo, *Democracy and Freedom* (Melbourne, 1919), pp. 71–2; pp. 6–7; pp. 5–6, 55, 34; pp. 7, 63–4; p. 37; pp. 49, 2, 6.

39 E. Mayo, *Psychology and Religion* (Melbourne, 1922), pp. 16–17.

40 Mayo, *Democracy and Freedom*, p. 33; pp. 37 and 50; p. 30; pp. 39, 42; p. 49; p. 35; p. 65; pp. 13 and 42; pp. 43, 50 and 51–2; pp. 59 and 62–3; p. 73; pp. 71, 70 and 69.

41 Mayo, *Psychology and Religion*, pp. 9–10; pp. 14, 16–17 and 27; pp. 28–30; p. 33; p. 37.

42 E. Mayo, *The Human Problems of an Industrial Civilization* (Boston, 1933) and *The Social Problems of an Industrial Civilization* [1949], (London, 1975).

43 Mayo, *The Human Problems of an Industrial Civilization*, pp. 124, 143.

44 Mayo, *The Social Problems of an Industrial Civilization*, pp. xv, 7.

45 *Ibid.*, pp. 125 and 127.

46 Mayo, *The Human Problems of an Industrial Civilization*, p. 157.

47 Mayo, *The Social Problems of an Industrial Civilization*, pp. 116 and 129.

48 *Ibid.*, p. 115.

49 D. Modjeska, *Exiles at Home* (Sydney, 1981), pp. 112–15.

50 M. Barnard, 'How "Tomorrow and Tomorrow" came to be written', *Meanjin*, 29, 3 (1970), p. 328.

51 M. Barnard Eldershaw, *Tomorrow and Tomorrow and Tomorrow* (London, 1983), p. 367.

52 *Ibid.*, p. 168.

53 See chapters 3 and 4 of this study.

54 See chapter 2 of this study.

55 F. Eggleston, *Search for a Social Philosophy* (Melbourne, 1941), p. 8; V.G. Childe, *What Happened in History* (Harmondsworth, 1982), p. 288.

56 In using the terms 'the Australians', Barnard Eldershaw appear to be following Hancock's usage.

57 Barnard Eldershaw, *Tomorrow*, pp. 12, 9 and 10.

58 *Ibid.*, pp. 10–12; p. 11; p. 45.

59 Mayo, *Democracy and Freedom*; Eggleston, *Search for a Social Philosophy*.

60 Barnard Eldershaw, *Tomorrow*, pp. 91, 46 and 47.

61 C. Northcott (ed.), *Australian National Development* (Columbia, 1918), pp. 277 ff., and P.R. Cole, *Personal Efficiency* (Melbourne, 1936).

62 Barnard Eldershaw, *Tomorrow*, pp. 90–1.

63 *Ibid.*, p. 317; p. 339; pp. 289, 385 and 415; pp. 32–3.

64 See C.H. Spence, *A Week in the Future* [1888], (Sydney, 1987), p. 33.

65 *Ibid.*, p. 44 and Barnard Eldershaw, *Tomorrow*, p. 216.

66 Barnard Eldershaw, *Tomorrow*, pp. 32–3, 221–2 and 231; pp. 225, 228 and 440; pp. 35, 36 and 223.
67 *Ibid.*, pp. 443, 455.
68 *Ibid.*, pp. 15 and 24.
69 See chapter 4 of this study.
70 J. Anderson, 'Orage and the New Age circle' in J. Anderson, G. Cullum and K. Lycos (eds), *Art and Reality: John Anderson on Literature and Aesthetics* (Sydney, 1982), pp. 241–6. See also J. Roe, 'The historical imagination and its enemies', *Meanjin*, 43, 2 (1984).
71 J. Anderson, 'Foreword', *ibid.*, p. 3.
72 Barnard Eldershaw, *Tomorrow*, pp. 21, 379, 25 and 426–7; pp. 18, 8 and 444–5.
73 On Eggleston generally, see W. Osmond, *Frederic Eggleston: An Intellectual in Australian Politics* (Sydney, 1985).
74 F. Eggleston, *Reflections of an Australian Liberal* (Melbourne, 1953), pp. 1, 5, 203.
75 F. Eggleston, 'The Australian democracy and its economic problems', Eggleston Papers, National Library of Australia, Ms 423/20, pp. 565 and 568.
76 F. Eggleston, 'The mind of John Citizen', Eggleston Papers, National Library of Australia, Ms 423/20, p. 399; p. 403; p. 400; pp. 411–12.
77 F. Eggleston, *State Socialism in Victoria* (London, 1932), pp. 330–1; p. 323; p. 346.
78 F. Eggleston, 'Mind and community', Eggleston Papers, National Library of Australia, Ms 423/20, pp. 427, 431.
79 Eggleston, *Search for a Social Philosophy*, pp. 30, 31 and 18; pp. 42–4 and 46; p. 66; p. 70; pp. 57–8 and 74; p. 81; p. 78.
80 T.H. Green, *Lectures on the Principles of Political Obligation* (London, 1948), pp. 121–41; Mayo, *Democracy and Freedom*, p. 63.
81 Eggleston, *Search for a Social Philosophy*, pp. 318, 328–9, 304 and 8.
82 *Ibid.*, pp. 306, 313 and 322; pp. 325–6 and 348.

Epilogue and Conclusion: Cultural Liberalism Spurned?

1 See D. Walker, *Dream and Disillusion* (Canberra, 1976), pp. 44–50.
2 T.E. Hulme, *Speculations*, Herbert Read (ed.), (London, 1965).
3 M. Levenson, *A Genealogy of Modernism* (Cambridge, 1984), pp. 37–47, 80–102.
4 P. Lassere, *Le Romantisme Français* (Paris, 1907).
5 M. Levenson, *Genealogy*, p. 209.
6 See especially, T.E. Hulme, 'Humanism and the Religious Attitude' in *Speculations*, pp. 3–71.
7 On the relationship between Clark and McAuley, see S. Holt, *Manning Clark and Australian History 1915–1963* (St Lucia, 1982), pp. 101–3.
8 *Ibid.*, p. 131.
9 C.M.H. Clark, *The Quest for Grace* (Ringwood, 1990), p. 142; p. 199; pp. 122 and 143.
10 C.M.H. Clark, *Occasional Writings and Speeches* (Melbourne, 1980), pp. 3–4.
11 *Ibid.*, p. 19.
12 Clark, *The Quest for Grace*, pp. 44–5.
13 Clark, *Occasional Writings and Speeches*, pp. 80–1.
14 C.M.H. Clark, *A History of Australia, Volume I, From the Earliest Times to the Age of Macquarie* (Melbourne, 1962), pp. 15, 352, 56, 380.

15 *Ibid.*, pp. 22–3; p. 162; p. 146 and pp. 367 ff.; pp. 324 and 352; p. 109.
16 J. McAuley, *The End of Modernity* (Sydney, 1959), p. viii; p. v.
17 J. McAuley, 'Culture and counter culture: a personal view', *Quadrant*, XX, 9 (1976), pp. 12–20. See also J. McAuley, 'Politics and counter culture', *Twentieth Century*, 26 (1972), pp. 259–64.
18 R. Conway, *Conway's Way* (Blackburn, 1988), pp. 152–3.
19 D. Green, 'Letters from a young poet', *Quadrant*, XXI, 3 (1977), pp. 19–20.
20 J. McAuley, 'Music' in L. Kramer (ed.), *James McAuley* (St Lucia, 1988), pp. 12–13.
21 McAuley makes use of Voegelin in his review of Denis de Rougement, 'Passion and society', *Quadrant*, 1, 3 (1957), pp. 90–1.
22 On McAuley in the early 1940s, see D. Balzidis, 'James McAuley's radical ingredients', *Meanjin*, 39, 3 (1980), pp. 374–82, and D. Horne, *The Education of Young Donald* (Sydney, 1967), pp. 228 ff.
23 J. McAuley, 'My New Guinea', in Kramer (ed.), *James McAuley*, pp. 28 and 22.
24 McAuley, *The End of Modernity*, p. vii.
25 *Ibid.*, pp. 3, 4, 7 and 25; pp. 4–5; pp. 11–12; pp. 30 and 35–6; p. 88; p. 38.
26 See E. Mayo, *Democracy and Freedom* (Melbourne, 1919), pp. 23 ff.; E. Burgmann, *The Regeneration of Civilization* (Melbourne, 1943), pp. 75–90.
27 McAuley, *The End of Modernity*, p. 57.
28 R.T. Wallis, *Neoplatonism* (New York, 1972), p. 173.
29 J. McAuley, 'Journey into Egypt' in Kramer, (ed.), *James McAuley*, p. 182.
30 McAuley, *The End of Modernity*, pp. 148, 157–8.
31 See C. Taylor, *Sources of the Self: The Making of the Modern Identity* (Cambridge, 1989) and A. MacIntyre, *After Virtue* (London, 1981), and for a general discussion S. Mulhall and A. Swift, *Liberals and Communitarians* (Oxford, 1992).
32 For 'negative liberty', see I. Berlin, *Four Essays on Liberty* (Oxford, 1969), pp. 118–72.
33 H. Emy, 'Australian politics in the nineties: from liberalism to conservatism', *Quadrant*, XXXV, 12 (1991), p. 10.
34 C. Birch, *On Purpose* (Sydney, 1990). For Ronald Conway, see especially *The Great Australian Stupor* (Melbourne, 1971), and *The Rage for Utopia* (Sydney, 1992).
35 See D. Kemp, 'Liberalism and conservatism in Australia', in B. Head and J. Walter (eds), *Intellectual Movements and Australian Society* (Melbourne, 1988), pp. 322–62. Also see R. Manne, 'The future of conservatism', and J. Stone, 'The future of clear thinking', *Quadrant*, XXXVI, 1–2 (1992), pp. 49–64.

Bibliography

Primary Sources

Manuscripts

Anderson, F., Papers, University of Sydney Archives.
Brereton, J. Le Gay, Letters to Duncan Hall, National Library of Australia.
Burgmann, E.H., Papers, National Library of Australia.
Eggleston, F.W., Papers, National Library of Australia.
Henderson G.C., Papers, Archives Department, Public Library of South Australia.
Irvine, R.F., Papers, National Library of Australia.
Mayo family, Papers, Archives Department, Public Library of South Australia.
Portus, G.V., Papers, Archives Department, Public Library of South Australia.
Taylor T.G., Papers, National Library of Australia.
Wood, G.A., Papers, University of Sydney Archives.

Journals and Newspapers

Age (1880, 1888).
Athenaeum, Sydney (1875, 1876).
AJPP (1923–1930).
Australian Economist (1888, 1889).
Bulletin (1888–1900).
Hermes (1895–1914).
Morpeth Review (1927–1934).
Quadrant (1957).

Printed Sources

Adams, F., *The Australians: A Social Sketch* (London, 1893).
Allen, L.H., *Gods and Wood-Things* (Sydney, 1913).
Allen, L.H., 'Possibilities of art in Australia', *Conservatorium Magazine* (October, 1917).
Anderson, F., 'The poetry of Matthew Arnold', *Centennial Magazine*, I, 2 (1888).

Anderson, F., 'A modern philosopher – Green of Balliol', *Union Book of 1902* (Sydney, 1902).

Anderson, F., *On Teaching to Think* (Sydney, 1903).

Anderson, F., 'Psychology and education', *Australian Journal of Education*, 2, 1 (1904).

Anderson, F., 'Liberalism and socialism', Presidential Address to Section G, *AAAS: Report of the Eleventh Meeting* (1908).

Anderson, F., *Sociology in Australia – A Plea for Its Teaching* (Sydney, 1912).

Anderson, F., *Liberty, Equality and Fraternity* (Sydney, 1922).

Anderson, F., 'The present religious situation', *AJPP*, I, 3 (1922).

Anderson, F., *Christian Liberty and Ecclesiastical Union* (Sydney, 1923).

Anderson, F., *The Religion of a Christian Student* (Sydney, 1930).

Anderson, J., *Studies in Empirical Philosophy* (Sydney, 1962).

Anderson, J., *Education and Inquiry*, D.Z. Phillips (ed.), (Oxford, 1980).

Anderson, J., *Art and Reality: John Anderson on Literature and Aesthetics*, J. Anderson, G. Cullum and K. Lycos (eds), (Sydney, 1982).

Armstrong, A.H., *Plotinus Enneads I*, 1–9 (Cambridge, Mass., 1966).

Arnold, M., *Culture and Anarchy* (Cambridge, 1971).

Atkinson, M., *The New Social Order: A Study of Post-War Reconstruction* (Melbourne, 1919).

Atkinson, M., *Australia: Economic and Political Studies* (London, 1920).

Badham, C., *Speeches and Lectures* (Sydney, 1890).

Barff, H.E., *A Short Historical Account of the University of Sydney* (Sydney, 1902).

Barnard, M., 'How "Tomorrow and Tomorrow" Came to be Written', *Meanjin*, 29, 3 (1970).

Barnard, M., *A History of Australia* (North Ryde, 1978).

Barnard Eldershaw, M., *Tomorrow and Tomorrow and Tomorrow* [censored edn, 1947], (London, 1983).

Barrett, J., *The Twin Ideals: An Educated Commonwealth* (London, 1918).

Bean, C.E.W., *In Your Hands Australians* (London, 1918).

Board, P., *Report Following Upon Observations of American Education* (Sydney, 1909).

Board, P., 'Mental science and education', *AAAS: Report of the Twelfth Meeting*, J. Shirley (ed.), (Brisbane, 1910).

Board, P., 'History and Australian history', *Journal and Proceedings of the Royal Australian Historical Society*, 3, 6 (1916).

Board, P., 'Australian citizenship', *Journal and Proceedings of the Royal Australian Historical Society*, 5, 4 (1919).

Board, P., 'Public education in a unified Australia', *AJPP*, IV, 3 (1926).

Board, P., 'Economic and social values in education', *AAAS: Report of the Eighteenth Meeting* (Perth, 1928).

Bragg, W.H., 'Address', *AAAS: Report of the Twelfth Meeting*, J. Shirley (ed.), (Brisbane, 1910).

Brennan, C.J., *Prose*, A.R. Chisholm and J.J. Quinn (eds), (Sydney, 1965).

Brennan, C.J., *Poems (1913)* (Sydney, 1972).

Brennan, C.J., *Christopher Brennan*, T. Sturm (ed.), (St Lucia, 1984).

Brown, W.J., *The New Democracy* (London, 1899).

Burgmann, E.H., 'Review: the Platonic tradition in English religious thought', *Morpeth Review*, 1 (1927).

Burgmann, E.H., 'The necessity of religion', *Morpeth Review*, 11 (1930).

Burgmann, E.H., 'What is Man?', *Morpeth Review*, 12 (1930).

Burgmann, E.H., *Religion in the Life of the Nation* (Morpeth, 1930).

Burgmann, E.H., *God in Human History* (Morpeth, 1931).

Burgmann, E.H., 'Life or death', *Morpeth Review*, 2, 16 (1931).

Burgmann, E.H., 'Our present discontents', *Morpeth Review*, 2, 15 (1931).

Burgmann, E.H., 'The Christian attitude to Russian Communism', *Morpeth Review*, 2, 20 (1932).

Burgmann, E.H., 'Geneva, Moscow and Jerusalem', *Morpeth Review*, 3, 27 (1934).

Burgmann, E.H., 'The churches and the New Age', *Morpeth Review*, 3, 26 (1934).

Burgmann, E.H., *The Regeneration of Civilization* (Melbourne, 1942).

Burgmann, E.H., *The Education of an Australian* (Sydney, 1944).

Childe, V.G., *The Dawn of European Civilization* (London, 1925).

Childe, V.G., *History* (London, 1947).

Childe, V.G., *Social Evolution* (London, 1954).

Childe, V.G., *Society and Knowledge* (London, 1956).

Childe, V.G., *The Prehistory of European Society* (London, 1962).

Childe, V.G., *How Labour Governs*, F.B. Smith (ed.), (1923), (Melbourne, 1964).

Childe, V.G., *Man Makes Himself* (London, 1966).

Childe, V.G., *What Happened in History* (Harmondsworth, 1982).

Childe, V.G., *The Aryans* (New York, 1987).

Childe, V.G., 'Letter to R.P. Dutt', 4 April 1931, *Hummer*, 29 (1990).

Church, R.W., *The Oxford Movement* (London, 1892).

Clark, C.M.H., *A History of Australia, Volume I, From the Earliest Times to the Age of Macquarie* (Melbourne, 1962).

Clark, C.M.H., *Occasional Writings and Speeches* (Melbourne, 1980).

Clark, C.M.H., *The Quest for Grace* (Ringwood, 1990).

Cole, P.R., *Herbart and Froebel: An Attempt at a Synthesis* (Teachers College, Columbia, New York, 1907).

Cole, P.R., *A History of Educational Thought* (London, 1931).

Cole, P.R., 'The development of an Australian social type', *Journal and Proceedings of the Royal Australian Historical Society*, 18, 2 (1932).

Cole, P.R., *Personal Efficiency* (Melbourne, 1936).

Coleridge, S.T., 'On the constitution of church and state', *Collected Works*, J. Colmer (ed.), 10 (Princeton, 1976).

Collis, E.H., *Lost Years: A Backward Glance at Australian Life and Manners* (Sydney, 1948).

David, T.W.E., 'The aims and ideals of Australasian science', *AAAS: Report of the Tenth Meeting*, G.M. Thomson (ed.), (Dunedin, 1904).

Eckhart M., *A Modern Translation*, R.B. Blakney (tr.), (New York, 1941).

Eggleston F., *State Socialism in Victoria* (London, 1932).

Eggleston F., *Search for a Social Philosophy* (Melbourne, 1941).

Eggleston F., *Reflections of an Australian Liberal* (Melbourne, 1953).

Garran, R.R., *Prosper the Commonwealth* (Sydney, 1959).

Green, H.M., *Christopher Brennan* (Sydney, 1939).

Green, T.H., *Lectures on the Principles of Political Obligation* (London, 1941).

Griffith, S., 'A plea for the study of the unconscious vital processes in the life of communities', *AAAS: Report of the Sixth Meeting* (Sydney, 1895).

Hancock, W.K., *Australia* (London, 1930).

Hancock, W.K., *Politics in Pitcairn and Other Essays* (London, 1947).

Hancock, W.K., *Country and Calling* (London, 1954).

Hancock, W.K., *Today, Yesterday and Tomorrow* (Sydney, 1973).

Higgins, H.B., *Robert Browning: His Mind and Art* (Melbourne, 1906).

Higgins, H.B., *Shakespeare's Aims and Ideals* (Melbourne, 1907).

Higgins, H.B., *A New Province for Law and Order* (Sydney, 1922).

Hughes, R., *C.J. Brennan: An Essay in Values* (Sydney, 1934).

Hughes, W.M., 'The limits of state interference', *AAAS: Report of the Eleventh Meeting*, W. Hawkin (ed.), (Adelaide, 1908).

Hughes, W.M., *The Case for Labour* [1910], (Sydney, 1970).

Hulme, T.E., *Speculations*, H. Read (ed.), (London, 1965).

Huxley, T., *Science and Education* (New York, 1897).

Irvine, R.F. (ed.), *The Place of the Social Sciences in a Modern University* (Sydney, 1914).

Irvine, R.F. (ed.), *National Organization and National Efficiency* (Melbourne, 1915).

Irvine, R.F. (ed.), 'Town planning: is it a necessity?', *Building* (12 April 1917).

James, W., *The Varieties of Religious Experience* (Glasgow, 1960).

Knibbs, Sir George, 'Science and its service to man', *AAAS: Report of the Sixteenth Meeting*, W.R.B. Oliver (ed.), (Wellington, 1924).

Lang, J.D., *Freedom and Independence for the Golden Lands of Australia* (London, 1852).

Lassere, P., *Le Romantisme Français* (Paris, 1907).

Lawrence, D.H., *Kangaroo* [1923] (Harmondsworth, 1987).

Livy, *The Early History of Rome*, A. de Selincourt (tr.), (Harmondsworth, 1971).

McAuley, J., *The End of Modernity* (Sydney, 1959).

McAuley, J., 'Politics and counter-culture', *Twentieth Century*, 26 (1972).

McAuley, J., 'Culture and counter-culture: a personal view', *Quadrant*, XX, 9 (1976).

McAuley, J., *James McAuley*, L. Kramer (ed.), (St Lucia, 1988).

MacCallum, M., *George Meredith: Poet and Novelist* (Sydney, 1892).

MacCallum, M., *Tennyson's Idylls of the King and the Arthurian Story for the XVIth Century* (Glasgow, 1894).

Masson, O., *The Scope and Aims of Chemical Science and its Place in the University* (Melbourne, 1887).

Mayo, G.E., *Democracy and Freedom* (Melbourne, 1919).

Mayo, G.E., *Psychology and Religion* (Melbourne, 1922).

Mayo, G.E., *The Human Problems of an Industrial Civilization* (Boston, 1933).

Mayo, G.E., *The Social Problems of an Industrial Civilization* [1949], (London, 1975).

Menzies, R.G., *The Place of the University in the Modern Community* (Melbourne, 1939).

Mitchell, W., *Structure and Growth of Mind* (London, 1907).

Mitchell, W., *The Two Functions of the University and their Cost* (Adelaide, 1917).

Montesquieu, *De L'Esprit des Lois* [1748], (Paris, 1974).

Morgan, L., *Ancient Society* (New York, 1907).

Muscio, B., 'The Hegelian dialectic', *Mind*, ns, xxiii, 92 (1914).

Muscio, B., *Lectures on Industrial Psychology* (Sydney, 1917).

Muscio, B., 'The mechanical explanation of religion', *Monist*, xxviii, 1 (1918).

Muscio, B., 'The meaning of philosophy (i)', *AJPP*, I, 4 (1923).

Muscio, B., 'Our philosophical heritage', *AJPP*, II, 3 (1924).

Muscio, B., 'Dr Haldane's religion', *AJPP*, III, 2 (1925).

Muscio, B., 'A philosopher in search of his soul', *AJPP*, IV, 2 (1926).

Newman, J.H., *Oxford University Sermons* (London, 1887).

Northcott, C.H. (ed.), *Religion and Politics* (Sydney, 1907).

Northcott, C.H. (ed.), *Australian National Development* (Columbia, 1918).

Northcott, C.H. (ed.), *Factory Organization* (London, 1928).
Pearson, C.H., *National Life and Character* (London, 1894).
Piddington, A.B., *Worshipful Masters* (Sydney, 1929).
Portus, G.V., *The Cult of Kultur* (Newcastle, 1915).
Portus, G.V., *Australia: An Economic Interpretation* (Sydney, 1933).
Portus, G.V., *Happy Highways* (Melbourne, 1953).
Portus, G.V., *The University in Australia* (Fisher Library, University of Sydney, nd).
Ross, L., *William Lane and the Australian Labor Movement* (Sydney, 1935).
Rousseau, J.J., *The Social Contract and Discourses*, G.D.H. Cole (tr.), (London, 1973).
Scott, W., *What is Classical Study?* (Sydney, 1885).
Scott, W., 'On fixing a minimum wage', *AAAS: Report of the Sixth Meeting* (Sydney, 1895).
Smith, G.E., *Human History* (London, 1930).
Smith, J., *Select Discourses* [1660], (New York, 1979).
Spence, C.H., *A Week in the Future* (Sydney, 1987).
Spence, W.G., *Australia's Awakening* (Sydney, 1909).
Stephens, A.G., *Chris Brennan* (Sydney, 1930).
Stephens, A.G., *A.G. Stephens: Selected Writings*, L. Cantrell (ed.), (Sydney, 1977).
Stephensen, P.R., *The Foundations of Culture in Australia* (Sydney, 1935).
Strong, H.A., *Address to the Students Attending the Classical Lectures* (Melbourne, 1879).
Taylor, T.G., 'Geography and Australian national problems', *AAAS: Report of the 1923 Meeting* (Wellington, 1924).
Taylor, T.G., *Our Evolving Civilisation* (Toronto, 1946).
Taylor, T.G., *Australia: A Study of Warm Environments and their Effect on British Settlement*, 5th edn, (London, 1949).
Taylor, T.G., *Journeyman Taylor* (London, 1958).
Tocqueville, A. de, *Democracy in America*, vol. 2, J.P. May and M. Lerner (eds), (New York, 1968).
Tucker, T.G., *The Place of Classics in Education* (Melbourne, 1886).
Tucker, T.G., *Things Worth Thinking About* (Melbourne, 1909).
Windeyer, W., 'Tennyson's In Memoriam', *Sydney University Magazine* (January 1855).
Wise, B.R., *The Commonwealth of Australia* (London, 1909).
Wise, B.R., *Industrial Freedom: A Study in Politics* (London, 1892).
Wollheim, R. (ed.), *Hume on Religion* (London, 1963).
Wood, G.A., 'The Miltonian ideal', *Historical Essays by Members of the Owens College, Manchester*, T.F. Tout and J. Tait (eds), (London, 1902).
Wood, G.A., *St Francis of Assisi* (Sydney, 1908).
Woolley, J., *Lectures Delivered in Australia* (London, 1862).

Other Papers and Reports.

Inaugural Ceremony of the University of Queensland (Brisbane, 1911).
Final Report of the Royal Commission on the Government, Administration, Teaching and Finances of the University of Melbourne (Melbourne, 1904).
Inauguration of the University of Queensland (Brisbane, 1909).
Record of the Jubilee Celebrations of the University of Sydney (Sydney, 1902).
Report of the Royal Commission on the Establishment of a University, Western Australian Parliament, Votes and Proceedings (Perth, 1910).

Report of the Commissioners on Agricultural, Commercial, Industrial and Other Forms of Technical Education (Sydney, 1905).
Parliamentary Debates, Commonwealth of Australia (1901–1902).
Union Book of 1902 (Sydney, 1902).
University of Sydney Calendars (1900–1920).

Secondary Sources

Books

Bailyn, B., *The Ideological Origins of the American Revolution* (Cambridge, Mass., 1967).
Baker, A.J., *Anderson's Social Philosophy* (Sydney, 1979).
Baumer, F.L., *Modern European Thought* (New York, 1977).
Berlin, I., *Four Essays on Liberty* (Oxford, 1969).
Birch, C., *On Purpose* (Sydney, 1990).
Blondel, M., *L'Action* [1892], (Paris, 1973).
Bollen, J.D., *Protestantism and Social Reform in New South Wales 1890–1910* (Melbourne, 1972).
Bracher, K.D., *The Age of Ideologies: A History of Political Thought in the Twentieth Century* (London, 1984).
Brown, P., *The Cult of the Saints* (London, 1981).
Brown, S.J., *Thomas Chalmers and the Godly Commonwealth* (Oxford, 1982).
Bruce, B.B., *A New Class?* (New York, 1981).
Burgmann, V. and Lee, J. (eds), *A People's History of Australia*, vols. 1–4 (Melbourne, 1988).
Burrow, J., *Evolution and Society* (Cambridge, 1966).
Butler, M., *Romantics, Rebels and Reactionaries* (Oxford, 1981).
Butlin, N.G., *Investment in Australian Development 1861–1900* (Cambridge, 1964).
Butterfield, H., *The Origins of Modern Science* (London, 1957).
Campbell, D., 'Culture and the colonial city: a study in ideas, attitudes and institutions: Sydney 1870–1890', PhD thesis (University of NSW, 1982).
Castles, S., Kalantzis, M., Cope, B. and Morrisey, M., *Mistaken Identity: Multiculturalism and the Demise of Nationalism in Australia* (Sydney, 1988).
Clark, A., *Christopher Brennan* (Melbourne, 1980).
Clark, C.M.H., *A History of Australia*, vol. 5 (Melbourne, 1981).
Conway, R., *The Great Australian Stupor* (Melbourne, 1971).
Conway, R., *The End of Stupor?* (Melbourne, 1983).
Conway, R., *Conway's Way* (Blackburn, 1988).
Conway, R., *The Rage for Utopia* (Sydney, 1992).
Crane, A.R. and Walker, W.G., *Peter Board: His Contribution to the Development of Education in New South Wales* (Melbourne, 1957).
Crawford, R.M., *A Bit of a Rebel* (Sydney, 1975).
Croce, B., *Philosophy, Poetry, History: An Anthology of Essays*, C. Sprigge (ed. and tr.), (Oxford, 1966).
Davie, G., *The Democratic Intellect: Scotland and her Universities in the Nineteenth Century* (Edinburgh, 1961).
Docker, J., *Australian Cultural Elites: Intellectual Traditions in Sydney and Melbourne* (Sydney, 1974).
Dutton, G., *Snow on the Saltbush* (Ringwood, 1984).
Etzioni-Halevy, E., *The Knowledge Elite and the Failure of Prophecy* (London, 1985).

Evans, R., *Loyalty and Disloyalty* (Sydney, 1987).

Finkielkraut, A., *The Undoing of Thought*, D. O'Keeffe (tr.), (London, 1988).

Foster, L., *High Hopes: The Men and Motives of the Australian Round Table* (Melbourne, 1986).

Freeden, M., *The New Liberalism: An Ideology of Social Reform* (Oxford, 1978).

Fuller, T. (ed.), *The Voice of Liberal Learning: Michael Oakeshott on Education* (Yale, 1989).

Gardner, W.J., *Colonial Cap and Gown* (Christchurch, 1979).

Gathercole, P., Irving, T. and Melleuish, G., *Childe and Australia* (St Lucia, 1995).

Gay, P., *The Enlightenment: An Interpretation, Vol. I, The Rise of Modern Paganism* (London, 1973).

Gellner, E., *Muslim Society* (Cambridge, 1981).

Gellner, E., *Nations and Nationalism* (Oxford, 1983).

Gellner, E., *Culture, Identity and Politics* (Cambridge, 1987).

Gellner, E., *Plough, Sword and Book: The Structure of Human History* (London, 1988).

Goldmann, L., *Le Dieu Caché* (Paris, 1959).

Goodwin, C.D., *Economic Enquiry in Australia* (Durham, NC, 1966).

Gouldner A., *The Future of Intellectuals and the Rise of the New Class* (New York, 1979).

Grave, S.A., *A History of Philosophy in Australia* (St Lucia, 1984).

Gray, J., *Liberalism* (Milton Keynes, 1986).

Gray, J., *Liberalisms* (London, 1989).

Green, S., *Prehistorian: A Biography of V.G. Childe* (Bradford on Avon, 1981).

Haese, R., *Rebels and Precursors: The Revolutionary Years in Australian Art* (Ringwood, 1988).

Hall, J., *Powers and Liberties: The Causes and Consequences of the Rise of the West* (Harmondsworth, 1986).

Hartz, L. (ed.), *The Founding of New Societies* (New York, 1964).

Harvie, C., *The Lights of Liberalism* (London, 1976).

Hawthorn, G., *Enlightenment and Despair: A History of Social Theory*, 2nd edn (Cambridge, 1987).

Hayek, F.A., *Law, Legislation and Liberty* (London, 1982).

Hazzard, S., *Coming of Age in Australia* (Sydney, 1985).

Head, B. and Walter, J. (eds), *Intellectual Movements and Australian Society* (Melbourne, 1988).

Henretta, J., *The Evolution of American Society* (Lexington, 1973).

Herf, J., *Reactionary Modernism* (Cambridge, 1984).

Heyck, T.W., *The Transformation of Intellectual Life in Victorian England* (London, 1982).

Higonnet, P., *Class, Ideology and the Rights of Nobles During the French Revolution* (Oxford, 1981).

Hirst, J., *The Strange Birth of Colonial Democracy* (Sydney, 1988).

Holt, S., *Manning Clark and Australian History 1915–1963* (St Lucia, 1982).

Horne, D., *The Education of Young Donald* (Sydney, 1967).

Horne, D., *Ideas for a Nation* (Sydney, 1989).

Hughes, H.S., *Consciousness and Society: The Reorientation of European Social Thought 1870–1930* (Frogmore, 1974).

Hutcheson, F., *An Inquiry into the Original of our Ideas of Beauty and Virtue* [1726], (New York, 1971).

Inglis, F., *Radical Earnestness: English Social Theory 1880–1980* (Oxford, 1982).

Jonas, H., *The Gnostic Religion* (Boston, 1963).

Joyce, R.B., *Samuel Walker Griffith* (St Lucia, 1984).

Kelley, D., *The Beginning of Ideology* (Cambridge, 1981).

Kelly, P., *The End of Certainty* (Sydney, 1992).

Kern, S., *The Culture of Time and Space 1880–1918* (London, 1983).

Knights, B., *The Idea of the Clerisy in the Nineteenth Century* (Cambridge, 1978).

Levenson, M., *A Genealogy of Modernism* (Cambridge, 1984).

Luft, D.S., *Robert Musil and the Crisis of European Culture 1880–1942* (Berkeley, 1980).

MacIntyre, A., *After Virtue* (London, 1981).

MacIntyre, A., *Whose Justice? Which Rationality?* (London, 1988).

MacIntyre, A., *Three Rival Versions of Moral Enquiry: Encyclopaedia, Genealogy and Tradition* (Notre Dame, Indiana, 1990).

Macintyre, S., *The Oxford History of Australia, Volume 4, The Succeeding Age* (Melbourne, 1986).

Macintyre, S., *A Colonial Liberalism* (Melbourne, 1991).

McKernan, S., *A Question of Commitment: Australian Literature in the Twenty Years after the War* (Sydney, 1989).

McLeod, H., *Religion and the People of Western Europe* (Oxford, 1981).

Mann, M., *The Sources of Social Power*, vol. 1 (Cambridge, 1986).

Manne, R. (ed.), *The New Conservatism in Australia* (Melbourne, 1982).

Meaney. N. (ed.), *Under New Heavens* (Sydney, 1989).

Miller, P., *The New England Mind: The Seventeenth Century* (Cambridge, Mass., 1954).

Milner, A., *Contemporary Cultural Theory* (Sydney, 1991).

Modjeska, D., *Exiles at Home* (Sydney, 1981).

Molnar, T., *The Twin Powers: Politics and the Sacred* (Grand Rapids, 1988).

Morse, D., *Perspectives on Romanticism* (London, 1981).

Morse, D., *Romanticism: A Structural Analysis* (London, 1982).

Mulhall, S. and Swift, A., *Liberals and Communitarians* (Oxford, 1992).

Munro, C., *Wild Man of Letters: The Story of P.R. Stephensen* (Melbourne, 1984).

Munz, P., *Our Knowledge of the Growth of Knowledge: Popper or Wittgenstein* (London, 1988).

Nadel, G., *Australia's Colonial Culture* (Melbourne, 1957).

Nairn, B., *Civilising Capitalism: The Labour Movement in New South Wales 1870–1900* (Canberra, 1970).

Nairn, B. and Serle, G. (eds), *Australian Dictionary of Biography*, vols 7 and 9 (Melbourne, 1979, 1986).

Newsome, D., *Two Classes of Men* (London, 1974).

Nisbet, R., *The Sociological Tradition* (New York, 1966).

Oakeshott, M., *Rationalism in Politics* (London, 1967).

O'Farrell, P., *Vanished Kingdoms: Irish in Australia and New Zealand, A Personal Excursion* (Sydney, 1990).

Osmond, W., *Frederic Eggleston: An Intellectual in Australian Politics* (Sydney, 1985).

Palmer, V., *The Legend of the Nineties* (Melbourne, 1954).

Passmore, J., *A Hundred Years of Philosophy* (Harmondsworth, 1968).

Peckham, M., *Beyond the Tragic Vision* (New York, 1962).

Penrose, R., *The Emperor's New Mind: Concerning Computers, Minds and the Laws of Physics* (London, 1990).

Pocock, J.G.A., *The Machiavellian Moment* (Princeton, 1975).

Pocock, J.G.A., *Virtue, Commerce and History* (Cambridge, 1985).

Pons, X., *A Sheltered Land* (Sydney, 1994).

Pratt, A., *David Syme* (London, 1908).

Prickett, S., *Romanticism and Religion* (Cambridge, 1976).

Ratnapala, S., *Welfare State or Constitutional State?* (Sydney, 1990).
Richter, M., *The Politics of Conscience: T H Green and His Age* (London, 1964).
Rickard, J., *H B Higgins: The Rebel as Judge* (Sydney, 1984).
Rickard, J., *Australia: A Cultural History* (Melbourne, 1988).
Ritchie, J. (ed.), *Australian Dictionary of Biography*, vol. 12 (Melbourne, 1990).
Roe, J., *Beyond Belief* (Sydney, 1986).
Roe, M., *Nine Australian Progressives: Vitalism in Bourgeois Social Thought* (St Lucia, 1984).
Rorty, R., *Contingency, Irony, and Solidarity* (Cambridge, 1989).
Rowse, T., *Australian Liberalism and National Character* (Melbourne, 1978).
Schama, S., *Citizens: A Chronicle of the French Revolution* (Harmondsworth, 1989).
Schumpeter, J., *Capitalism, Socialism and Democracy* (London, 1987).
Searle, G.R., *The Quest for National Efficiency* (Oxford, 1971).
Selleck, R.J.W., *The New Education* (London, 1968).
Serle, G., *The Creative Spirit in Australia: A Cultural History* (Richmond, 1987).
Shaftesbury, Earl of (Antony), *Characteristics of Men, Manners, Opinions, Times* [1711], J. Robertson (ed.), (Indianapolis, 1964).
Shann, E., *An Economic History of Australia* (Cambridge, 1930).
Sheldrake, R., *The Presence of the Past* (London, 1988).
Smith, B., *The Death of the Artist as Hero* (Melbourne, 1988).
Smith, F.B. and Goldberg, S.L., *Australian Cultural History* (Cambridge, 1988).
Sorel, G., *Reflections on Violence*, T.E. Hulme (tr.), (London, 1915).
Stabile, D., *Prophets of Order* (Boston, 1984).
Stone, N., *Europe Transformed 1878–1919* (Glasgow, 1983).
Stretton, H., *Political Essays* (Melbourne, 1987).
Taylor, C., *Sources of the Self: The Making of the Modern Identity* (Cambridge, 1989).
Thomas, M., *Australia in Mind* (Sydney, 1989).
Thurley, G., *The Romantic Predicament* (London, 1983).
Trahair, R., *The Humanist Temper: The Life and Work of Elton Mayo* (New Brunswick, 1984).
Tregenza, J., *Professor of Democracy: The Life of Charles Henry Pearson* (Melbourne, 1968).
Trigger, B., *Gordon Childe: Revolutions in Archaeology* (London, 1980).
Turner, G., *National Fictions* (Sydney, 1986).
Tylor, E.B., *Primitive Culture*, 2 vols (Boston, 1874).
Vincent, A. and Plant, R., *Philosophy, Politics and Citizenship: The Life and Thought of the British Idealists* (Oxford, 1984).
Walker, D., *Dream and Disillusion* (Canberra, 1976).
Wallis, R.T., *Neoplatonism* (New York, 1972).
Walter, J. (ed.), *Australian Studies: A Survey* (Melbourne, 1989).
Weil, S., *The Need for Roots* (London, 1978).
White, R., *Inventing Australia: Images and Identity 1788–1980* (Sydney, 1981).
Wiener, M., *English Culture and the Decline of the Industrial Spirit, 1850–1980* (Cambridge, 1981).
Williams, R., *Culture and Society* (Harmondsworth, 1971).
Wise, T., *The Self-Made Anthropologist: A Life of A.P. Elkin* (Sydney, 1985).

Articles

Aspinwall, B., 'The Scottish religious identity in the Atlantic World 1880–1914', *Religion and National Identity*, S. Mews (ed.), (Oxford, 1982).

Balzidis, D., 'James McAuley's radical ingredients', *Meanjin*, 39, 3 (1980).

Beilharz, P., 'Welfare and citizenship in Australia after World War II: a parting of ways', *Australian Quarterly* (Spring 1991).

Bourke, H., 'Sociology and the social sciences in Australia 1912–1928', *Australian and New Zealand Journal of Sociology*, 17, 1 (1981).

Bourke, H., 'Industrial unrest as social pathology: the Australian writings of Elton Mayo', *Historical Studies*, 20, 79 (1982).

Bourke, H., 'Intellectuals for export: Australia in the 1920s', *Australian Cultural History*, F.B. Smith and S.L. Goldberg (eds).

Burns, R., 'Flux and fixity: M.B. Eldershaw's *Tomorrow and Tomorrow*', *Meanjin*, 29, 3 (1970).

Callaghan, P.S., 'Idealism and arbitration in H.B. Higgins' *New Province for Law and Order*', *Journal of Australian Studies*, 13 (1983).

Carroll, J., 'The post-Humanist university: three theses', *Salisbury Review*, 7, 2 (1988).

Carter, D., 'Current history looks apocalyptic: Barnard Eldershaw, Utopia and the literary intellectual, 1930s/1940s', *Australian Literary Studies*, 14, 2 (1989).

Connell, R.W., 'Images of Australia', *Quadrant*, XI, 2 (1968).

Conway, R., 'The end of the great Australian stupor?', *Interchange*, 32 (1983).

Davie, G., 'John Anderson in Scotland', *Quadrant*, XXI, 7 (1977).

Emy, H., 'Australian politics in the nineties: from Liberalism to Conservatism', *Quadrant*, XXXV, 12 (1991).

Frow, J., 'The social production of knowledge and the discipline of English', *Meanjin*, 49, 2 (1990).

Gray, J., 'The politics of cultural diversity', *Salisbury Review*, 7, 1 (1988).

Green, D., 'Letters from a young poet', *Quadrant*, XXI, 3 (1977).

Green, D., 'Training our leaders: the university and society', *Age Monthly Review*, December 1987–January 1988.

Hempenstall, P., 'The bush legend and the red bishop: the autobiography of E.H. Burgmann', *Historical Studies*, 77 (1981).

Hempenstall, P., 'An Anglican strategy for social responsibility: the Burgmann solution', *Anglican Social Strategies from Burgmann to the Present*, J. Moses (ed.), (St Lucia, 1989).

Hume, L.J., 'Another look at the cultural cringe', *Political Theory Newsletter*, 3, 1 (1991).

Irving, T.H., 'New light on *How Labour Governs*: rediscovered political writings by V. Gordon Childe', *Politics*, 23, 1 (1988).

Kemp, D., 'Liberalism and conservatism in Australia', *Intellectual Movements and Australian Society*, B. Head and J. Walter (eds), (Melbourne, 1988).

Leach, R.W., 'A need for radical history', *Australian Studies*, 11 (1989).

Manne, R., 'The future of conservatism', *Quadrant*, XXXVI, 1–2 (1992).

Meaney, N., 'Reflections on Hancock's *Australia*', *Australian Historical Association Bulletin*, 43 (1985).

Melleuish, G., 'The philosophy and theology of John Woolley', *Journal of Religious History*, 12, 4 (1983).

Melleuish, G., 'From certainty to alienation: the development of Romanticism in colonial New South Wales', *Melbourne Historical Journal*, 15 (1983).

Melleuish, G., 'Beneficent providence and the quest for harmony: the cultural setting for colonial science in Sydney 1850–1890', *Journal and Proceedings, Royal Society of New South Wales* 118 (1985).

Melleuish, G., 'Daniel Deniehy, Bede Dalley and the ideal of the natural aristocrat in colonial New South Wales', *Australian Journal of Politics and History*, 33, 1 (1987).

Melleuish, G., 'Liberal intellectuals in early twentieth century Australia: restoring the religious dimension', *Australian Journal of Politics and History*, 35, 1 (1989).

Melleuish, G., 'Justifying commerce: the Scottish Enlightenment tradition in colonial NSW', *Journal of the Royal Australian Historical Society*, 76, 2 (1989).

Melleuish, G., 'Vere Gordon Childe: evolutionary historian', *Quadrant*, XXXIII, 1–2 (1989).

Melleuish, G., Review: S.L. Goldberg and F.B. Smith (eds), *Australian Cultural History*, B. Head and J. Walter (eds), *Intellectual Movements and Australian Society*, J. Rickard, *Australia: A Cultural History*, in *Australian Journal of Politics and History*, 35, 2 (1989).

Melleuish, G., 'Keeping the shutters firmly closed: the social laboratory, liberal intellectuals and the growth of the Protectionist mentality', *Australia as a Social and Cultural Laboratory?*, G. Melleuish (ed.), (Australian Studies Centre, University of Queensland, 1990).

Melleuish, G., 'Australia and the Servile State', *Political Theory Newsletter*, 3, 2 (1991).

Melleuish, G., 'The case for civilisation: an Australian perspective', *Thesis Eleven*, 34 (1993).

Melleuish, G., 'Australian individualism and Australian liberty' in *Identifying Australia in Postmodern Times*, Livio Dobrez (ed.), (Canberra, 1994).

Melleuish, G., 'Utopians and sceptics: competing images of democracy in Australia', in G. Stokes (ed.), *Australian Political Ideas* (Sydney, 1994).

Melleuish, G., 'The place of Vere Gordon Childe in Australian intellectual history', in P. Gathercole, T.H. Irving and G. Melleuish (eds), *Childe and Australia* (St Lucia, 1995).

Morgan, P., 'A world of one's own: traditions and divisions in Australian life', *The New Conservatism in Australia*, R. Manne (ed.), (Melbourne, 1982).

Moses, J., 'Australia's academic garrison 1914–1918', *Australian Journal of Politics and History*, 36, 3 (1990).

Roe, J., 'The historical imagination and its enemies', *Meanjin*, 43, 2 (1984).

Roe, M., 'The new outlook', *Childe and Australia*, P. Gathercole, T. Irving and G. Melleuish (eds), (St Lucia, 1995).

Rowse, T., 'Liberalism and Hancock's *Australia*', *Arena*, 44–45 (1976).

Rubinstein, W.D., 'Elites in Australian history', *The New Conservatism in Australia*, R. Manne (ed.), (Melbourne, 1982).

Rubinstein, W.D., 'Men of wealth', *Australian Cultural History*, S.L. Goldberg and F.B. Smith (eds), (Cambridge, 1988).

Sherington, G., 'Education and enlightenment', *Under New Heavens*, N. Meaney (ed.), (Sydney, 1989).

Sherratt, A., 'V. Gordon Childe: Archaeology and Intellectual History', *Past and Present*, 125 (1989).

Stone, R., 'The future of clear thinking', *Quadrant*, XXXVI, 1–2 (1992).

Turney, C., 'Scholar and writer – P.R. Cole', *Pioneers of Australian Education*, C. Turney (ed.), (Sydney, 1983).

Index

Adams, Francis, 67
Allen, L.H., 96
Anderson, Francis, 21, 82–3, 87–95; on
    Matthew Arnold, 89; on education, 88,
    89, 141; on Free Trade, 95, 133; on
    T.H. Green, 88, 90; on human/social
    progress, 89, 90–1, 91–3, 95; *Liberty,
    Equality and Fraternity*, 90–1, 128; on
    Personality, 91, 92, 93, 94; Philosophy
    Lectures at University of Sydney, 91–4;
    on the real, 87–8; on religion, 87–8,
    89–90, 91, 95; on the state, 93–4, 148, 149
Anderson, John, 46, 107, 136, 149; as
    liberal, 167
Arnold, Matthew, 58–9; *see also* Anderson,
    Francis
Atkinson, Meredith, 118
Australia: Anglicising of, 46–7, 104, 105;
    cultural influences on, 46, 48, 104;
    D.H. Lawrence's view of, 47–8; as radical
    fragment, 28; as a Social Laboratory, 39;
    see also Culture, Australian; 'Modern
    Australia'; modernity, in Australia
Australian Economic Association: and co-
    operation, 32; and free trade, 30
Australian Settlement, 40

Backhouse, Judge, 65
Badham, Charles, 62–5, 66, 82; on culture,
    63; on myth, 64–5; and Oxford
    Movement, 56; views of contemporaries
    on 64–5; *see also* Brennan, Christopher
Barnard, Marjorie, 127, 160; on George
    Arnold Wood, 161; *see also Tomorrow and
    Tomorrow and Tomorrow*
Barnard Eldershaw, M.: *see Tomorrow and
    Tomorrow and Tomorrow*

Barrett, James, 41, 42, 67, 69, 71, 77
Baumer, Franklin, 33
Bean, C.E.W., 42
Bergson, Henri, 129, 131; and vitalism,
    176–7
Birch, Charles, 187
Bracher, Karl Dietrich, 33
Blondel, M.: on human action, 12
Board, Peter, 72–5, 76, 77; on citizenship,
    73; on education, 72–3, 74; on history,
    73–4
Bragg, Professor W.H., 41, 70
Brennan, Christopher, 51, 65, 83, 97–101,
    141; and Charles Badham, 101; on fact
    and idea, 97–8; and Gnosticism, 98, 100;
    as 'myth', 97, 100–1; on spiritual
    evolution, 98–100; *see also* McAuley,
    James
Brown, Jethro: *The New Democracy*,
    40–1
Brown, Peter: on Hume and religion, 11
Burgmann, Ernest, 127, 128, 133, 137–48;
    on church and state, 145–7; as Cultural
    Liberal, 140; *The Education of an
    Australian*, 140, 142–3; and Hancock's
    Australia, 138, 143; on individual
    development, 141–2; and *Morpeth
    Review*, 138; on Personality, 139, 142,
    144; as Platonist, 138–9; *The Regeneration
    of Civilization*, 140, 144–7; on social
    development, 143–7; on spiritual
    development, 139

Caird, Edward, 82
Carroll, John: on culture, 10; on humanist
    university, 50–1
Chalmers, Thomas, 83

222

Childe, Vere Gordon, 107, 126–36; *The Dawn of European Civilization*, 92; education, 27; *How Labour Governs*, 127; on human and social progress, 128, 129, 130, 131–6; on knowledge as practice, 128, 130–1, 134, 135; *Man Makes Himself*, 129, 130; on National Socialism, 135, 162; *The Pre-History of European of European Society*, 135; as realist, 126–8; *Social Evolution*, 131; *Society and Knowledge*, 130; *What Happened in History*, 131

civic humanism, 17, 20, 57, 72, 76, 193 note 49; and science, 42, 68–72, 79; and universities, 42, 50

civilisation, *see* Burgmann, Ernest; Childe, Vere Gordon; Mayo, G. Elton

Clark, C.M.H. (Manning), 104, 177–81; and Catholicism, 179, 180; education, 47; and Evangelicalism, 177–8, 179–81; *A History of Australia*, 177, 179–81; on MacCallum, 83; *The Quest for Grace*, 178, 179

Cole P.R., 68, 75–7, 141; 'Australian Social Type', 76; on culture, 75–6; *History of Educational Thought*, 75

Coleridge, S.T.: 'On the Constitution of the Church and State', 57–8

Conway, Ronald, 45, 187; on McAuley, 181

cultural traditions, 11, 12–15, 16; Alasdair MacIntyre on, 13; Michael Oakeshott on, 13–14

culture, 12, 13, 14, 16, 17, 67, 68, 69–70, 77, 102; Arnold on, 58–9; Badham on, 63; Cole on 75–6; differing conceptions of, 10, 11; Irvine on 78; H.A. Strong on, 65; T.G. Tucker on, 65–6; and universities, 50, 55, 67, 103; *see also* Cultural Traditions; *kultur*, Liberalism, Cultural; Utilitarianism

culture, Australian: Radical nationalist conception of, 2–5, *see also* Palmer, Vance; criticisms of, 5–6; as 'invention', 7–9; *see also* White, Richard

Culture of Rationalism, 17, 23–4

David, Edgeworth, 41, 42, 68–9, 71

degeneration, 33, 34, 35, 40, 149; and arbitration, 44; and progress, 162; *see also Tomorrow and Tomorrow and Tomorrow*, Pearson, Charles Henry

de Tocqueville, Alexis, 21, 59–60

Docker, John, 6, 51

efficiency: and culture, 69, 75–6; National, 34, 39, 78, 79; and science, 42; *see also* Northcott, Clarence

Eggleston, Sir Frederic, 17, 117, 168–75; on 'Christian Ethic', 173–4; as liberal, 168; 'The Mind of John Citizen', 169–70; on National Socialism, 162, 174; on 'Personality', 168, 169, 173, 174; 'self-contained' man, 48, 169, 170, 171; *Reflections of an Australian Liberal*, 168; *Search for a Social Philosophy*, 171–5; on social evolution, 171–4; on the state, 168–9, 170, 171

Eldershaw, Flora, 127, 160; *see also Tomorrow and Tomorrow and Tomorrow*

ethos, 56–9; and Oxford University 56; University of Sydney, 56–7, 60–2, 95–6

Emy, Hugh, 187

Etzioni-Halevy, Eva, 23

Finkielkraut, Alain: on Culture, 10

Froebel, F., 68, 75, 76

Gardner, W.J., 64

Garren, Robert, 64–5

Gellner, Ernest, 15, 127; on historical development, 8, 18–9; on intellectuals, 23; on modernity, 19

Gnosticism, 52–3, 54; and Christopher Brennan, 97, 98; Hans Jonas on, 52–3; *see also* McAuley, James

Gouldner, Alvin, 23–4

Gray, John, 11, 12, 18; on Liberalism, 20

Green, H.M., 95

Green, T.H., 19, 20–21, 57, 59; *see also* Anderson, Francis

Griffith, Sir Samuel, 39, 40; on John Woolley, 56, 61

Hall, John, 23, 33

Hancock, W.K., 104, 107, 115–26, 127, 128, 136; *Australia*, 115–26, on the 'Australians', 121–6; *Country and Calling*, 115; education, 46–7; influence of Commonwealth idealism on, 116, 117, 119, 125–6; influence of Machiavellian realism on, 116, 117, 119, 126; and irony, 120; on justice *versus* realism, 123–6; and Livy, 120–1; on Pelagius and Augustine, 118–19; *Politics in Pitcairn*, 121; on protection, 123–4; *Today, Yesterday and Tomorrow*, 119; *see also* Rowse, Tim

Hartz, Louis, 27–8

Hayek, F.A., 188; on *kosmos* and *taxis*, 34–5, 128–9

Henderson, G.C., 41

Herbart, J.H., 68, 75

Herf, J., 48–9

Hermes, 95–6

Higgins, H.B., 44–5
Horne, Donald, 6, 9, 14
Hughes, H. Stuart, 33
Hughes, W.M., 43–4
Hulme, T.E., 176–7
Hume, David, 10, 11

Idealism, 106–8; *see also* Anderson, Francis;
    Burgmann, Ernest; Eggleston, Sir
    Frederic
Irvine, R.F., 22, 67, 77–80; and culture, 78,
    81; 'New Humanism', 78–9; on
    sociology, 78; on the state, 79–80, 148

James, William, 45, 131
Jones, Henry, 95

Kern, Stephen, 34
Knibbs, Sir George, 69, 70
Knowledge, theory of: *see* Childe, Vere
    Gordon; Mayo, G. Elton
kultur, 46, 103, 150, 156

Labor Party, 43
Lawrence, D.H.: *Kangaroo*, 47–8, 55, 60,
    105
Le Gay Brereton, John, 96
Levenson, Michael, 176–7
liberalism, 20, 21, 22, 33; and
    communitarianism, 186–7; Pearson on,
    36; and the state, 20, 34
liberalism, in Australia, 20, 21, 22, 48
Liberalism, Cultural, 24–5, 51, 68, 74, 128,
    137; and Burgmann, 140, 147–8, 175;
    and Childe, 128, 136; and Clark, 186;
    and contemporary liberalism, 186–7,
    188; contemporary relevance, 188–9;
    and contemporary universities, 187–8;
    defined, 17; and degeneration, 160–1;
    and Eggleston, 168, 174–5; and
    Hancock 118; and McAuley, 183, 185–6;
    and modernity, 19, 176; and
    republicanism, 188; and *Tomorrow and
    Tomorrow and Tomorrow*, 167–8; as
    tradition, 81, 101–2, 189–90;
    transformation of, 103–4, 107; and
    World War I, 103–4
liberalism, Free Trade, 26, 29–32, 48
    101–2; and Childe, 133; as kosmos, 34;
    see also Australian Economic Association;
    Wise, B.R.
liberalism, Protectionist, 26, 32–5, 48,
    101–2; as *taxis*, 34; *see also* protectionism;
    protectionist mentality; Syme, David
Liberals, Cultural, 51, 104; and Idealism,
    106–7; as Pelagians, 119; and rationality,
    163; and Realism, 106–7; and servile
    state, 149; *see also* Liberalism, Cultural

McAuley, James, 177, 181–6; and Brennan,
    177, 181–2; and Catholicism, 177, 181,
    182, 183, 184, 185; *The End Of Modernity*,
    6, 177, 181, 182–3; and Gnosticism,
    177–8, 181, 183, 184, 185; on liberalism,
    181; and modernity, 182, 183–4, 185;
    and traditional order, 182–3; *see also*
    Conway, Ronald
MacCallum, Mungo, 69, 82–3, 84–5; On
    'Idylls of the King', 83–5; on ideal of
    university, 85; and Romanticism, 85
MacIntyre, Alasdair, 187; on Augustine,
    119; on cultural traditions, 13, 51; on
    Hume, 10
Macintyre, Stuart, 22
Mann, Michael, 23
Masson, Orme, 69
Mayo, G. Elton, 71, 104, 129, 148–60; on
    civilisation, 149, 150, 153, 156, 159;
    Democracy and Freedom, 150–6; *The
    Human Problems of an Industrial
    Civilization*, 158; organic view of society,
    149, 153, 154, 155, 156; *Psychology and
    Religion*, 156–7; on religion, 156–7, 159;
    *The Social Problems of an Industrial
    Civilization*, 158, 159, 160; on the 'social
    will', 151, 152, 154; on the state, 148,
    149, 154, 155, 156, 158; theory of
    knowledge, 127, 128, 151–2, 154, 158
Meaney, N., 16
Menzies, R.G., 105
Mitchell, William, 67
'Modern Australia', 1, 2, 6
modernism, 176–7
modernity, 18–19; in Australia, 26–8; *see
    also* Liberalism, Cultural; McAuley,
    James
Molnar, Thomas, 101
Morgan, Lewis, 131–2
Morgan, Patrick, 45–6, 105
Murdoch, Walter, 108
Muscio, Bernard, 71, 107, 108–9; on
    Keyserling's *Travel Diary of a Philosopher*,
    109; as realist, 108–9
Musil, Robert, 55
myth, 59–60, 61–2; of Badham, 64–5, 101;
    and Brennan, 100–1

Naylor, Professor, 69–70
New Age: and Orage Circle, 176–7
new class, 23–4
Nicholson, Sir Charles, 54, 61
Northcott, Clarence, 107, 109–15;
    Australian National Development, 110–14:
    on Australian social development,
    110–13; and Franklin Giddings, 111; on
    Personality, 112; as realist, 109–10;

'social ideal', 111–12; social efficiency, 112, 113–14

Oakeshott, Michael, 14; on cultural traditions, 12, 13
Osmond, Warren, 17, 52
Oxford Movement, 56; see also Badham, Charles
Oxford University: Stephen Prickett and David Newsome on, 56

Palmer, Vance, 149, 176; Legend of the Nineties, 2–5, 47; view of culture, 2–5, 6
Palmer, Vance and Nettie, 117, 161
Pearson, Charles Henry, 22, 28, 35–8, 148–9; National Life and Character, 35–8; on the state, 35, 36, 37, 38
Personality: see Burgmann, Ernest; Eggleston, Sir Frederic; Anderson, Francis; Northcott, Clarence
Piddington, A.B., 64, 65, 82
Plato, 59; allegory of the cave, 52, 55
Platonism, 52, 54, 55; and Christopher Brennan, 97; and James McAuley, 184–5
Plotinus, 52, 55, 185
Portus, G.V., 48, 71, 133
post-modernity, 2–3
progress, human and social: see Anderson, Francis; Burgmann, Ernest; Childe, Vere Gordon; Eggleston, Sir Frederic; Northcott, Clarence; science
protectionism/protectionist ideology, 38–40, 46, 48–9, 67; Bulletin as advocate of, 38–9; and Labour, 42–5; see also Hancock, W.K.
protectionist mentality, 26, 45–8; and World War I, 104

Realism, 106–8; see also Muscio, Bernard; Hancock, W.K.; Childe, Vere Gordon; Northcott, Clarence; Taylor, Griffith
religion: see Anderson, Francis; Brennan, Christopher; Clark, C.M.H.; Eggleston, Sir Frederic; James, William; Liberalism, Cultural; Mayo, G. Elton
Rickard, John, 16
Roe, Jill, 35
Roe, Michael, 22, 23, 103
Romanticism, 17, 53–4, 56; and Christopher Brennan, 97–101; Marilyn Butler on, 53, 54; B. Croce on 53; Lucien Goldmann on, 53; 'lost vision', 53; David Morse on, 54; Morse Peckham on, 53–4; Geoffrey Thurley on, 54; and University of Sydney, 95–6; see also MacCallum, Mungo

Ross, Lloyd, 47
Rousseau, J. J., 57, 58
Rowse, Tim, 22, 106; Australian Liberalism and National Character, 6, 20–1; on Burgmann, 137; on Hancock, 117

Santamaria, B.A., 181
Schama, Simon, 18
science: as basis of social progress, 41–2; and civic humanism, 68–72; and culture, 66–8, 69; and universities, 50, 66–8
Scott, Walter, 32, 66
Shann, Edward, 117
Sherington, Geoffrey, 105
Sherratt, Andrew, 127, 128, 136
Smith, B. and Goldberg, S., 16
Smith, Bernard, 48
Smith, Grafton Elliot, 132–3
social sympathy, 30, 32, 45
Spence, Catherine Helen, 165
Spence, W.G., 42, 127
state: in Australia, 20, 21, 28; Hughes on, 43–4; ideal of, 58; Servile State, 5, 148–9; 'State Socialism', 31, 36, 37; see also Anderson, Francis; Eggleston, Sir Frederic; Irvine R.F., Mayo, G. Elton; Pearson, Charles Henry
Stenhouse Circle, 51
Stephens, A.G., 42, 65, 101
Stephensen, P.R., 104; on Australian culture, 4; education, 47
Stone, Norman, 33, 34
Stretton, Hugh, 11
Strong, H.A., 65
Stuart, Anderson, 69
Syme, David, 22, 32–3, 41; on laissez-faire, 32

Taylor, Charles, 187
Taylor, Griffith, 70–1, 133; conflict with F.A. Todd, 71; as realist, 110
Todd, F.A., 71
Tomorrow and Tomorrow and Tomorrow, 137, 160–8; as exploration of degeneration, 161, 163, 164, 165; on liberty and imagination, 161–2, 166–7, 168; on rationality and irrationality, 162–3, 164, 165; two possible pictures of twentieth century Australia, 161
Tucker, T.G., 65–6

university: American model of, 67, 72, 75, 77; and civic humanism, 42, 50; and differing conceptions of knowledge, 67, 82; German model of, 41, 77; humanist, 50–1; idea of, 55, 57, 58, 61, 67–8; and

university: cont.
   science, 42, 50; Wisconsin as ideal, 77;
   see also culture; ethos; Liberalism
   Cultural; MacCallum, Mungo;
   Romanticism, science
University of Melbourne: Report of Royal
   Commission into, 70
University of Queensland: Inaugural
   Ceremony, 41
University of Sydney: and Cultural
   Liberalism, 51, 54; ethos and myth,
   60–2; and Platonism, 55; *see also* Ethos;
   Romanticism
utilitarianism, 72–3; and culture 69, 70, 78

Walker, David, 103
Weil, Simone, 59, 60

West, John, 29–30, 33
White, Richard, 105, *Inventing Australia*,
   6–9; on culture, 6–9, 10, 11
Wiener, Martin, 46
Wilson, J.T., 66
Windeyer, William, 61–2
Wise, B.R., 30–2, 33; *The Commonwealth of
   Australia*, 32; *Industrial Freedom: A Study
   in Politics*, 30–1; on Protection, 31
Wood, George Arnold, 82–3, 85–7; on
   English history, 87; on St Francis of
   Assisi, 86; on Miltonian Ideal, 86; on
   Savonarola, 86; on Tennyson, 86; *see also
   Tomorrow and Tomorrow and Tomorrow*
Woolley, John, 51, 56, 60, 61, 67, 82;
   compared to Burgmann, 137–8; George
   Nadel on 137